QUESTIONS AND ANSWERS

LINGUISTIC CALCULATION

Published by Reidel in cooperation with KVAL.

VOLUME 1

QUESTIONS AND ANSWERS

Edited by

FERENC KIEFER

D. Reidel Publishing Company

A MEMBER OF THE KLUWER ACADEMIC PUBLISHERS GROUP

Dordrecht / Boston / Lancaster

Library of Congress Cataloging in Publication Data
Main entry under title:

CIP

Questions and answers.

(Linguistic calculation ; v. 1)
Papers from a conference held in Visegrád, Hungary, in May 1980.
Includes index.
1. Grammar, Comparative and general–Interrogative–Congresses.
2. Semantics–Congresses. 3. Language and logic–Congresses.
4. Information storage and retrieval systems–Congresses. I. Kiefer, Ferenc. II. Series.
P299.I57Q38 1983 415 83-9544
ISBN 90-277-1503-3

Published by D. Reidel Publishing Company,
P.O. Box 17, 3300 AA Dordrecht, Holland

Sold and distributed in the U.S.A. and Canada
by Kluwer Academic Publishers
190 Old Derby Street, Hingham, MA 02043, U.S.A.

In all other countries, sold and distributed
by Kluwer Academic Publishers Group
P.O. Box 322, 3300 AH Dordrecht, Holland

Printed in The Netherlands

TABLE OF CONTENTS

FERENC KIEFER / Introduction 1

LENNART ÅQVIST / On the "Tell Me Truly" Approach to the Analysis of Interrogatives 9

MONIKA DOHERTY / The Epistemic Meaning of Questions and Statements 15

GÜNTHER GREWENDORF / What Answers Can Be Given? 45

EVA HAJIČOVÁ / On Some Aspects of Presuppositions of Questions 85

ROLAND R. HAUSSER / The Syntax and Semantics of English Mood 97

JAAKKO HINTIKKA / New Foundations for a Theory of Questions and Answers 159

J. HOEPELMAN / On Questions 191

ARAVIND K. JOSHI / Varieties of Cooperative Responses in Question-Answer Systems 229

MANFRED PINKAL / Questions of Believing 241

PETR SGALL / Relevance of Topic and Focus for Automatic Question Answering 257

HANS KARLGREN and DONALD E. WALKER / The Polytext System - A New Design for a Text Retrieval System 273

INDEX 295

Ferenc Kiefer

Introduction

In almost all principled accounts of questions questions are related to the corresponding answers. Zellig Harris (Harris 1978:1), for example, maintains that "...all interrogative sentences can be derived, by means of the independently established transformations of the language, from sentences which assert that someone is asking about a disjunction of statements which are the relevant possible answers to that interrogative." This amounts to the claim that a yes-no question such as *Will John stay?* is derived from *I ask you whether John will stay* and a wh-question such as *Who came* is derived from something like *I ask you whether A came or B came or... or X came.*

Though in generative grammar interrogatives are not derived from the corresponding declaratives, the semantic interpretation of questions is akin to the syntactic source of questions posited by Harris. Jerrold J.Katz and Paul M.Postal (Katz-Postal 1964:113-117) state a reading rule for Q, the interrogative constituent, which boils down to (1) in the case of yes-no questions and to (2) in the case of wh-questions.

(1) Tell me which of the following is true: John will stay or John will not stay.
(2) Tell me which of the following is true: A came or B came or ... or X came.

Thus, the semantic interpretation of questions makes reference to the set of possible answers represented here by a disjunction of statements.

In logical analyses of questions answers appear quite naturally in the accounts. For questions do not represent propositions and therefore they cannot be assigned truth values. Answers, on the other hand, are formally declarative sentences and do represent propositions and thus can be true or false. It does not come as a surprise, then, that for a logician the meaning of a question is most naturally the set of all its possible answers. In other words, on this approach, a question denotes the set of propositions which are possible answers to it. One may also take a somewhat more restricted view and maintain that the meaning of a questions is the set of all its true answers. This approach is often

Ferenc Kiefer (ed.), Questions and Answers, 1–8.

referred to as the *propositional approach* to the semantics of questions. A yes-no question is identified with a set consisting of two propositions, one being the negation of the other, an alternative question with a set of propositions representing the alternatives, and, finally, a wh-question with a set of propositions which represent all the possible answers to the question, where ''possible answer'' means that the question word is replaced by an individual constant. If the meaning of a question is identified with its true answers only true propositions may count as possible answers.

The second approach, often called *categorial approach*, assumes that questions are functions from categorial answers to propositions. On this approach the yes-no question *Will John stay?* is analyzed as

$\lambda x_m(x_m(\text{John will stay}))$

where the variable x_m stands for ''yes'' or ''no''. And a question such as *Who came?* can be analyzed as

$\lambda x_{NP}(x_{NP}\ \text{came})$

This approach is based on the observation that the question word must be replaced in the answer by a constituent belonging to the same category and that an answer turns a question into a proposition. Notice that on the categorial approach questions are not identified with propositions though propositions are the final outcome of the analysis.

There is also a third approach which may be called *the epistemic-imperative approach*. On this approach the question *Will John stay?* is analyzed as

Bring it about that I know that John will stay or that I know that John will not stay.

For the alternative question *Will John or Bill stay?* we get the

Bring it about that I know that John will stay or that I know that Bill will stay.

And, finally, the wh-question *Who came?* is analyzed as

Bring it about that I know who came.

Questions can thus formally be represented by means of the imperative operator ! and the epistemic predicate K (=know). Thus, for example, for alternative questions with two alternatives the following identity holds:

?(p,q) = !(Kp v Kq)

where ? is the question operator and p and q represent the two alternatives. (Cf. Hoepelman, this volume).

The set of possible answers will essentially depend on the logic on which the logic of questions is based. In other words, in logical systems the class of answers is determined by the question and, vice versa, the question is uniquely determined by the class of answers.

The relationship between question and corresponding answer seems to be quite straightfroward, not to say simple, in logical analyses. However, the logical paradise is quickly lost, as Henry Hiż puts it (Hiż 1978:XII), when we inquire into the precise relationship between logical structures and actual questions in natural language. Leaving aside the question of how to derive natural language questions from logical forms—which poses particular problems of its own—it has to be determined what constitutes, semantically and pragmatically speaking, a question-answer pair in natural language. In grammar most accounts stipulated thus far would only allow for direct answers to a question. Though the notion of direct answer depends on the approach chosen, most accounts would consider the full answer *Yes, John will stay* and the elliptical answers *Yes, he will* and *Yes* as direct answers to the question *Will John stay?*. In the case of a question such as *Who came?* the set of direct answers would consist of *John came* and *John*.

The first problem arises if we consider ''yes'' and ''no'' as representing direct answers. Answering the question *Won't John stay?* with ''no'' amounts to the assertion that John will stay. The dialog

(3) Won't John stay?
No, he will stay.

however, is ill-formed. This means that ''no'' cannot stand for ''it is not the case that''. Similarly, the dialog

(4) Won't John stay?
Yes, he won't stay.

too, is deviant, which means that ''yes'' cannot stand for ''it is the case that''.

The above observations show quite clearly that ''yes'' and ''no'' cannot be considered to be reduced (elliptical) direct answers.

The main problem, however, is that none of the notions of direct answer as defined in the various logical approaches is satisfactory. Notice that the intuition on which the epistemic- imperative approach is based is that answers must be informative. Unfortunately, however, the notion of the informativeness of an answer has not as yet been explicated within this framework. Consider, for example, the question *Who lives in Budapest?* It would be quite absurd to interpret this question as asking for the enumeration of all of the about two million inhabitants of Budapest. Though for every person x who lives in Budapest *x lives in Budapest* would constitute a true answer to the above question, it seems completely pointless to identify the set of such answers with the meaning of the question *Who lives in Budapest?* Similarly, for every person x, *x lives in Budapest* is a possible answer. But again it would be pointless to identify the meaning of said question with the set of all possible answers. What one needs, among other things, is, of course, a contextually restricted notion of true answer or possible answer. Similar considerations hold for the categorial approach to the semantics of questions as well.

Or, to take another example, let us assume that somebody asks the question *Where is the Eiffel Tower?* in Paris. *The Eiffel Tower is in Paris* counts both as possible and true answer. Nevertheless its informativeness is zero. In the epistemic-imperative approach the interpretation ''Bring it about that I know where the Eiffel Tower is'' does not say anything about which answer satisfies the question, that is, when do I know where the Eiffel Tower is. What seems to be important, then, is to have a notion of ''pragmatically significant answer''. It is worth while noting that though questions indicate knowledge-desiderata, ''the answers need not necessarily eliminate those desiderata in the sense that the questioner then knows the particular information after the answer has been given; often it is already sufficient for him to have some basis for an assumption, supposition, hypothesis, etc. The amount of knowledge that will be sufficient for him in each case depends upon what purposes he has and upon what he already knows.'' (Grewendorf, this volume) In other words, the analysis of questions must be able to express degrees of knowledge and not only complete knowledge.

Yet another problem arises if one considers questions such as *Who is*

Sylvia? In order to provide an informative answer to this question the knowledge-situation of the questioner has to be taken into account. An answer such as *John's wife* may be quite adequate, in other cases, however, the questioner may use the above question to ask for information about Sylvia's past, about her character, etc. This brings out a further point. The informativeness of the question may depend on the speaker's purposes or projects. Maybe, this aspect of questions becomes even more apparent with the question *Where is the Eiffel Tower?* asked in Paris. Under normal circumstances, the speaker's purpose may be assumed to be getting to the Eiffel Tower. Therefore, to simply locate the Eiffel Tower would not be sufficiently informative and helpful. But an answer in which the questioner is told how to get to the Eiffel Tower is certainly both informative and helpful.

An adequate account of answers has thus to take into account at least the following aspects of questions: (i) the speaker's purposes (''teleological relativity''), (ii) the speaker's state of knowledge at the time the question is asked and (iii) the relativeness in the elimination of knowledge desiderata. (Cf. Grewendorf, this volume).

An adequate answer concept has also to take into consideration cases when the speaker asks the wrong question. He may, for example, have incorrect presuppositions about certain states of affairs. Let us, for example, assume that John is a bachelor but he has a girl friend. Consider now the following question: *What is John's wife like?* By answering this question with *John is not married* the answerer corrects the questioner's wrong presupposition about John. However, he may also answer with *You mean John's girl friend. She is quite O.K.*, etc. By taking into consideration the speaker's purposes and his state of knowledge, even wrongly put questions can be answered properly.

Sometimes it may not be clear what the speaker's purposes are. In such cases the answerer may provide several responses, among other things, ''suggestive indirect responses''. (Cf. Joshi, this volume).

The general moral to be drawn from the above considerations is that answerhood is essentially a pragmatic notion. In traditional semantic systems there is no way to tell when a question is answered. The only thing one can say semantically about answers is which, for each question, are the contextually independent possible answers.

As we saw above, the clarification of the contextual restrictions is a very important line of research. Its importance is not exhausted by its theoretical value. Practical applications (for example, question answering systems), too, presuppose an adequate account of questions and answers.

With what I have said I do not want to suggest that the semantics of questions and answers is less important than the inquiry into their pragmatic aspects. In fact, pragmatics presupposes semantics. A proper semantic account of questions and answers is a prerequisite for a proper pragmatic account.

There are still quite a few unsolved questions in the semantics of questions. Some of them are clearly demonstrated by the papers of the present volume.

This seems to be the right place to say a few words about the papers of this volume. In May 1980 a conference was held in Visegrád, Hungary, sponsored by KVAL, on questions and answers. The aim of the conference was to bring together representatives of various disciplines: logicians, philosophers, computer scientists and linguists to discuss theoretical as well as practical aspects of questions and answers in the hope that each discipline would benefit from the findings of the other. The present volume contains a selection of the papers presented at the Visegrád conference.

Lennart Åqvist discusses the formal consequences of a proposal made by David and Stephanie R.Lewis according to which the imperative- epistemic analysis of questions is to be replaced by an imperative-assertoric one, that is, the assertoric operator ''You tell me truly that...'' is to be substituted for the epistemic operator ''I know that...'' generally used in the imperative-epistemic accounts of questions.

Monika Doherty deals with the epistemic meaning of questions and statements. The epistemic meaning of a sentence is that part of sentence meaning that identifies an epistemic attitude. Epistemic attitudes concern the existence of the state-of-affairs referred to by the sentence. Doherty's main claim is that questions and statements differ from each other in essential aspects of their epistemic meaning.

What answers can be given is the topic of Günther Grewendorf's paper. After an insightful overview of the most interesting recent proposals about what constitutes an answer, he makes an attempt to explicate the notion of ''pragmatically significant answer''.

Eva Hajičová inquires into the problem of how the presuppositions of questions are interrelated with the topic-focus articulation of questions.

Roland Hausser's paper presents a grammatical (syntactic and semantic) treatment of the major syntactic moods in English. Answers are considered to represent a special mood, the so-called responsive mood. Mood is a purely syntactico-semantic category. The English expressions of various moods are analyzed solely in terms of the constituent words and a mood-marker. Responsives are accounted for in connection with interrogatives. Answers (responsives) must be compatible with the interrogative (the constituent of the responsive must agree with the category of the wh-word of the interrogative) and they are context-dependent (because they depend in their truth-value on the interrogative relative to which they are interpreted). The analysis is carried out in the framework of Montague grammar.

Jaakko Hintikka elaborates on certain points of his epistemic logic (he introduces a three-valued logic, he formulates new conditions on modal sets and modal systems, etc.). The revised epistemic logic is then used to present a new account of questions and answers.

A new logical approach to the semantics of questions is presented in Jaap Hoepelman's paper. The author claims that it possible to assign truth values to questions. The propositional operator ? is interpreted as "It is the question whether". The semantics of ? is given in Lukaszewicz's three valued logic. Hoepelman's theory seems to be able to handle a number of phenomena which could not be accounted for adequately thus far (negative questions, the scope of questions, the use of "yes" and "no" in answers, etc.).

Aravind K.Joshi briefly reviews the cooperative responses desirable in question-answer systems. The paper is primarily concerned with question-answer systems which are designed for interacting with data bases. Most of the responses described in Joshi's paper have to do with the situation when there is a disparity between the user's view of the structure and content of the data base and that of the system. Joshi attempts to place the type of interactions at hand in a more general framework for handling misconceptions.

Questions of believing are the topic of Manfred Pinkal's paper in a three-fold sense: First, the paper is concerned with some questions of belief semantics. Second, belief questions of the type *Do you believe that John loves Mary?* are analyzed. Third, various theoretical remarks are made, all based on belief questions and their corresponding answers.

Petr Sgall discusses the relevance of topic and focus for automatic question answering. Topic and focus play an important role in the semantics of questions and they may determine what counts as an appropriate answer to a question. The observations made with respect to natural language dialogs can be carried over to automatic question-answering systems enriching thereby their efficiency.

The last paper of the volume, that by Hans Karlgren and Donald E.Walker, puts questions and answers in a broader perspective. The paper describes a new design for a text retrieval system called ''The Polytext System''. Retrieval in this system means ''the process of locating in a set of given texts those texts or text passages that contain information relevant to a given query.'' After a brief outline of the Polytext System the authors discuss the advantages which this system has over existing retrieval systems. Though the paper is not directly concerned with questions and answers it is made clear that the study of questions and answers, an adequate account of dialogs, is a necessary prerequisite for a workable Polytext System.

Hungarian Academy of Science
Institute of Linguistics

Stockholm, August 27, 1982

References

Harris, Z.: The Interrogative in a Syntactic Framework, in: Hiż 1978.
Hiż, H. (ed.): Questions, D. Reidel Publ. Co., Dordrecht, 1978.
Katz, J. J., Postal, P. M.: An Integrated Theory of Linguistic Descriptions, The M.I.T. Press, Cambridge (Mass.), 1964.

Lennart Åqvist

On the ''tell me truly'' approach to the analysis of interrogatives

In their 1975 **Theoria** review of Raymond Olson and Anthony Paul (eds.) **Contemporary philosophy in Scandinavia** —hereafter referred to as Lewis (1975), see the bibliograpy at the end of the present paper— David and Stephanie R. Lewis give a very perceptive critical and constructive account of my theory of interrogatives as summarized in Åqvist (1972) and first set forth in Åqvist (1965). Most interestingly, they propose to replace the imperative-epistemic analysis of questions by an imperative-assertoric one, obtained from substituting throughout the **assertoric** operator ''You tell me truly that...'' for the **epistemic** operator ''I know that'' used in my original translation scheme for interrogatives of various types. The Lewis convincingly show that such a revised analysis is preferable to mine for a number of reasons; it leads e.g. (1) to a better treatment of certain interesting problem cases discussed on pp. 48—51 in Lewis (1975), (2) to a way of handling examination questions that is clearly superior to the rather **ad-hocish** treatment proposed in Åqvist (1969), and (3) to a useful application to questions in police interrogations for the purpose of eliciting confessions—a topic that seems so far to have been fairly neglected by interrogative theorists.

In this short note I want to explore a bit further the ''tell me truly'' approach, as I shall call the revised translation scheme preferred by the Lewis; in particular, I will consider what kind of formal framework or machinery it leads to. My starting point will be an analysis of the meaning of the assertoric operator ''You tell me truly that...''. As a historical observation I recall that the ''tell me truly'' approach was suggested already by Belnap (1969) p. 122 f., where he argues for the view that questions involve **linguistic** requests (imperatives) rather than or alongside epistemic ones.

Let us consider two relatively simple questions, viz.

(1) Is Linguistic Philosophy still alive?
(2) When will the train arrive?

Writing **P** for the statement ''Linguistic Philosophy is still alive'' we

Ferenc Kiefer (ed.), Questions and Answers, 9–14.

take the form of the yes-no question (1) to be

(1a) Is it the case that **P**?

The imperative-epistemic and imperative-assertoric (à la Lewis) translations of (1a) then become, respectively

(1b) Let it be the case in the immediate future that either I know that **P** or I know that not-**P**!
(1c) Let it be the case in the immediate future that either you tell me truly that **P** or you tell me truly that not-**P**!

The qualification ''in the immediate future'' is inspired by the Lewis (1975) remark in the first paragraph on p. 48—it nicely agrees with the Åqvist and Hoepelman (1978) thesis to the effect that genuine imperatives and obligation-statements are essentially future-oriented in character; see e.g. Spohn (1975) pp. 249—250 for a similar view.
Again, let us write **Fx** for ''The train will arrive at **x**'' and take the form of the fill-in-the -blank question (2) to be

(2a) For which time **x** is it the case that **Fx**?

Then, the imperative-epistemic and imperative-assertoric translations of (2a) are, respectively

(2b) Let it be the case in the immediate future that, for some time **x**, I know that **Fx**!
(2c) Let it be the case in the immediate future that, for some time **x** , you tell me truly that **Fx** !

Now, how are we to understand the operator ''you tell me truly that...'' which plays a crucial role in the translations (1c) and (2c)? The Lewis suggest the following type of definition (p. 50): **X** tells **Y** truly that **P**/**Fx**/ iff **X** tells **Y** that **P** /**Fx**/, and **P** /**Fx**/. Although pretty happy with this definition as it stands, I would like to have something more here: an explication of the import of the locution ''tell **that**'', which occurs in the **definiens.** What does it mean in turn? In answer to that question we suggest the following patterns of analysis:

D1. **X** tells **Y** that **P**/**Fx**/ iff there is a sentence **S** such that (i) **X** presents

S to **Y**, and (ii) **S** asserts that **P/Fx/**.

D2. **X** tells **Y** truly that **P/Fx/** iff there is a sentence **S** such that (i) **X** presents **S** to **Y**, (ii) **S** asserts that **P/Fx/**, and (iii) **S** is true.

The first important ingredient in these definitions is then a three-place relation of **presentation** (addressing, communicating, or what have you) which goes in direction **from** one interlocutor **X** (a "sender") via a sentence **S** (a "message") **to** a second interlocutor **Y** (a "receiver", an "addressee")' We think that no adequate theory of pragmatics can dispense with such a basic relation of presentation and that efforts should be made to characterize it axiomatically within such a theory.

The second ingredient in our suggested analysis of "telling that" is captured by clause (ii) to the effect that the sentence **S** is to **assert that P/Fx/**, which notion can be defined as follows:

D3. **S** asserts that **P/Fx/** iff **S** is true if and only if **P/Fx/**.

In the context at hand, then, to **assert that** means to **be true if and only if.** For the time being, let it just be pointed out that I take the connective "if and only if" in the **definiens** of D3 to express an appropriate kind of **strict** equivalence rather than a "merely material" one.

We now go back to the question (1a) and consider its imperative-assertoric (à la Lewis) translation (1c). Applying D2 and D3, the latter is then turned into

(1d) Let it be the case in the immediate future that
either there is a sentence **S** such that (i) you present **S** to me, (ii) **S** is true if and only if **P**, and (iii) **S** is true,
or there is a sentence **S** such that (i) you present **S** to me, (ii) **S** is true if and only if not-**P**, and (iii) **S** is true.

Applying the same procedure to the imperative-assertoric translation (2c) of question (2a), we obtain:

(2d) Let it be the case in the immediate future that, for some time **x**, there is a sentence **S** such that (i) you present **S** to me, (ii) **S** is true if and only if **Fx**, and (iii) **S** is true.

Summary of our argument so far: starting with the example questions (1) and (2), we took their logical form to be rendered by (1a) and (2a), respectively, and, following the Lewis (1975) direction, translated them into (1c) and (2c). Again, applying the analysis of ''telling that'' and ''telling truly that'' embodied in D1—D3, we arrived at (1d) and (2d) as our final translations of the respective interrogatives with which we started out. In view of the plausibility of these translations it looks like a worth while project to generalize them to other kinds of questions dealt with in my earlier work in the area. One might also expect the ''tell me truly'' approach to provide a neater and more direct theory of the question-answer relationship than my original approach. These and other related matters will have to be left aside in the present paper, though.

I now switch to the problem as to what kind of formal framework is called for by the ''tell me truly'' approach. I shall examine the problem by briefly dealing with the interpretation of (i) the imperative operator, (ii) the presentation predicate, and of (iii) the truth predicate, all of which appear as syntactical elements in the translations (1d) and (2d).

(i) The locution ''let it be the case in the immediate future that'' could be interpreted as synonymous with the compound operator SHALL $\oplus$ in the Åqvist and Hoepelman (1978) system of deontic tense logic, where $\oplus$ is an operator for the ''next moment'' in discrete time. If that is a reasonable suggestion, it also partially answers the question of framework: we need a general pragmatic-semantic machinery of modal tense logic involving **enriched trees** in the sense of branching structures based on discrete, linear and infinitely open-ended time (on the signed integers, if you like) together with an optimality-expressing choice-function enabling one to handle such deontic operators as SHALL; see Åqvist and Hoepelman (1978) sect. 7. The nodes in an enriched tree can then be thought of as **possible points of speech** or **contexts of communication** .

(ii) As for our predicate of presentation, we interpret it as denoting a matching three-place relation of the sort mentioned above. An interesting condition on that relation is to the effect that at every node in the tree there is a unique sender (denoted by the first person pronoun ''I'') who presents a unique sentence or message (denoted e.g. by the phrase ''this sentence'') to a unique receiver (denoted by the second person pronoun ''you''). This condition can be made more plausible if we admit an ''empty sentence'' representing **silence** among the well formed sentences of our formal language; then, contexts where a respondent refuses to answer a question by simply remaining silent can be handled as cases of his presenting the ''empty sentence'' to the questioner.

(iii) A remarkable feature of the formulations (1d) and (2d) is their containing existentially quantified **variables over sentences** as well as a one-place **predicate of sentences** ''is true''. This is surprising, since (1d) and (2d) are obviously themselves sentences of an **object-language L** that we should describe syntactically and interpret semantically via truth conditions relatively to **models** built on our enriched trees. Thus, it appears that our object-language **L** will have to contain its own truth predicate, seemingly contrary to the Tarski lesson we learnt on our mother's knee. Well, rather than engaging in small talk about deep matters here, I just point out the existence of a recent and still current discussion of languages containing their own truth predicates, presumably beginning with Kripke (1975) and with contributions such as Martin and Woodruff (1976), Kindt (1976), Kindt (1979) and Davis (1979). If there is anything I miss in this fascinating discussion, it is an application to languages of **modal** predicate logic, because that is what the ''tell me truly'' approach calls for on my present reconstruction of it.

September 1980

Uppsala Universitet
Filosofiska Institutionen

Bibliography

Åqvist, L. (1965): **A new approach to the logical theory of interrogatives** . Uppsala. Fresh edition 1975, TBL Verlag Gunter Narr, Tübingen.

Åqvist, L. (1969): Scattered topics in interrogative logic, in J. W. Davis **et al** . (eds.) **Philosophical Logic** . Reidel, Dordrecht-Holland, pp. 114-121.

Åqvist, L. (1972): On the analysis and logic of questions, in Olson and Paul (1972), pp. 27-39.

Åqvist, L and Hoepelman, J. Ph. (1978): Some theorems about a ''tree'' system of deontic tense logic. Forthcoming in an anthology on deontic logic ed. by Risto Hilpinen.

Belnap, Nuel D., Jr (1969): Åqvist's corrections-accumulating question-sequences, in J. W. Davis **et al** . (eds.) **Philosophical Logic** . Reidel, Dordrecht-Holland, pp. 122 -134.

Davis, L. (1979): An Alternate Formulation of Kripke's Theory of Truth. **Journal of Philosophical Logic 8** (1979), pp. 289-296.

Kindt, W. (1976): Über Sprachen mit Wahrheitsprädikat, Ms. University of Bielefeld, to appear in Ch. Habel and S. Kanngiesser (eds.), **Sprachdynamik und Sprachstruktur** , Tübingen.

Kindt, W. (1979): The introduction of truth predicates into first-order languages, in F. Günthner and S. J. Schmidt (eds.), **Formal Semantics and Pragmatics for Natural Languages** . Reidel, Dordrecht-Holland, pp. 359-371.
Kripke, S. (1975): Outline of a Theory of Truth. **Journal of Philosophy 72** (1975), pp. 690-716.
Lewis, David and Stephanie R. (1975): Review of Olson and Paul (1972): **Theoria xli** (1975), pp. 39-60.
Martin, R. L. and Woodruff, P:W. (1976): On Representing ''True in **L** '' in **L** , in A. Kasher (ed.), **Language in Focus** . Reidel, Dordrecht-Holland.
Olson, R. and Paul, A. (1972): **Contemporary philosophy in Scandinavia** . The Johns Hopkins Press, Baltimore and London.
Spohn, W. (1975): An Analysis of Hansson's Dyadic Deontic Logic. **Journal of Philosophical Logic 4** (1975), pp. 237-252.

Monika Doherty

The epistemic meaning of questions and statements

A study of questions and answers—or, more generally, questions and statements—may yield widely differing findings, depending on the overall aim one pursues. It is one thing to look for the pragmatic criteria distinguishing the various sorts of questions and statements, or selecting certain statements as adequate answers to certain questions. It is another thing to look for the most basic semantic elements distinguishing questions from statements, or rather the linguistic means used to express the one and the other. Although the latter may seem a comparatively simple task, it becomes quite intricate when questions and statements are seen as part of a system of linguistic means, whose paradigmatic and syntagmatic interdependencies become apparent in the way they interact with each other, i.e. in their respective contextual properties.

I want to claim that those syntactic and phonological means which are in themselves sufficient to characterize a sentence as a question or as a statement belong to a set of syntactic, lexical and phonological means which serve to express attitudes (''attitudinal means''), in particular those concerning the existence of the state-of-affairs referred to by a sentence: ''epistemic attitudes''. The set contains sentence negation, sentence adverbs, modal verbs, particles, verbs of thinking, question tags, contrastive stress, etc., all of which contribute to the expressions of epistemic attitudes. A sentence may sometimes contain several of these attitudinal means; if it is an independent sentence, it will always contain at least two of them: one specifying an attitude and another one determining the speaker's relationship towards it.

Although there does not yet exist a systematic description of epistemic attitudes as expressed by the various linguistic means mentioned, the fact that certain linguistic means do serve to express such attitudes would hardly be disputed. But the proposed separation of attitudinal means into those that specify attitudes and those that determine the speaker's relationship towards them will have to be argued for at some length as it is something which has not been thought of before. I want to show in the following that the syntactic and phonological means characterizing questions and statements are just those formal elements

Ferenc Kiefer (ed.), Questions and Answers, 15–44.

which determine the speaker's relation towards the attitude expressed by a sentence.

I do not want to say that these elements are restricted to an epistemic function; at least questions seem to have an additional intentional meaning—which will, however, not be dealt with in this paper. For the sake of simplicity, I will also restrict myself to ''yes-no'' questions—the difference between ''yes-no'' questions and ''wh-''questions being no part of their respective epistemic characteristics anyway.

I will also argue in favour of a differentiation of attitudinal means (including those which determine the speaker's relation towards the attitude) into two structural classes: ''propositional'' and ''non-propositional'' means to come to terms with a significant formal difference corresponding to a number of alternative contextual properties (see 2.3).

The set of elements and rules presented has been developed as part of a general attempt at a systematic representation of

(i) the basic semantic elements constituting that part of the meaning of a sentence which identifies an epistemic attitude: ''the epistemic meaning'' of a sentence;

(ii) the semantic structures those elements may enter into (i.e. the syntactic relations they can have to each other and to the other parts of the meaning of a sentence).

The criterion for the assumptions made was their inner coherence, their descriptive adequacy and explicative power regarding the paradigmatic and syntagmatic properties of epistemic means. They were not linked in detail to any of the prevailing linguistic theories.

1. Simple sentences

1.1 Epistemic attitudes

The question as to which linguistic means express epistemic attitudes can to a certain extent be answered intuitively. Surely, nobody would deny that a speaker using a sentence like

(1) I think that Jane has left.

or

(2) Jane has probably left.

expresses with it an epistemic attitude. The relevant linguistic means helping him to do so is in (1) ''think that'', in (2) ''probably''. To stream-line the following arguments, I will say that sentences with ''think that'' or ''probably'' express epistemic attitudes. In retracting from what the speaker means to what the sentence or a part of it means, I can say that not only a sentence like (1) but also a sentence like

(3) Pat thinks that Jane has left.
or
(4) Pat thought that Jane had left.

expresses an epistemic attitude. The difference between (1) and (3) is obvious: in (1) it is the speaker, in (3) it is some Pat who holds the view that Jane has left. In either case it is the individual referred to by the grammatical subject of ''think that''.

The difference between (3) and (4) lies in the time at which the individual referred to by the grammatical subject holds the view: in (3) the time coincides with the time at which the sentence is uttered, in (4) it precedes the time of utterance.

In regard to the person holding the view (3) and (4) are alike. That also (1) and (2) are alike in this respect is less obvious. Yet the difference is only a difference in explicitness. Either sentence attributes the epistemic attitude to the speaker. In (1) this is brought about by the pronoun ''I'', in (2) by some rule specifying the bearer of the epistemic attitude in the absence of any other form of specification (see 1.4).

Although it is contrary to traditional views, I want to claim that also sentences like

(5) Jane has not left.

(6) Jane has left.

contain epistemic means: the ''not'' in (5) and the affirmative form of (6), i.e. the absence of any other epistemic means.[1]

As these two forms of epistemic attitudes share a lot of linguistic properties despite their semantic antonymity, I want to coordinate them terminologically by calling them the negative and positive forms of a sentence. The negative and positive forms of a sentence express attitudes in much the same way as sentence adverbs. It is again the speaker who is identified with the bearer of the attitudes in (5) and (6).

The claim that the positive form expresses an epistemic attitude has two rather far-reaching consequences:

(A) Any sentence expresses an attitude.

(If it does not contain another attitudinal means it must necessarily be interpreted as having a positive form.)

(B) Sentences like (1), (3) and (4)—which shall be called ''attitudinal sentences''—contain two epistemic attitudes.

This becomes more obvious when one compares them with sentences like

(7) I do not think that Jane has left.

(8) Pat thinks probably that Jane has left.
etc.

One of the two epistemic attitudes expressed by all these sentences is specified by ''think that'' and attributed to the person referred to by the grammatical subject of the attitudinal verb, the other is specified by the positive or negative form of the matrix sentence or the sentence adverb and attributed to the speaker.

For the time being I will restrict myself to the epistemic meaning of simple sentences and return to complex ones under 2.

Epistemic attitudes are attitudes towards propositions. The linguistic means expressing propositions are sentences. Sentences specify with their meanings the conditions that have to be met to make a proposition true in regard to a given state-of-affairs. Propositions can be considered as functors mapping possible worlds onto truth values.[2]

In a sentence like (2), (5) or (6) the attitude expressed is directed towards the proposition expressed by the remaining constituents of the sentence. We can therefore say that the meaning of all three sentences contains a proposition and an attitude directed towards this proposition. (that the two do not yet exhaust the meaning of a sentence will be shown in 1.2).

Let me symbolize the propositional meaning of a sentence by ''p'' and the attitudinal meaning of a sentence by ''A''. The logical relationship between A and p can then be said to be of the form: A(p), with A being an attitudinal predicate taking p as its argument.

''A'' is in all three sentences an epistemic attitude of the speaker (hence ''A_S''), specifying his view as to whether p is true or not true (i.e. as to whether the state-of-affairs identified by p exists in regard to a certain present, past, future, real or imaginary situation). In (6) the speaker holds a positive view, considering p to be true: pos_S (p); in (5) he holds a negative view, considering p not to be true: neg_S (p); in (2) he holds a positive, yet uncertain view, considering p to be probably true: $PROB_S$ (p):.[3]

1.2 Attitudinal mood

The statement that A is a speaker's attitude holds for (6), but not for the positive view determined by the positive form of the sentence

(9) Has Jane left?

As it is, (6) has the form of a statement, (9) that of a question, or more precisely: (6) is a declarative sentence and (9) an interrogative sentence. (Even if one neglects possible pragmatic variations, there is no necessary correspondence between questions and interrogatives, statements and declaratives; see 1.5) I will jointly refer to the declarative and interrogative form of a sentence as ''sentence mood'' (SM).

Sentence mood is an obligatory syntactic category for any independent sentence: except imperatives[4], there is no independent sentence—whatever its internal make-up may be like (reductions and or various verb forms notwithstanding)—which would not be either of the declarative or of the interrogative form.

As the comparison of (6) and (9) shows, a difference in sentence mood leads to a difference in the epistemic meaning of a sentence. It is only the declarative sentence which attributes the attitude expressed to the speaker. We can therefore assume that it is the function of the declarative SM to attribute the attitude expressed to the speaker.

To attribute an attitude to the speaker could simply mean to determine that the speaker h a s the attitude. Although this would be enough to distinguish the epistemic meaning of declaratives from that of interrogatives like (9), it is not enough to distinguish the epistemic meaning of declaratives from an interrogative sentence like

(10) Has Jane not left?

In addition to the negative attitude expressed by the negative form of (10), which is not attributed to the speaker, (10) expresses a positive attitude, which is attributed to the speaker. It has been the speaker's view that Jane has left, at least until the time of uttering (10) when he begins to admit also the possibility of the opposite.

The difference between (6) and (10) makes it clear that the attitudinal meaning of a sentence

1. need not be restricted to one attitude even if the sentence seems to contain only one attitudinal means,
and
2. the interrogative SM does not exclude a speaker's attitude altogether. It merely prevents the attitude expressed explicitly from being attributed to the speaker.

Although (6) and (10) can be said to express a positive attitude of the speaker, the extent to which the speaker commits himself to this view is obviously different. In (6) he holds the view that p is true without any reservations, excluding the alternative view altogether; in (10) the speaker does not any longer exclude the alternative view, in fact, he begins to have his doubts as to whether his positive view is really correct.

One can say that (6) presents a linguistic form committing the speaker to the attitude expressed without any reservations whereas (10) presents a linguistic form which does not exclude the expression of a speaker's reservation as to its validity.

The reservation implied by (10) is due to the interrogative SM, i.e. to the epistemic feature shared by sentences like (10) and (9).

The difference in the speaker's commitment in regard to an attitude expressed by a sentence is primarily determined by the mood of the sentence. I will call the speaker's commitment to the attitude determined by the SM the ''attitudinal mood'' (AM) of a sentence, and the unreserved commitment determined by the declarative SM the ''assertive mood''[5], juxtaposing it to the ''non-assertive mood'' determined by the interrogative SM. The positive attitude of the spaker is asserted by the declarative SM in (6), but not asserted by the interrogative SM in (10).

The hypothesis that any independent sentence will be either of the declarative or the interrogative form can now be restated as

(C) Any independent sentence expresses either an assertive or a non-assertive mood.[6]

AM must be seen as an obligatory attitudinal predicate of any independent sentence, taking A(p) as its argument. Thus the meaning of each independent sentence is of the general form: AM(A(p)). Each sentence expresses an attitude towards p and an AM which determines whether the speaker asserts A(p) or does not assert it.

*1.3 Presupposed attitudes**

Sentence (10) contains a negative and a positive attitude with neither attitude being asserted, but the positive attitude being attributed to the speaker. Now consider a sentence like

(11) Jane has n o t left.

with a contrastive emphasis on ''not''. (11) is clearly a case in which the speaker repudiates a view alternative to the one he himself holds. That is also (11) expresses two attitudes:

1. the negative attitude (expressed by ''not'') asserted by the speaker as his attitude through the assertive mood of the sentence: neg_s (p), and
2. a positive attitude attributed to someone else: $pos_{not\text{-}s}$ (p)[7] and not asserted by the assertive mood of the sentence.

Or take a sentence like

(12) Jane needn't have left.

which also expresses two attitudes: a negative speaker's attitude which

* In the meantime I have had reason to differentiate between ''presupposed attitude and ''implied attitude'', with the latter applying to all cases discussed in this paper so that I have to ask the patient reader to replace any occurrence of ''presuppose'', pressupposed'', ''presupposition'' by ''imply'', ''implied'' and ''implication''.

is asserted and directed towards the modality expressed by ''need'' and a positive speaker's attitude saying that p (Jane has left) is true. (12) is said to presuppose or at least imply (the truth of) p. Although the speaker necessarily shares the positive view that amounts to a presupposition or implication of p (as in (12)) we cannot say that the speaker asserts the positive view in (12) any more than we can say that the speaker asserts the positive view in (11). (12) and (11) show clearly that

(D) Only one attitude can be asserted by the assertive mood of a sentence.[8]

Yet we cannot conclude that the speaker's commitment to the attitude not asserted by the assertive AM is the same as to the attitude not asserted by the non-assertive AM. To clarify the issue, I will say that the AM of a sentence binds or does not bind the attitude expressed by that sentence. The attitude which is bound by the AM is asserted or not asserted by the speaker. The attitude which is not bound by the AM is "presupposed" by the speaker. The speaker presupposes a state-of-affairs in which someone holds a certain view towards p.

Any independent sentence must contain some linguistic means determining an asserted or non-asserted attitude. The asserted or non-asserted attitude is an obligatory part of the meaning of an independent sentence. A presupposed attitude is only an optional part of the meaning of an independent sentence.

A sentence like (6) does not presuppose any attitude; (11) presupposes a positive attitude attributed to someone else. Symbolizing the presupposition of an attitude towards p with Pres (A(p)), one can represent the meaning of (11) as

(11) Pres ($pos_{not\text{-}s}$ (p)) Ass (neg_s (p)).

The difference between the attitude presupposed by (11) and that presupposed by (12) is not only a difference in regard to the speaker's involvement in it. If the presupposition of an attitude towards p amounts to the presupposition of p, the attitude presupposed can only be of the type ''the speaker knows that p''[9], i.e. the attitude which is explicitly expressed in a sentence like

(13) I know that Jane has left.

The presupposition of (12) could be represented as

(12) Pres (KNOW$_S$ (p)) Ass (neg$_S$ ... (p))

As the asserted attitude takes a modality as its argument, it cannot be represented with the means developed so far. The dots indicate the missing modal part of the argument.[10]

1.4 Rules specifying the bearer of an attitude

The distinction between attitudes bound by the AM and attitudes presupposed carries over to sentences with a non-assertive AM. In saying that the negative attitude expressed by (10) is bound to the non-assertive mood of the sentence, and that the positive attitude expressed by (10) is presupposed, we can generalize on the way in which the bearer of an attitude is specified:

A 1 The attitude bound to the assertive AM is attributed to the speaker.

A 2 The attitude bound to the non-assertive AM is attributed neither to the speaker nor to anyone else. (The speaker's relation to it is indifferent.)

A 3 The attitude presupposed is attributed to the speaker in the context of the non-assertive AM.

A 4 The attitude presupposed is attributed to someone else in the context of the assertive AM (if it is alternative to the attitude asserted by the speaker).

A 1 covers the explicit attitude of all declarative sentences: (2), (5), (6), (11), (12); A 2 the explicit attitudes of the interrogatives (9) and (10); A 3 the additional attitude expressed in (10); A 4 the additional attitude expressed in (11).

((13) does not present an alternative attitude to the one bound by the assertive AM insofar as the argument of the asserted attitude is a modality leaving it open whether p is true or not true.)

A 1—4 cover also all declarative and interrogative attitudinal sentences, determining the bearer of the attitudes bound by their AM.

1.5 The case of a semantic difference between the syntactic and the phonological means determining AM

None of the rules introduced so far covers a sentence like

(14) Jane has left?

which obviously expresses a negative attitude of the speaker in addition to the non-asserted positive attitude:

(14) Pres (neg_s (p)) non-Ass (pos_v (p))

(''v'' represents the unspecified bearer of the positive attitude, implying the speaker's indifference.)

The syntactically determined SM of (14) is clearly declarative. Yet it is not interpreted as an assertive AM, as in the syntactically analogous example (6), but as a non-assertive AM. The only difference between (6) and (14) lies in their punctuation, i.e. fullstop in (6) and question-mark in (14). A fullstop is generally considered to indicate a statement, a question-mark a question. Although this would correctly apply also to (14) it does not allow to distinguish between (14) and (9) (Has Jane left?).

As I see it, there are two means to determine the AM of a sentence, i.e. its interpretation as a statement or a question. There are the syntactic means: word-order and the like (sentence mood), and there are the phonological means: certain intonational patterns which are represented by punctuation in spelling. Ignoring the difference between the intonational patterns of ''yes-or-no'' questions and ''wh-''questions, one could speak of an assertive intonation (being typical of statements) and an interrogative intonation (i.e. one for the ''yes-no'' question, another one for the ''wh''-question). In (6) and (9) the syntactic and phonological means coincide in their meanings, in (14) they differ.

The interpretation of (14) shows that the case in which the syntactic and phonological means of the AM differ causes a) the syntactically determined AM to be reinterpreted in favour of the phonologically determined AM and b) an alternative attitude of the speaker to be added to the meaning of the sentence. The latter can also be seen as a result of the reinterpreted AM, which in its assertive form binds a speaker's attitude.

The interpretation of the syntactic means in (14) is in its result similar to that of (6), i.e. the attitude asserted is the speaker's attitude. The phonological means of (14) cause the assertive AM to be reinterpreted as non-assertive, lowering at the same time the degree of the speaker's commitment towards A from an asserted attitude to a presupposed one, and turning the attitude attributed to the speaker into its alternative.

There are certain conditions under which the last change may be prevented, e.g. a question tag:

(15) Jane has left, hasn't she?

or a particle like ''doch'' in German:

(16) Jane ist doch abgereist?

The speaker's attitude presupposed in (15) and (16) is positive in accordance with the attitudinal meaning of the tag and of ''doch''.[11]

The reinterpretation can also take place in the other direction, i.e. from a non-assertive AM to an assertive AM. A typical example of this is an exclamation like

(17) Is that beautiful!

With the syntactic means determining a non-assertive AM, the phonological means an assertive AM—besides an emphatic interpretation.

That the emphatic interpretation is an extra element can be seen in sentences like

(18) Is that beautiful?!

where the intonation is emphatic but non-assertive. In (17) the speaker asserts the positive attitude expressed by the positive form of the sentence, in (18) he does not assert it. In both sentences the emphatic intonation introduces an alternative attitude which is in the context of the non-assertive AM attributed to the speaker (see A 3), otherwise to anybody else who might disagree with him (a variation of A 4).

(17) Pres (neg $_{v=\text{not-s}}$ (p)) Ass (pos$_s$ (p))

(with ''v = not-s'' indicating that the speaker does not presuppose anybody in particular, but, in no case, holds the view himself.)

(18) Pres (neg_S (p)) non-Ass (pos_S (p))

The alternative attitude presupposed by the emphatic intonation in (17) coincides with the alternative attitude presupposed by the reinterpretation of the AM. Although the analogy between (14) and (17) concerning the alternative attitude presupposed by the reinterpreted AM is veiled by the attitude presupposed by the emphatic intonation, there is no reason to assume any other difference between (14) and (17) than the one due to the final assertiveness of (14) as opposed to the final non-assertiveness of (17).

1.6 Rules determining the AM of a sentence

What has been said so far about the means determining the AM of a sentence can be generalized in

AM 1 The AM of a sentence is determined by syntactic means (sentence mood) and by phonological means (sentence intonation.)

AM 2 If there is a correspondence between sentence mood and sentence intonation the declarative determines the assertive mood, the interrogative the non-assertive mood of the sentence.

AM 3 If sentence mood and sentence intonation do not correspond, the AM determined by sentence mood is reinterpreted in accordance with sentence intonation.

AM 4 In the case of AM 3, the attitudinal meaning of a sentence is extended by a presupposed attitude alternative to the one bound by the AM.

2. Complex sentences

The following shall spell out the analogies and differences between the epistemic meaning of simple statements and questions and that of complex attitudinal sentences whose object clause is interpreted to a certain extent analogously to a statement or to a question.

2.1 The speaker's attitude

I have already pointed out that a sentence like

(3) Pat thinks that Jane has left.

expresses not only Pat's attitude towards the propositional meaning of the sub-clause but also the speaker's attitude towards the propositional meaning of the whole sentence, i.e. the attitudinal state-of-affairs attributed to Pat. In (3) the speaker's attitude is positive. In

(8) Pat thinks probably that Jane has left.

it is positive but uncertain. The declarative SM determines an assertive AM in either case. The speaker asserts the positive attitude in (3) and the attitude specified as PROB in (8):

(3) Ass (pos_S (p)) (8) Ass ($PROB_S$ (p))

Exchanging the declarative sentence mood in (3) for the interrogative one, we get

(19) Does Pat think that Jane has left?

a case in which the positive attitude towards Pat's attitudinal state-of-affairs is not asserted.

Exchanging the positive sentence form in (3) for the negative one, we get

(20) Pat does not think that Jane has left.

a negative attitude towards Pat's attitudinal state-of-affairs asserted by the speaker.

Exchanging the positive sentence form in (19) for the negative one, we get

(21) Doesn't Pat think that Jane has left?

a negative attitude towards Pat's attitudinal state-of-affairs which is not asserted by the speaker, who holds a positive view himself:

(20) Ass (neg_S (p))

(21) not-Ass (neg_V (p)) Pres (pos_S (p))

We can also combine the declarative SM with an interrogative intonation and get

(22) Pat thinks that Jane has left?

where the attitudes expressed towards Pat's attitudinal state-of-affairs are distributed exactly opposite to (21). The positive attitude is the one bound by the non-assertive AM, the speaker himself holds a negative view:

(22) non-Ass (pos_V (p)) Pres (neg_S (p))

2.2 The "propositional speaker's" attitude

The attitude towards the propositional meaning of the sub-clause has in all these cases been specified by "think that" and attributed to "Pat", the person referred to by the grammatical subject of the epistemic verb. Quite a lot of epistemic verbs or verbal expressions follow the pattern of "think". Yet there are also verbs like "wonder", which have to be used in a different way.

A sentence like

(23) Pat wonders whether Jane has left.

differs from a sentence like (3) not only in regard to Pat's attitude being specified as "wonder". The proposition expressed by the attitudinal sentence (3) identifies a state-of-affairs in which Pat's attitude towards the truth of Jane's having left is assertive. (As the person referred to by the grammatical subject of the attitudinal sentence does not himself assert the attitude attributed to him with this sentence, I will speak of an assertive attitude, vs. the asserted attitude attributed to the speaker by the AM of a sentence.)

The proposition expressed by (23) identifies a state-of-affairs in which Pat's attitude towards the truth of Jane's having left is non-assertive.

(3) and (23) determine not only Pat's attitude towards the propositional meaning of the sub-clause, they determine also an AM binding this attitude. The AM binding Pat's attitude in (3) is assertive. The AM binding it in (23) is non-assertive.

As the different attitudinal moods go with the different verbs, I will classify verbs like "think" as "assertive predicates" and verbs like "wonder" as "non-assertive predicates". "Think" expresses a specific epistemic attitude (basically positive, yet hypothetical) and an assertive AM, in short: the assertive attitude THINK. (As I do not attempt to analyze the attitude expressed any further, I will simply use capital letters to symbolize the difference between the words, e.g. ''think'' and the attitudes expressed, e.g. THINK.)

''Wonder'' expresses a positive attitude and a non-assertive AM, in short: a non-assertive positive attitude.[12]

If an AM is expressed by the predicate of an attitudinal sentence, I will symbolize the difference by a subscript: AM_p. Whereas the AM of an independent sentence, i.e. its linguistic status as a question or a statement, is determined by syntactic and phonological means, the AM_p of an attitudinal sentence, i.e. the linguistic status of its sub-clause as an indirect question or an 'indirect statement', is determined by lexical means.

As the attitude towards the propositional meaning of the sub-clause is always attributed to the person referred to by the grammatical subject of the attitudinal sentence, I will call the bearer of this attitude the ''propositional speaker'' (abbreviated as ''ps''). ''Speaker'' should not be taken literally here as verbs of thinking identify attitudinal state-of-affairs without any reference to their verbalization. It is merely meant to shorten the awkward ''attitude of the propositional bearer of attitude''.

The propositional speaker may be anybody, including the speaker of the attitudinal sentence (cf. (1)).[13]

The propositional speaker's attitude in (3) and (8) is specifed by ''think''. It is attributed to the person referred to as ''Pat''. The propositional argument in (3) can now be replaced by the assertive attitude of Pat towards the propositional meaning of the sub-clause (hence ''p_{sub}''):

(3) $Ass\ (pos_s\ (Ass_p\ (THINK_{ps}\ (p_{sub}))))$

Analogously, (23) could be represented as

(23) $Ass\ (pos_s\ (non\text{-}Ass_p\ (pos_{ps}\ (p_{sub}))))$

Impersonal subjects are interpreted as identical in reference with ''I'' if the AM is assertive. In a sentence like

(24) It is not certain that Jane has left.

it is the speaker who holds the negative attitude towards the attitudinal state-of-affairs as well as the propositional speaker's attitude specified as CERTAIN:

(24) Ass $(neg_s(Ass_p\ (CERTAIN_{ps=s}\ (p_{sub}))))$

However, if the AM_p is non-assertive the propositional speaker's attitude is attributed to nobody in particular (as the speaker's relationship to the attitude bound by the non-assertive AM is indifferent):

(25) Is it certain that Jane has left?

non-Ass $(pos_v\ (Ass_p\ (CERTAIN_{ps=v}\ (p_{sub}))))$

Impersonal structures may serve to express also a non-assertive AM_p:

(26) It is questionable whether Jane has left.

$Ass(pos_s\ (non\text{-}Ass_p\ (pos_{ps=s}\ (p_{sub}))))$

with "questionable" determining the propositional speaker's attitude as positive and non-assertive, and the assertive AM attributing it to the speaker.

2.3 Propositional and non-propositional epistemic means

Before continuing with the semantic analysis of attitudinal sentences, I want to turn to a difference between the epistemic meaning of simple and complex (attitudinal) sentences which they exhibit only under certain conditions. As sentences like

(27) Is it probable that Jane has left?
and
(28) It is not probable that Jane has left.

show, the attitude PROB may appear in the argument of a non-asserted positive attitude (27), and in that of an asserted negative attitude (28). Yet this does not apply to PROB when used in a simple sentence; neither

(29) *Has Jane probably left?
or
(30) *Jane has not probably left.

are considered well-formed.

The difference extends to some other classes of context; cf.

(31) *Jane has indeed probably left.

(32) *Jane has p r o b a b l y left.[14]

(33) It is indeed probable that Jane has left.

(34) It is p r o b a b l e that Jane has left.

As I have shown elsewhere (DOHERTY, 80), the contextual restrictions underlying the deviancy of (29)—(32) can be generalized in form of a selection rule concerning all opaque epistemic attitudes (attitudes by which the speaker can assert the truth of p only to a certain extent)—provided they are not expressed by the epistemic means of attitudinal sentences:

SR 1 Opaque attitudes may not form the argument of any other epistemic attitudes.

whether the latter are explicitly expressed as in (30) and (31), or merely implied as in (29) and (32), which are both related to an epistemic attitude alternative to the one they specify explicitly).

As (27) and (28), (33) and (34) show, SR 1 does not apply if the means specifying the opaque attitude is part of an attitudinal sentence, where it is itself part of a propositional meaning and therefore part of the natural argument of attitudes. The difference in the contextual properties of opaque attitudes in simple sentences as opposed to complex (attitudinal) sentences cannot be explained if one considers attitudes generally as operators mapping propositions onto propositions—notwithstanding the difference in the formal means which serve to express them. Although it has become a generally accepted custom to identify the entire meaning of a sentence with a proposition (determining the conditions for its truth value), the difference in the contextual properties of opaque attitudes in simple and complex (attitudinal) sentences suggests that the epistemic attitude which is expressed through a sentence adverb is itself not part of another proposition (which could, in turn, become the argument of another attitude). However much debatable this may be, I propose to distinguish epistemic means into those which identify attitudinal states-of-affairs, placing an attitude within a propositional structure (i.e. attitudinal sentences) and those which identify attitudes non-propositionally (i.e. sentence adverbs and the like). The former shall be ''propositional attitudinal means'' expressing attitudes propositionally, the latter ''non-propositional attitudinal means'' expressing attitudes non-propositionally.

Now we can say that SR 1 applies to non-propositional opaque attitudinal means but not to propositional ones.

2.4 Primary and secondary propositional means

The propositional speaker's attitude is directed towards the truth of p_{sub}. In all the examples used so far the propositional speaker considers p to be true. In

(35) Pat thinks that Jane has not left.

the propositional speaker, Pat, considers p_{sub} not to be true.
In

(36) Pat thinks that Jane has probably left.

Pat considers p_{sub} to be probably true.

A comparison of (3), (35) and (36) shows that the argument of THINK contains more than the propositional meaning of the subclause. It contains also an epistemic meaning directed towards p_{sub}, determined in (3) as a positive attitude, in (35) as a negative attitude, in (36) as a positive, yet uncertain attitude specified as PROB.

Concerning the attitudes expressed towards the proposition ''Jane has left'', the sub-clauses of the attitudinal sentences (3), (35) and (36) share their meaning with the independent sentences (6), (5) and (2).

They differ from the independent sentences in regard to the person specified as the bearer of the attitude (i.e. ps or s).

We can now extend the statement that any independent sentence contains a propositional meaning and an attitude to sub-clauses of attitudinal sentences.[15]

If the non-propositionally expressed attitude is part of an independent sentence, it is directly bound to the AM of the sentence; if it is part of a sub-clause of an attitudinal sentence, it is itself in the argument of the propositionally expressed attitude, which is in turn bound to the AM_p. Ignoring the difference between the propositional and the non-propositional expression of the attitude specified as PROB, (36) could be paraphrased as

(37) Pat thinks that it is probable that Jane has left.

with (37) separating the attitudinal and the propositional part of the argument of THINK into two sub-clauses.

(37) expresses the attitude PROB propositionally, (36) expresses it non-propositionally. However, as an epistemic attitude cannot but be directed towards a proposition, yet THINK is directed towards PROB in (37), I will assume that the attitude PROB is also in (36) part of a propositional structure, comparable to the one of (37).

It is, of course, not the adverb itself that accounts for the analogy in the interpretation of (36) and (37). Adverbs can only be used as non-propositional means, in contrast to adjectives, which may also be used propositionally (see (37)). The adverb itself is in (36) just as non-propositional as in (2). It is the attitudinal sentence which provides the non-propositional attitudinal means in its argument with a propositional-like quality.

To distinguish between an expression which is propositional due to its own linguistic nature and an expression which acquires its propositional quality from a context with a ''propositionalising'' effect, I will call the latter a ''secondary propositional expression'' as opposed to a ''primary propositional expression''. The analogy between (29) and (28), i.e. between a primary propositional expression (''it is probable'') and a secondary propositional expression (''probably'') in the sub-clause of a propositionalising attitudinal sentence, is limited. The secondary propositional expression is subject to exactly the same restrictions as the non-propositional one, i.e. to SR 1 (which does not apply to the primary propositional expression); cf.

(38) *Pat thinks that Jane has not probably left.

(39) Pat thinks that it is not probable that Jane has left.

(40) *Pat wonders whether Jane has probably left.

(41) Pat wonders whether it is probable that Jane has left.

The similarities between (38) and (40), (30) and (29) on the one hand and (39) and (41), (28) and (27) on the other show that the propositionalising effect of attitudinal sentences does not minimize the basic differences between expressions which are propositional and expressions which are non-propositional by their own nature.

The propositionalising effect of an attitudinal sentence shall be put down as:

AS 1. An attitudinal sentence propositionalises the non-propositional expression from its sub-clause into a secondary propositional expression by introducing an attitudinal variable x (with x being some attitude towards p_{sub} to be specified by the meaning of the attitudinal expression from the clause, ''a_{sub}'', as ''A_{sub}''.

I will represent the general form of the argument of the propositional speaker's attitude expressed by the epistemic predicate of an attitudinal sentence as:

$(x/x(p_{sub})/ \text{ is } A_{sub})$

read the expression in slanted lines as ''x is an attitude towards p_{sub}'').

The meaning of (36) can now be represented as:

(36) $Ass(pos_s (Ass_p (THINK_{ps} (x/x(p_{sub})/ \text{ is PROB}))))$

i.e. the speaker asserts a positive attitude towards Pat's assertive thinking that p_{sub} is probable.

The meanings of (3) and (35) are similar to (36) except that PROB is replaced by positive resp. negative. The meaning of

(42) It is probable that Jane has left.

contains a propositionally expressed attitude directed towards the positive attitude determined by the positive sentence form of the sub-clause:

(42) $Ass(pos_s\ (Ass_p\ (PROB_{ps=s}\ (x/x(p_{sub})/$ is positive))))

In (37) the same meaning is expressed by the two sub-clauses, sub and sub[1]:

(37) $Ass(pos_s\ (Ass_p\ (THINK_{ps}\ (Ass_{p_{sub}}(PROB_{ps_{sub}=s}$ $(x/x(p_{sub},)/$ is positive))))))

2.5 Propositional speaker's attitude modified by speaker's attitude

In a sentence like (3) (Pat thinks that Jane has left.) the propositional speaker's attitude is determined by the integration of the meanings of ''think'' and the positive form of the sub-clause; in a sentence like (35) (Pat thinks that Jane has not left.) the propositional speaker's attitude is determined by ''think'' and the negative form of the sub-clause.

However, in a sentence like (20) (Pat does not think that Jane has left.) the propositional speaker's attitude is not only determined by ''think'' and the positive form of the sub-clause but also by the negation of ''think'', which determines the speaker's attitude in the first place (see 2.2):

(20) $Ass(neg_s\ (Ass_p\ (THINK_{ps}\ (x/x(p_{sub})/$ is positive))))

Whereas the negation in (35) concerns the attitude in the argument of Pat's thinking, the negation in (20) concerns Pat's thinking itself. In (35) it is Pat who holds a negative view as to Jane's having left, in (20) it is the speaker who holds a negative view as to Pat's thinking that Jane has left. Yet, the difference seems only a minor one, still more so if one considers analogous sentences in which the propositional speaker is identical with the speaker of the attitudinal sentence:

(43) I think that Jane has not left.

(44) I don't think that Jane has left.

The similarity is underlined by the fact that adverbs like ''probably'' which may not be negated are not much better in the sub-clause of a negated attitudinal sentence; cf (38) with

(45) *I think that Jane has not probably left.

(46) *I don't think that Jane has probably left.[16]

Logically seen, it cannot be the same if the propositional speaker holds the assertive view that the state-of-affairs identified by p_{sub} does not exist, or if the speaker holds the view that the attitudinal state-of-affairs (i.e. the propositional speaker's assertive attitude that p_{sub} is true) does not exist. Although the latter must be true in the case in which the propositional speaker holds the view that p_{sub} is not true (when he cannot but exclude the view that p_{sub} is true), it would also have to be true when the propositional speaker has an indifferent view as to whether p_{sub} is true or not. Yet, due to the assertiveness of ''think that'', neither (20) nor (44) can be interpreted as expressing a non-assertive view of the propositional speaker. The propositional speaker may think that Jane has not left or he may think something else—he cannot think that Jane has left, and he cannot be indifferent concerning the truth of p_{sub}, either. If he does not hold a negative view towards p_{sub} directly, he cannot but hold it per implication.

(35) and (43) identify the same attitudinal state-of-affairs explicitly that (28) and (44) identify implicitly.

However, whether the speaker's negative attitude towards p implies the propositional speaker's negative attitude towards p_{sub} depends on the AM and the epistemic verb of the attitudinal sentence. Since its negated attitude is not asserted by the speaker, the question

(21) Doesn't Pat think that Jane has left?

does not imply a negative attitude of Pat. On the contrary, the speaker himself presupposes a positive attitude towards p, i.e. Pat's attitude being positive:

(21) Pres (pos_s (Ass_p ($THINK_{ps}$ (x/x (p_{sub})/ is positive))))
non-Ass (neg_v (Ass_p($THINK_{ps}$ (x/x (p_{sub})/ is positive))))

Similarly, a statement with an interrogative intonation presupposes a negative attitude of the speaker towards p, implying a negative attitude of the propositional speaker towards p_{sub} :

(22) Pat thinks that Jane has left?

(22) Pres (neg_s (Ass_p ($THINK_{ps}$ (x/x(p_{sub})/ is positive))))
non-Ass (pos_v (Ass_p($THINK_{ps}$ (x/x (p_{sub})/ is positive))))

The analogy between the speaker's attitude and the propositional speaker's attitude is transferred into the attitudinal meaning presupposed by a negated question or a reinterpreted statement. The positive question expressing the speaker's indifference towards p does not imply anything about the propositional speaker's attitude:

(10) Does Pat think that Jane has left?

(47) Does Pat think that Jane has not left?

2.6 Attitudinal sentences with ''know''

Sentences like

(48) Pat knows that Jane has not left.

(49) Pat does not know that Jane has left.

where ''think'' is replaced by ''know'' differ even more. The speaker's negative attitude towards p does not carry over to the propositional speaker's attitude at all. Moreover, unlike (43) and (44), (48) and (49) express alternative states-of-affairs: in (48) Jane has not left and Pat knows this, in (49) Jane has left and Pat does not know this.

In either sentence it is the speaker who knows the truth about p_{sub}. This difference is not only due to the epistemic verb but also to ''that''. Like some other verbs ''know'' may be used as an assertive or a non-assertive predicate (seen from the speaker's point-of-view). In

(50) Pat knows whether Jane has left.

the positive attitude of the sub-clause is not asserted although Pat d o e s have an assertive view concerning the truth of p_{sub}. He either knows that Jane has left or he knows that Jane has not left. In

(51) Pat does not know whether Jane has left.

Pat does not know whether p_{sub} is true or not. Whether the speaker knows the truth about p_{sub} or not is left open in either case.[17]

''Know that'' determines the speaker's assertive attitude and ''know whether'' determines the speaker's non-assertive attitude towards p_{sub};[18] either form determines the propositional speaker's attitude towards p_{sub} depending, as in all attitudinal sentences, on the positive or negative attitude of the speaker (towards p).

However, as any attitudinal state-of-affairs cannot but be presented from the speaker's point-of-view, the outcome is uneven. Firstly, "know that" and "know whether" determine the propositional speaker's assertive attitude only in the context of an assertive AM. Unlike (50), neither

(52) Does Pat know whether Jane has left?
or
(53) Does Pat know that Jane has left?

express an assertive attitude of the propositional speaker towards p_{sub}. On the other hand, ''know that'' determines the speaker's attitude towards$_{sub}$ also in the context of a non-assertive AM. In regard to the speaker's attitude towards p_{sub} the question

(54) Does Pat know that Jane has not left?

has the same meaning as (48), notwithstanding their differences, concerning the assertiveness or non-assertiveness of the speaker's attitude towards p.

We can say that ''know that'' presupposes an assertive attitude of the speaker towards p_{sub}. Secondly, the cases determining the speaker's assertive attitude towards p_{sub} specify that attitude by ''know'' and the attitudinal expression of the sub-clause, the case determining the propositional speaker's assertive attitude towards p_{sub} leaves that attitude unspecified (besides saying that the propositional speaker knows the truth about p_{sub}). (49) determines the speaker's attitude towards p_{sub} by ''know'' and the positive form of the sub-clause:

Pres (KNOW$_s$ (x/x(p_{sub})/ is positive))))
Ass (neg$_s$ (Ass$_p$ (KNOW$_{ps}$ (x/x(p_{sub})/ is positive))))

(48) and (54) determine the speaker's attitude towards p_{sub} by ''know'' and the negative form of the sub-clause:

(54) Pres (KNOW$_s$ (x/x (p_{sub})/ is negative))
non-Ass (pos$_v$ (Ass$_p$ (KNOW$_{ps}$ (x/x (p_{sub})/ is negative))))

(55) Pat does not know that Jane will probably leave.

determines the speaker's attitude towards p_{sub} by ''know'' and ''probably'':

Pres (KNOW$_s$ (x/x (p_{sub})/ is PROB))
Ass (neg$_s$ (Ass$_p$ (KNOW$_{ps}$ (x/x (p_{sub})/ is PROB))))[19]

The propositional speaker's attitude towards p_{sub} is identical to the speaker's attitude towards p_{sub} only if the speaker asserts a positive attitude towards p (as in (48)). (50) is the case in which only the propositional speaker knows the truth about p_{sub}. The propositional speaker's attitude is specified by ''know'' but not by the attitudinal expression of the sub-clause. I will represent the open choice between the positive attitude expressed and its alternative by KNOW-WH-:

(50) Ass (pos$_S$ (Ass$_P$ KNOW-WH-$_{ps}$ (x/x (p_{sub})/ is positive))))

where KNOW-WH- Is meant to extend the attitude towards p $_{sub}$ given by its alternative, i.e. by (x/x(p_{sub})/ is negative).

2.7 Summarizing attitudinal sentences

What has been said about attitudes as expressed by attitudinal sentences can be summarized as follows:

Attitudinal sentences contain epistemic means which express attitudes propositionally and epistemic means which express attitudes non-propositionally. They determine the AM binding the speaker's attitude towards the propositionally expressed attitudinal state-of-affairs according to the rules specified in AM 1—Am 4.

Attitudinal sentences specify the speaker's attitude towards p by the attitudinal expression dominating the predicate of the matrix sentence. They determine the propositional speaker's attitude by a combination of linguistic means: first of all, it is the syntactic predicate of the matrix sentence which determines the propositional speaker's attitude (in relation to the attitude towards p_{sub} specified according to AS 1), as well as the AM_p binding it.

However, the propositional speaker's attitude towards p_{sub} does not only depend on the verb of the attitudinal sentence and the attitudinal expression of the sub-clause but also on the speaker's attitude towards p. With verbs like ''think'', e.g. the attitude determined by the expression of the sub-clause is changed into its alternative if the speaker's attitude towards p (whether asserted or presupposed) is negative.

Verbs like ''know'' presuppose the attitude KNOW in relation to the attitude towards p_{sub} (as determined by the expression of the sub-clause) for the speaker himself if followed by ''that''; if followed by ''whether'', they relate the propositional speaker's attitude to the attitude towards p_{sub} (as expressed by the attitudinal means of the sub-clause) or its alternative.

3. Some more technical deliberations and once more the most important claims about the epistemic meaning distinguishing questions and statements

Although the paper does not make any explicit claim on the ways in which the epistemic meaning is to be mapped onto the forms expressing it, some general principles follow from what has been said about the semantic structure and the epistemic means determining its various elements.

Assuming an interpretative position, AM 1—4 specify the conditions correlating the relevant syntactic and phonological means of a sentence, i.e. sentence mood and sentence intonation to AM. A 1—4 specify the conditions determining the bearer of an attitude; as they depend on the AM of a sentence they might as well be thought of as integrating A and AM.

Provided the syntactic representation of the surface structure of an independent sentence contains a node specifying its SM (and a node for epistemic means specifying the attitude bound by it, as e.g. sentence adverb (SA), including sentence negation and a zero-form spelled out as a positive attitude in the absence of any other epistemic means), it seems to me one could do without whatever deep structure there might otherwise be necessary. The information needed: what sort of sentence (dependent or independent, and, if the former, what class of clause), what sort of adverb and in what syntactic relation to which other epistemic means within the same clause and beyond it, etc. could all be given by the lexico-syntactic characteristics of the surface structure (and the phonological representation added to it).

The interpreting rules could work their way up, starting from the syntactically lowest epistemic means (e.g. the right-most adverb with a semantic property ''epistemic'') in the lowest clause.[20] The interpreting process would have to be accompanied by an evaluating process which guarantees that any overt or implied contradictions in the epistemic meaning of a sentence are identified through specific selection rules (as e.g. SR 1) or via general logical relations (as e.g. the mutual exclusion of antonymous semantic elements), marking the respective combinations of epistemic means as deviant.

As a more elaborate account of the interpreting and evaluating processes concerning the specific semantic and syntactic properties of epistemic means will have to take into consideration a lot more data than could be presented within this paper, I will contend myself with these sketchy remarks on the intricate problem of relating sentence structure and sentence meaning in detail. Whatever specific technical procedures we may develop to correlate the epistemic meaning of a sentence to the means constituting it, they will have to meet the most important claims of this paper:

—Any independent sentence expresses with its sentence mood and the corresponding sentence intonation an attitudinal mood, which binds the attitude expressed explicitly. Statements are characterized by the assertive attitudinal mood, which commits the speaker to asserting with the sentence the attitude bound by the attitudinal mood; questions are characterized by the non-assertive attitudinal mood, which commits the speaker to an indifferent position regarding this attitude.

—The attitudinal mood of a sentence decides upon the bearer of any attitude expressed—whether the attitude is bound or not bound by the attitudinal mood.

—Attitudinal sentences are, in addition to the above, characterized by a propositional attitudinal expression, specifying (the propositional speaker's attitude towards p_{sub} and) an assertive or non-assertive attitudinal mood: AM_p (binding it).

Humboldt Universität
Sektion Anglistik-Amerikanistik

Notes

[1] The meaning of sentences like (5) and (6) is generally considered to be nothing but a proposition (in the case of (6) a negated proposition). Although sentences like (5) and (6)—if used in sub-clauses like (i) If Jane has left...
may indeed express nothing but a proposition, they will always express a proposition and an attitude towards it if used independently.

[2] R. Stalnaker (1974), e.g., says that the linguistic means of a sentence determine its meaning, which together with the context in which the sentence is used determines a proposition. The proposition in its turn determines together with a possible world a truth value.

[3] Any epistemic attitude will in some way or other be determined either as someone's positive or someone's negative attitude concerning the truth of p. To speak of someone's attitude towards p as expressed by certain linguistic means does, of course, not necessarily mean that the person referred to really h a s the attitude. It merely says that the linguistic means attribute the attitude to that person whether the speaker uses them sincerely and adequately or not.

[4] Imperatives may be considered an additional type of SM. However, they differ from declarative sentences only through the form of their verb and a special form of reduction. Otherwise there is not much more of a difference between sentences like
(i) Report to the headmaster at once!
and
(ii) The teacher wants that you report to the headmaster at once.
than between sentences like (3) and (6). Even if one holds on to the traditional differentiation and considers an imperative as a sentence mood of its own, one must concede that the intentional attitude in (i) is specified as the speaker's attitude in the same way as the epistemic attitude in (6) is specified as the speaker's attitude. (The intentional attitude in (ii) is attributed to the person referred to by the grammatical subject of ''want'' just as the epistemic attitude in (3) is attributed to the person referred to by the grammatical subject of ''think''.) Despite their difference concerning the attitude expressed, declaratives and imperatives can be classed together and opposed to interrogatives, which do not attribute the attitude expressed to the speaker.

[5] Although ''assertion'' may be considered a speech-act, I do not want to elaborate on any performative aspect attitudinal expressions may have. The assertion or non-assertion of an attitude is to be understood merely as an epistemic relationship determining the speaker's position in regard to A(p).

[6] As the imperative does not restrict the speaker's commitment towards the intentional attitude expressed, it can be grouped together with the declarative as a sentence mood determining an assertive attitudinal mood.

[7] ''Not-s'' covers quite a variety of different cases including those in which the speaker himself has an alternative attitude to the one he has at the time in which he utters the sentence. It may also apply to a case in which the speaker rejects an alternative view not attibuted to anyone in particular (see example (18)).

[8] The claim that only one attitude may be asserted is not meant to exclude cases in which the attitude asserted is made up of a combination of the meaning of several attitudinal means as e.g. in
(i) Jane has probably r e a l l y left.

[9] The relation between Pres(KNOW(p)) and Pres(p) is that of an implication as KNOW(p) implies p (but p does not imply KNOW(p).

[10] The meaning of any complex expression is made up from the meanings of the expressions constituting it, integrated according to the syntactic relations the individual expressions have to each other. The syntactic relations between attitudinal expressions corresponds in most cases to that of their linear order whithin a sentence; e.g. the syntactic relation between the two adverbs in
(i) Jane has probably r e a l l y left.
is: probably(really(p)).
[11] If attitudes are expressed not by means of their own but by a certain constellation of means (which otherwise do not express these attitudes), they are expressed by a marked use of those means. The use of a question with a negation or of a declarative sentence with an interrogative intonational pattern can be considered such cases as the alternative attitude presupposed by them is not expressed by any of the means outside of those constellations. Attitudes expressed by the marked use of linguistic means are even more context dependent than any other attitudes. As demonstrated by (16) and (17) they may disappear altogether if the interpretation of the context determines anything contrary to them.
[12] There are also epistemic verbs expressing negative attitudes as e.g. ''deny''. In
(i) Pat denies that Jane has left
the propositional speaker's attitude is negative. The meaning of epistemic verbs may even contain presupposed attitudes as e.g. ''doubt''. In
(ii) Pat doubts whether Jane has left. Pat's negative attitude is clearly presupposed and not bound by the non-assertive AM_p. There is a correspondence between the assertiveness or non-assertiveness of an epistemic predicate and the connector ''that'' or ''whether'', with ''that'' following the assertive and ''whether '' following the non-assertive predicate. As to the epistemic predicates as ''know'' and ''say'' which may be followed by either connector compare 2.6.
[13] Speech-act theoreticians as J. R. Searle (1969) concentrate on the case in which the propositional speaker is identical with the speaker, i.e. on the performative use of ''illocutionary force indicating devices''. I do, however, not see any reason for treating these cases separately as they share the characteristics of a l l attitudinal sentences. Peculiarities as e.g. the unusual character of a question like
(i) Do I think that Jane has left?
rest on criteria taken from extra-linguistic knowledge.
[14] The evaluation may not be shared by all speakers of English.
[15] There are some more classes of sub-clauses which express an attitude towards their propositional meaning as e.g. the causal clause in
(i) We've dropped the plan because it will probably be raining. Unlike an attitudinal sentence (i) does not provide any means comparative to the AM_p of an attitudinal sentence. Nor is the attitude expressed by the sentence adverb of the sub-clause bound by the assertive AM of the whole sentence; cf.
(ii) Have you dropped the plan because it will probably be raining?

Despite the non-assertive AM of the whole sentence, (ii) continues to specify the attitude towards p_{sub} by ''probably'' (which would be excluded if ''probably'' were bound by the non-assertive AM (see (31) above). The attitude expressed by adverbial sub-clauses can only be presupposed as being known by the speaker (cf. (55) below).
[16] There are some more properties of sentences like (46) pointing to the influence of the negation in the matrix sentence on the sub-clause. If a question-tag is used with the sub-clause in (46) it has to be of the form used after negated sentences:
(i) I don't think that Jane has left, has she?

R. Lakoff (1969) tock this to prove her assumption that sentences like (47) were the result of a transformation from (45) to (46) raising the negation from the sub-clause into the matrix-sentence. In my opinion, (45) and (46) are identical in meaning only per implication and cannot be thought of as being transformationally related (provided there are any sentences at all which are transformationally related to each other).

[17] Sentences like

(i) Pat knows where Jane has gone.

are interpreted analogously to sentences with ''know whether'', i.e. only the propositional speaker knows the answer to the element asked about by the question word.

[18] The only exception to this is the case in which the propositional speaker is identical with the speaker:

(i) I know whether Jane has left.

Yet the meaning of (i) is not identical with that of

(ii) I know that Jane has left.

The difference between (i) and (ii) is the same as that between (50) and (48).

[19] In presupposing that the speaker knows the truth about p_{sub} , ''know that'' provides the condition for ''probably'' to be used within the argument of a negated predicate.

[20] As the bearer of an attitude is finally determined only when the phonological information about the AM of a sentence is available, it might be just as good to move from top to bottom, carrying the relevant information about the AM downwards, in some cases even to where the propositional speaker is specified. Consider a sentence like

(i) It is certain that Jane has left?

in which the propositional speaker can be interpreted identical to the speaker provided the AM is assertive. Since it will take a lot more reasoning to opt for an interpreting direction opposite to the generally accepted one, I will for the time being ignore any evidence against the latter.

References

M. Doherty, Grundlagen einer Theorie über sprachliche Ausdrucksmittel epistemischer Einstellungen, (unpublished dissertation B), Berlin 1980.

R. Lakoff, A Syntactic Argument for Negative Transportation, in: Papers from the Fifth Regional Meeting of the Chicago Linguistic Society, 1969, pp. 140—147.

J. R. Searle, Speech Acts, Cambridge 1969.

R. Stalnaker, Pragmatics, in: J. Petöfi, D. Franck (Hrsg.) Präsuppositionen in Philosophie und Linguistik, Frankfurt/M. 1973, pp. 389—408.

Günther Grewendorf

What answers can be given?

Nobody asks – politicians answer.

(0) Introduction[0]

The question in the title is, of course, too general. We can consider answers from different points of view, and thus the above "can" is to be modifed with an "if". The aspect to be dealt with in this study is actually one which, as we should properly expect, is most obvious with respect to the analysis of questions and answers: It is the question of when the answers to questions are acceptable, sensible or proper at least in the sense that the questioner does not have to check up on what question he has actually asked. In this sense, many answers which according to current question theories should be answers, are unfortunately such that they *cannot* be given as answers.

As to the aspect which is of interest here, questions like the one in the title were usually answered with the comment that the questioner must learn from the answer which of the alternatives contained in the question is actually the case. This pairing of the answer concept with the *elimination* of knowledge-desiderata has made it necessary for the analysis of answers to explicate those epistemic concepts by means of which such an analysis was supposed to be undertaken. In part (i) of this study I will therefore discuss the theories of Hintikka/Åqvist, Kaplan and Boër/Lycan, whose epistemic concepts might qualify as a basis for the analysis of answers. It will become apparent that only Boër/Lycan's theory takes into account the aspect of the "teleological relativity" of "knowing who" which is essential for a theory of answers. Although in the following this aspect is illustrated predominantly with examples of who-questions, it should become clear that it can also be shown with other kinds of wh-questions.

It is clear that question theory and answer theory are bound together inseparably. A given answer to the question of what a question is always determines a particular answer to the question of what an answer is. And a given conception of what might qualify as an answer always determines a particular conception of what a question is. In part (ii) I will show by means of my analysis of the question theories of Karttunen, Higgin-

Ferenc Kiefer (ed.), Questions and Answers, 45–84.

botham/May and Boër, the various ways in which conceptions of answers have determined concepts of question semantics. The problem involved here is just that the inconsistency of the "semantic point of view" creates dilemmas for these theories which may lead to the conclusion that the pragmatic aspect of answers has nothing at all or everything to do with question semantics. Since the latter has disastrous results for a question syntax, this alternative is no longer available.

Taking into account the results of part (i) and (ii), part (iii) will attempt to explicate the concept of a pragmatically significant answer on a *pragmatic* level. For this purpose, a concept of informativeness of answers relevant to question theory will be defined with the aid of subjective probability theory. Use will also be made of decision theory in order to be able to reconstruct in part (iv) how a rational and well-meaning answerer makes his choice between the alternatives made available by questions.

(i) Knowing who is who

Let us assume that I ask the question

(1) Who is Mary's seducer?

and I get the answer

(2) Mary's seducer is Mary's seducer.

Undoubtedly, I have been given a *true* answer. But have I been given an answer *at all?* Now, if it is the point of an answer that the questioner can in some sense "do something" with the answers, then it is not at all clear whether (2) actually is an answer. We can say in any case that (2) is certainly not a satisfactory, significant or acceptable answer. Accordingly, one would demand of an adequate question theory that it should not allow answers of type (2) as significant answers. Such a question theory must then, in addition to certain substitution restrictions, include the requirement that answers must be *informative*.

Lennart Åqvist (1975) has developed a question theory according to which questions are analyzed as requests for the elimination of a knowledge-desideratum. Such a deontic/epistemic theory of questions makes possible the integration of this quest for informativeness in the epistemic part of the theory. Thus, if questions are interpreted as requests by the questioner to be provided with certain knowledge, then one can formulate heuristically that precisely those sentenes are permitted as answers which eliminate the knowledge-desideratum expressed in the question. Consequently, Åqvist's basic idea for his explication of the concept of a direct answer is as follows:[1] A sentence S is a direct answer to my question Q, if from the truth of S and from the fact that I know that S is true, the truth of the epistemic statement contained in the formalized question follows. Thereby, however, the problem of the informativeness of answers is shifted to the problem of the truth-conditions for epistemic statements.

Now, what happens in case (1) if we get the answer

(3) Cupido is Mary's seducer.

According to Åqvist, on the basis of this answer the questioner knows that Cupido is Mary's seducer. But does he thereby know *who* Mary's seducer is? That this is not the case is shown as follows: Given that I know that Mary's seducer is a certain Cupido, but do not know who this mysterious Cupido is; given further that I do not know that Mr. Feuerbach is a seducer, but I know who Mr. Feuerbach is (I meet him every morning in the underground and know where he works etc.), however, I do not know that Cupido and Mr. Feuerbach are identical. In this case the inference from

(4) I know that Cupido is a seducer.

to

(5) There is someone of whom I know that he is a seducer.

is not permitted. Necessary for the validity of this inference is the additional premise

(6) I know who Cupido is.

that is, a premise which says that I know the "identity" of the individual designated by "Cupido". Åqvist has thus included such a "I know who ... is" condition in his semantic rules for the existential generalization and universal specification in sentences which contain an epistemic operator.

We are now in a position to say that the only real motivation for Åqvist's use of Hintikka's epistemic logic appears to be that it makes possible, with the help of the formalization of "I know who B is", the expression of the fact *that answers must be informative.* Thereby the problem of the informativeness requirement for answers, the problem of the logical analysis of identification questions, as well as the problem of the semantic rules for existential generalization and universal specification in sentences with an epistemic operator are reduced to the question of the *adequacy of the formalization of utterances of the form* "I know who B is".

As the first modern philosopher (or linguist) Jaakko Hintikka tackled the problem of "knowing who"[2]. In his explication attempt which was taken over by Åqvist, he starts from a critique of Quine's conception according to which epistemic operators are to be regarded as "referentially transparent"[3] if there is quantification into the context of such operators. Since this conception has the unpleasant consequence that

(7) S knows that the dictator of Chile is the dictator of Chile.
(7′) K_s (D=D)

and

(8) The dictator of Chile is Pinochet.
(8′) D=B

entail the statement

(9) S knows that the dictator of Chile is Pinochet.
(9′) K_s(D=B)

and that (9) entails the statement

(10) S knows who the dictator of Chile is.
(10′) $(\exists x)K_s(x=D)$

Hintikka started from a "referentially opaque" interpretation of epistemic operators and demanded for the derivation of (10) the additional premise

(11) S knows who Pinochet is.
(11′) $(\exists x)\ K_s(x=B)$

The question remains when S knows who Pinochet is. If in this case one also wants to block the derivation of (11) from

(12) S knows that Pinochet is identical with himself.
(12′) $K_s(B=B)$

with the demand for a premise analogous to (11), we see that this premise has to be just (11) itself, so that the resulting argument is an excellent case of question-begging.

Hintikka's prescription for this case consists of stipulating that in the case of quantification into epistemic contexts the variables range only over persons known to the epistemic subject. The existential quantifier is now to be read as "There is an x that is known to the epistemic subject S". Now, that an x is known to the epistemic subject S means nothing other than that this epistemic subject S knows who this x is. In accordance with this interpretation of quantification, (11′) would have to be read as "Of some x such that S knows who that x is, S knows that x is B". This means, however, that a formalization of (11) understood in this way would be circular *as an explication* of "knowing who".

It seems to me that the problem is that it is difficult to clarify what the truth-conditions for statements like (11) could look like. What one attempts to formalize with the help of (11′) is itself too much bound to pragmatic factors and not sufficiently explicated for it to become clear what is to be understood by (11′). In this context let us consider, say,

(13) S knows who the painter of the Scuola di San Rocco is.
(14) S knows who the inventor of the lightning conductor is.
(15) S knows who the murderer of B is.

We would certainly consider (13) and (14) to be true already if S could give the names of the appropriate people. But for (15) consider the following case: There are twenty people in a room and S knows that the murderer of B is among them. He even knows his name, but he cannot identify him, because he does not know what he looks like. Would we then consider (15) to be true?

Are statements of the form "S knows who B is" consequently ambiguous? (Could they possibly mean "S can remember B", "S can identify B", "S knows B's name", "S knows what function B has", "S knows what role B plays in field Y" etc.) We will see that this is not the case.

In his later works Hintikka has taken these observations into account and pointed out[4] that in the context of numerous propositional attitudes we have to distinguish between two "methods of individuation": "Individuation by acquaintance" depends upon the perspective from which the person who has the appropriate propositional attitude looks at a situation. In this sense, S knows who B is if he can locate him among his personal acquaintances, for example

(16) I know who B is.—He is the blond man who asked me for a light in the underground yesterday.

In the language of Hintikka's possible-world semantics: In all the epistemic alternatives consistent with my knowledge "B" stands for (the "world line" through) all the individuals who can be located by means of the stated relationship to S. In the case of "descriptive individuation" S can establish by giving the name, profession, age, etc. one definite individual for all the epistemic alternatives consistent with his knowledge.

Since the usual quantification into modal contexts only operates on well-defined individuals, it is clear that the normal "object" interpretation of quantifiers cannot be used for the formalization of examples like (16). Consequently Hintikka introduces "contextual" quantifiers which operate on "perspective objects". The truth-conditions for

(17) $(\exists_k x)\ K_s(x=B)$

are then the same as for

(18) S is acquainted with B.

that means that (17) is true if "S can locate B among his personal acquaintances".

It is clear that the ambiguity of "knowing who" specified with respect to the difference between descriptive and perspective individuation is here only shifted to the ambiguity and context dependence of "S is acquainted with B". Apart from the consequences which this modification of quantification has for the epistemic part of Åqvist's question theory, there appear to be two serious objections. The first one is that in view of the ambiguity and context dependence of "knowing who" Hintikka's "subjectivized ontological interpretation" of quantification has the consequence that we can no longer determine absolutely the range of individual variables in quantifications[5]. When we relativize the ranges of individual variables with respect to specific contexts or situations in various cases we face the consequence that the most important semantic concepts in Åqvist's question logic can no longer be determined precisely in the case of logical quantifiers. The second objection is that if we take this interpretation of quantification as a starting-point, then in a question theory all sentences which express a proposition of the kind

(19) There is an individual X, such that A knows something about X, without "knowing" X

or represent a corresponding question, cannot be formulated in this system.

A final point concerns the "=" in formalizations such as (10′) or (11′). As especially Steven Boër and William Lycan have shown[6], the potential regress of who-questions is *ultimately* not stopped by referential singular terms, but by names and definite descriptions used *attributively*. The reason for this is that only such attributive answers provide the kind of factual information which—if they convey the right kind of information—can stop the regress of "Who is ..." questions which threatens referential answers. If we do not want to devolve the problems of "knowing who" to individuation problems with respect to the range of individual variables, then this decision has the following consequence for a logical analysis of "knowing who": within the corresponding logical forms it isn't identity statements involving referential singular terms that matter but rather subject-predicate constructions, i.e. special kinds of *properties*.

A solution to the problems arising in individuation by acquaintance for an analysis of "knowing who" might be seen in some suggestions of David Kaplan's (1971). From the inadequacy of Quine's conception, Kaplan draws the conclusion that a term in an epistemic context can be exported only when not its denotatum but the term itself *as an object-language expression* stands in a particular relation to the epistemic subject: The terms must be "vivid" for the epistemic subject in the sense that a person exists who the epistemic subject associates as a reference object with the term in use. As an operational criterion for the vividness of a term with respect to an epistemic subject the following has been suggested:[7]

(20) A term t is *vivid* for an epistemic subject ES, when on the basis of his knowledge he is in a position to mark by himself the denotatum of t as t.

In accordance with Kaplan's suggestion an analysis of "S knows who B is" would look like this

(21) $\exists\alpha[R(\alpha, B, S) \wedge K_s \ulcorner\alpha=B\urcorner]$

where "$R(\alpha, B, S)$" is to be read as "term α represents B for S" which in turn should be the case if (i) α denotes B, (ii) α is (sufficiently) vivid, (iii) α is a name of B for S; "$K_s \ulcorner\alpha=B\urcorner$" is to be read as S knows-true a sentence of the form $\ulcorner\alpha=B\urcorner$.

It is clear that this analysis avoids the exportation problems illustrated in (7) through (11). From (21) and "B=C" we can no longer infer

(22) $\exists\alpha[R(\alpha, B, S) \wedge K_s \ulcorner\alpha=C\urcorner]$

However, the central question is: Do we have here an analysis of "knowing who" that is satisfactory for our purposes? We must answer this question negatively for the following reasons. If we examine Kaplan's characterizations of the vividness of a term, for example:

> "The notion of a vivid name is intended to go to the purely internal aspects of individuation"—it is "the conglomeration of images, names, and partial descriptions" to bring somebody before one's mind. "The vivid names 'represent' those persons who fill major roles in that *inner story* which consists of all those sentences which (the epistemic subject) believes."[9]

in spite of these certainly vague characterizations we can definitely say the following: An epistemic subject S already has a vivid name for a person D, when he can personally identify this person. In this case it follows from the fact that S knows-true $\ulcorner\alpha=D\urcorner$, that S knows who D is. But this is an unsatisfactory result. The reason is that the ostensive identifiability of a person D is in no way sufficient for knowing who D is. Let us assume a journalist is supposed to interview Franz Beckenbauer; he has already met him several times at press receptions, he has seen him in films etc., but he does not know that he is one of the best football (soccer) players in the world—does he really know who Franz Beckenbauer is? In other words, the inappropriateness of the concept of a vivid term for the analysis of "knowing who" seems to result from the fact[10] that the concept is relativized to the "inner life" of an epistemic subject and not to the *purposes* or as Boër/Lycan say, to the *projects,* relative to which one can say that someone knows who someone is.[11]

The last mentioned point is central in Boër/Lycan's (1975) analysis of "knowing who". Without taking over their—rather peculiar—formalism, I would like to sketch briefly the basic ideas in their analysis since they have also been essential for my analysis of the concept of a pragmatically significant answer (cf. section (iii) and (iv)) to a large extent.

The fact that neither the knowledge of the name, address, or profession, nor the knowledge of individuating physiognomic details, nor the capacity for ostensive identifiability are *per se* sufficient for knowing who someone is, leads Boër/Lycan to the conclusion that no type of identifying description is autocratically privileged in the sense that with it the potential regress of "Who is ..." questions must stop. Rejecting the amiguity thesis because

a) the ambiguity is difficult to locate,
b) the ambiguity would have monstrous proportions,
c) the ambiguity would infect all cognate locutions such as "remember who", "tell who" etc.,
d) they do not share the conception of verificationism,

they instead postulate a "hidden parameter" which must be represented in the logical analysis of "knowing who" by an expression expressing a purpose or project:

> "relative to a particular project, it is easy to frame a question-and-answer test for whether an *arbitrarily* chosen subject knows who some *N* is. For example, relative to the desirable task of throwing the murderer in jail, we can say in advance what test *anyone* would have to meet in order to be said to know who the murderer is." (p. 313)

In their logical analysis Boër/Lycan return to Kaplan's idea that object-language expressions play a privileged role in the identification of individuals, but this being privileged is now relativized to a teleological parameter, irrespective of the identity of the epistemic subject. In further contrast to Kaplan they take into account the fact that the potentially ad infinitum "Who is ..." question game can ultimately only be stopped by definite descriptions used *attributively*. Their analysis of "S knows who N is" thus looks like this,[12]given a referential reading of N:

(23) $\exists\varphi\exists\beta\,[\text{Imppred}\,(\varphi, N, P) \wedge \triangle(\beta, N) \wedge K_s \ulcorner \varphi!\beta \urcorner]$

and with an attributive reading of N:

(24) $\exists!x\exists\alpha\exists U\exists\varphi\,[Fx \wedge \triangle(\alpha,x) \wedge \triangle(\ulcorner \lambda yUy \urcorner, \lambda yFy) \wedge$
$\wedge\, \text{Imppred}\,(\varphi, x, P) \wedge K_s \ulcorner U\alpha \wedge \varphi!\alpha \urcorner]$

"Imppred (φ, N, P)" is to be read as "is an important predicate of N for purpose P" and the two further conjunction parts in (23) say that S knows-true a superficial sentence one term of which is used to pick out N whatever N's attributes might be, i.e. "$\triangle(\beta, N)$" is supposed to mean "β rigidly designates N"[13,14]; accordingly for the attributive reading of N (as "the F") in (24).

It remains to be clarified what it is supposed to mean that φ is an important predicate of N for purpose P. In order to clarify this, Boër/Lycan proceed from the idea that knowing who someone is relative to a purpose P means being able to locate this person uniquely in a certain frame of reference, i.e. being able "to pick him out *as* a member of some group in which the questioner has a special interest"[15]. However, to be able to place the corresponding person in a certain *category* determined by the particular purpose P (C(P)) is not enough, knowing who someone is relative to P is a matter of knowing which member of that category he is, i.e. one has to indicate the properties of this person that in a certain way are related to the property of membership in that category[16] (so-called C(P)-determinates) and which uniquely individuate him as a member of that category. That φ is an important predicate of N relative to P can now be analyzed in terms of some connection between φ and the C(P)-determinates of N: Such an important predicate is a rigid designator of a property which only N possesses and which is a C(P)-determinate of N.[17] (More exactly: φ is an important predicate of N relative to P iff ⌜λxφx⌝ is a rigid designator of a property which only N possesses and which is a C(P)-determinate of N.)

Boër/Lycan's analysis certainly contains some weaknesses. For example, they say that an important predicate should be an expression of the knower's "language of thought". Although this serves to free his knowledge from the relativization to a single-language competence, it is not really any clerarer than, for example, Kaplan's concept of vividness. A further problem is whether the requirement that a knower of who someone is must be able to locate that person uniquely in a certain frame of reference is too strong, that is, whether indefinite answers to who-questions such as

(25) Who was Aeschylus?
(26) Aeschylus was a famous Greek tragedian.

might also provide the appropriate knowledge. In spite of such objections, it nevertheless seems to me that Boër/Lycan's analysis works out for the first time the *teleological relativity* of knowing who.

Now, if Åqvist's demand is justified that an answer to a question Q should be a just sufficient epistemic condition for the truth of the epistemic statement contained in the formalization of Q, then we could conclude against the background of Boër/Lycan's analysis of knowing who that—with one exception—none of the question theories advanced up to now can claim adequacy, because none of these theories takes into account the teleological relativity of knowing who.[18] However, this conclusion naturally only applies to semantic theories of questions, since fully worked out pragmatic theories do not exist.[19] Two central questions can be raised here: (i) Must, therefore, the teleological relativity of knowing who in *semantic* analyses of questions be taken into account at all? (ii) Does Boër/Lycan's analysis of knowing who—either from a semantic or pragmatic point of view—provide a satisfactory basis for the purposes of a *question* theory, i.e. in particular, for an explication of the answer concept? I intend to deal with the first question next. Let us then consider how the more recent question theories proceed.

(ii) Inconsistencies in the semantic analyses of questions

First, let us consider Karttunen's (1977) extension of PTQ. On semantic grounds Karttunen assigns indirect questions to the category Q=t//t; for question-embedding verbs the category IV/Q is assumed correspondingly. A sentence such as

(27) John knows who runs.

is then derived as follows

(28) John knows who runs (4, (PTQ))

John | knows who runs (Question Embedding Rule)

knows | who runs (WH-Quantification Rule)

who | ?he_1 runs (Proto-Question Rule)

he_1 | runs (4, (PTQ))

with the intensional translation

(29) $know'(^{\wedge}b, \hat{p}[\exists x(^{\vee}p \wedge p = ^{\wedge} run_*'(x))])$

If, then, as Gazdar (1979) postulates, the object of semantics is that aspect of the meaning of sentences which is connected with truth-conditions, Karttunen's semantic analysis of (27) definitely does *not* provide the correct results.[20] If we assume that John, Mary and George are the only people who run, then, in accordance with this analysis, (27) is true if Bill knows about John, Mary, and George that they run. As we have seen in part (i), although this is a necessary condition for the truth of (27), it is, however, in no way sufficient: X can know that an individual has a certain property (e.g. running) without knowing who this individual is, and in this case we would not say that X knows who runs. Knowing who runs means, then, knowing about everyone who runs that he runs, as well as knowing about everyone who runs who he is. As we have seen the latter can only be clarified with reference to pragmatic factors such as purposes or projects; i.e. we have here pragmatic aspects which play a role for the truth-conditions, which, however, were not taken into account in Karttunen's analysis.[21]

At another point in Karttunen's semantics, pragmatic considerations do play a role; however, the consequences of this pragmatic influence are overlooked.

When we examine Karttunen's question theory, it is at first not clear why he derives all questions from so-called *proto-questions* which are constructed from declarative sentences. First it must be realized that, among other things, due to the factivizing character of question-embedding verbs Karttunen in contrast to Hamblin assumes that questions denote the set of propositions expressed by their *true* answers. If we now assume he would derive—as would be syntactically possible—who-questions from whether-questions with the help of a wh-quantification rule, this would for example yield for

(30) Who loves Mary?

(31) $\hat{p} \exists x [{}^{\vee}p \wedge [p = {}^{\wedge} love_{*}' ({}^{\vee}x, m) \vee p = {}^{\wedge} \neg love_{*}' ({}^{\vee}x, m)]]$

and would thus have the consequence that the question (30), for everyone who loves Mary, would denote the proposition that he loves her, and for everyone who does not love Mary, the proposition that he does not love her. Question (30) and question

(32) Who does not love Mary?

would then be semantically equivalent and

(33) John knows who loves Mary?

would be true if John knows for every person whether he loves Mary or not. This, however, according to Karttunen leads to the inacceptable conclusion

(34) "that, in order to know who dates Mary, John must have some knowledge about all the individuals including those he has never heard of and whose very existence is unknown to him."[22]

i.e. the truth-conditions for (33) would be the same as if Karttunen—like Hamblin—had taken as the denotatum for (30) the set of propositions expressed by the *possible* answers. Now, (34) is doubtlessly a *pragmatic* argument. Karttunen thus obtains from pragmatic considerations his semantic argument for the assumption of proto-questions and the derivation of wh-questions from them. If, however, pragmatic considerations can have semantic consequences in this way, then they must not be used only to reject the considerations criticized by Karttunen, they must also be employed with respect to Karttunen's own solution. Here pragmatic considerations of the type (34) would now have the consequence that wh-questions no longer denote the set of propositions expressed by their true answers but rather the set of propositions which—dependent on the context—*come into question* as true answers. That is, with respect to questions like

(35) Who has already read Shakespeare's "Hamlet"?
(36) Who can help me with this?
(37) Where is the Eiffel Tower? (asked in Paris)

similar considerations to those in (34) would lead to the result that the "question domain" of wh-questions would have to be restricted in each case—with the corresponding *semantic* consequences for Karttunen's theory. Similar semantic modifications would naturally also have to be applied to Hamblin's theory. In such a case, if this were done, i.e. if questions would not denote the set of propositions expressed by possible but rather by contextually possible answers, then—curiously enough—Karttunen's argument (34) for the derivation of wh-questions from proto-questions dissolves. (The avalanche started by this argument has carried the argument itself away.)

Karttunen—and as I see it, all other semantic analyses of this kind—thus find themselves in a dilemma. If pragmatic arguments such as (34) are abandoned, then the semantics is kept "pure", but in Karttunen's case this would have the consequence that a) the derivation of wh-questions from proto-questions is no longer necessary, and b) the semantics of wh-questions would also have to take into account the propositions expressed by false answers. Since Karttunen's argument, which relies on the factivizing role of question-embedding verbs, does not seem to me to be very sound, consider

(38) John indicated how that should be done, but unfortunately he did not understand anything about the subject.
(39) John told Mary which students passed the exam, but he was mistaken.

b) in particular would lead to a fundamental change in his semantics in Hamblin's sense.

If, in contrast, pragmatic arguments of the type (34) are used in conceiving the semantics, then the "pragmatic adequacy" of the semantics demands further reaching consequences than Karttunen has drawn.

A few such consequences were in fact drawn by Higginbotham and May (1981). For one thing, they wanted to avoid the implausible consequence of Karttunen's question semantics, namely that the question whether p is identical with the question whether q, if p and q are logically equivalent, and therefore, that the question

(40) What is the sum of 16 and 2?

is identical with the question

(41) What is the product of 3 and 6?

And they also want to define the concept of answer in such a way that it can take into account the aspect of "relevant information". They thus analyse a *wh-question* with the logical form

(42) For which x, $\psi(x)$

semantically as the set S of the possible assignments of truth-values to $[\psi^x_a]$ for all $a \in D$ where D is an appropriate domain. An *answer* to a question represented by (42) is then specified as a sentence which is incompatible with at least one element of S. The basic idea behind this theory is that a question represents "maximal ignorance concerning which elements of D are ψ" (and that S represents that ignorance) and that an answer relieves this ignorance, that is "eliminates a possible state of affairs hitherto left open". Answers that are not incompatible with only one element of S are *complete;* answers which are compatible with several elements of S are *partial.* The answer

(43) John saw Peter.

to the question

(44) Who saw Peter?

is then only complete if D contains only one element.

A great advantage of Higginbotham/May's analysis in contrast to Karttunen's theory is that it allows sentences of the type

(45) Fred did not see Peter.

as answers (namely *partial* answers) to questions of type (44). However, this advantage is dearly bought.

The drawback in Higginbotham/May's analysis is that it collides head-on with the argument that prevented Karttunen from deriving wh-questions from whether-questions: According to their question semantics questions like (44) are the same as such questions as

(46) Who did not see Peter?

And further: If the domain D remains the same in each case, then according to this semantics (44) is also the same as

(47) Who hit Peter?

This major defect might be remedied "contingently", by assuming different—contextually determined—question domains D for the questions in each case. But this would conflict with Higginbotham/May's thesis according to which

> "The question expressed ... for each choice of *D* is thus determined by its logical form ... and is indifferent to contextual matters, such as the speaker's motives in asking the question, whether the people in *D* have names, and, if so, whether they are known to the speaker ..."

An important factor for the restriction of the domain **D** in each case would certainly be whether the speaker knows the individuals in question or whether the hearer can assume that the speaker knows them, etc.

The above mentioned advantage of Higginbotham/May's theory, that it allows the definition of partial answers, was motivated by a pragmatic consideration: The answer (45) provides the questioner with information obviously relevant to question (44). The point of view that questions are "suspensions of judgements" and answers are reliefs of ignorances is basic to the whole analysis. The semantic decision to regard questions as sets of functions of the indicated type is determined by pragmatic considerations of this kind. The difficulties indicated with respect to this semantics thus either result from the fact that pragmatic considerations have *not been carried through consistently to their conclusion,* i.e. as far as the contextually determined restrictions of the question domain (above all by means of the question purpose and knowledge of the participants), or from the fact that pragmatic factors have any influence *at all* on the semantic determinations.

From these two alternatives—the elimination of the pragmatic point of view from semantics or basing semantics on pragmatics—S. Boër has chosen the second in his Cresswellian semantics of questions. Boër proceeds from the assumption that who- and whether-sentences are to be regarded as nominals, i.e. expressions of the category $\langle 0, \langle 0, 1 \rangle \rangle$. Like Cresswell, Boër assumes an underlying functor *who*^{q}, but in order to preserve the functor's iterative applicability, he deviates from Cresswell in assigning it to the category $\langle \langle 0,1 \rangle, \langle \langle 0,1 \rangle, 1, \rangle \rangle$, i.e. applied to the results of λ-abstraction, this functor produces predicates. In order to make this possible, however, Boër must, prior to the application of *who*^{q}, postulate a zero-morpheme $\Delta \in F_{\langle \langle 0,1 \rangle, 1 \rangle}$ which forms dummy predicates from sentences and is interpreted as follows:

(48) $V(\Delta)$ is a function ζ: $D_0 \rightarrow D_{\langle 0,1 \rangle}$ such that for any $a \in D_1$ and $p \in D_0$, $(\zeta(p))(a) = p$.

After the application of λ-abstraction to dummy predicates, the functor *who*^{q} can then be applied. Since, however, this functor produces *predicates* ($\langle 0, 1 \rangle$) and not *nominals* ($\langle 0, \langle 0, 1 \rangle \rangle$) as assumed for indirect question sentences, Boër must assume an additional zero-morpheme $iq \in F_{\langle \langle 0, \langle 0,1 \rangle \rangle, \langle 0,1 \rangle \rangle}$ that forms predicates from indirect question sentences. In two provisional semantic rules Boër provides the following interpretations for *who*^{q} and *iq*: "*who*^{q} teases out the relevant property of PERSONS from the abstract within its scope, and *iq* acts as a complex quantifier having wide scope with respect to the intensional verb which takes the 'who'-clause as its complement,"[23] I state the rule for *iq* as:

(49) $V(iq)$ is a function ζ: $D_{\langle 0,1 \rangle} \rightarrow D_{\langle 0, \langle 0,1 \rangle \rangle}$ such that for any $\omega \in D_{\langle 0,1 \rangle}$, $\zeta(\omega)$ is a partial function
$\xi: \{\omega' \in D_{\langle 0,1 \rangle} \mid dom(\omega') \subset D_0\} \rightarrow D_o$ such that for any $\omega' \in dom(\xi)$ and any $w \in W$: $w \in \xi(\omega')$ iff
$\exists x \in dom(\omega) [w \in \omega(x)] \wedge \forall y \in dom(\omega) [w \in \omega(y) \equiv w \in \omega'(\omega(y))]$.

Since indirect question sentences are regarded semantically here as second-order properties, the following semantic solution becomes possible for the embedding of indirect question sentences.

The sentence

(50) John knows who runs.

is, extensionally speaking, regarded as the statement that the first-order property of propositions (cf. in (49) ω'), i.e. being known by John, belongs to the set of properties which represents the meaning of the indirect question sentence.

One advantage of this semantic analysis is that the inherent factivity of embedded indirect question sentences need not be regarded as a special function of the embedding verbs ("cross-over" phenomenon)[24]. Rather, it can be ascribed to the special semantics of the indirect question sentences themselves (cf. the last line in (49))[25]. Now, what about the teleological relativity in cases like (50)? Boër introduces it by means of the Cresswellian concepts of context property (understood as a function from the set of sentence tokens (which are in D_1) into the set of propositions) and open proposition (understood as a function from context properties into the set of propositions) in the semantic rules for *who*^{q} and *iq*. As a formal correlate of the property of being an important property (relative to a specified purpose) he defines a function Ω from $D_{\langle 0,1\rangle}$ into D_0 (the latter being now regarded as the set of all *open* propositions) that is intended to guarantee that a property ω is an important property relative to a certain context property η^* which, of course, specifies the classificatory purpose or the given project, i.e. Ω assigns to a property ω those open propositions θ for which the following holds:

(1) θ is defined on the set of those context properties that are in a context family generated by a context property η^*[26] where η^* represents exactly one classificatory purpose K with respect to the domain of ω[27].

(2) For any $\eta \in \text{dom}(\theta)$ and $w \in W$: $w \in \theta(\eta)$ iff ω counts in w as an important property relative to K.

The amended version of (49), i.e. the version that takes teleological relativity into account can now be formulated as follows:[28]

(49′) as in (49), except that it is now stated for ξ:
for every $\omega' \in \mathrm{dom}(\xi)$ is $\xi(\omega')$ an open proposition θ that is defined on the set of those context properties η for which
$\eta \in \bigcap_{\gamma \in \mathrm{rg}(\omega)} \mathrm{dom}(\gamma)^{29}$, where for every $\eta \in \mathrm{dom}(\theta)$ and $w \in W$: $w \in \theta(\eta)$
iff (a)–(c) obtain:

(a) $\exists x \in \mathrm{dom}(\omega)\ [w \in (\omega(x))(\eta)]$;
(b) $\forall y \in \mathrm{dom}(\omega)\ [w \in (\omega)y))(\eta) \equiv w \in (\omega'(\omega(y)))(\eta)]$;
(c) $\forall n \geqslant 2\ [[\mathrm{dom}(\omega) \subset D_1{}^n \wedge w \in (\omega(\langle a_1, \ldots, a_n \rangle))(\eta) \rightarrow$
$\forall i_{1<i\leqslant n}\ \exists \varphi \in D_{\langle 0,1 \rangle}\ [w \in (\Omega\ (\varphi))(\eta) \wedge w \in (\omega'(\varphi(a_i)))(\eta)]]^{30}$;

Applied to example (50), (49′) not only requires that an utterance of (50) be true in a world w relative to a contextually specified classificatory purpose *K* iff (a) somebody runs in w, and (b) for all people who run in w, John knows that they run in w, but the proviso (c) in (49′) additionally requires that John knows everyone who runs in w, relative to *K*, i.e. he knows an important property relative to *K* to be true of him in w.

I do not intend to go into the widely disputed details of wh-questions' semantics, such as the existential condition in (49) and (49′). This existential condition seems to me definitely unjustified in view of such examples as

(51) Who volunteers?
(52) Who is coming with?
(53) Who has survived the catastrophy?
(54) Who knows what the capital of Nicaragua is?

What I find more important in the semantics of *iq* is the question (and its consequences) of why Boër boosts the denotatum of indirect questions to the next highest level (to properties of properties). We find the same thing in Montague's analysis of terms—here the reason was *semantic:* the problem of denotation gaps in intensional contexts. In Boër's case the following grounds seem to be relevant: First, he wants to attach the inherent factivity of indirect questions to the semantic properties of the questions themselves, and not, as Karttunen does, to the properties of embedding verbs. But, in the first place, this factivity does not exist in all cases, cf.

(55) John asks who kissed Mary.
(56) John has no idea who ate up the cake.

In the second place, as example (39) shows, it can be cancelled in cases where it potentially exists. I conclude, therefore, that we are dealing here with a *pragmatic* phenomenon.

The second basis for this semantics is teleological relativity. Boër's semantic reversal of the syntactic situation in indirect question sentences permits a simple treatment with the help of Cresswell's concept of open propositions (i.e. with the help of Cresswell's "pragmatics"). In this case, too, we are dealing with a *pragmatic* argument.
Böer's semantics is thus grounded in pragmatic considerations. Important aspects of wh-questions are thereby taken care of, as we have seen. But the price of such an analysis is high: Boër's *syntax* of indirect question sentences flagrantly violates every kind of *naturalness principle.* In addition, Boër assumes a syntactic category for indirect question sentences that is purely semantically (and as we have seen indirectly pragmatically) motivated. But in order to derive this syntax, syntactic steps are required (e.g. dummy-predicate formation) which themselves are in no way semantically motivated. The *dilemma* arising when we semantically take into account the above-mentioned properties of "knowing who" seems to be the following: The more pragmatic considerations are integrated into the conception of a semantics, the more unnatural the syntactic consequences of the semantics.

Furthermore, Boër's solution to integrate teleological relativity into the *semantics* of *all* indirect who-questions is certainly too strong. While with "knowing who" it is relatively clear, what form teleological relativity should take (since it is clear what functions as ω' in (49)), this is not the case in

(57) Who wins depends on who is stronger.

and in the examples

(58) It is irrelevant who did it, what's decisive is that the window is broken.
(59) The National Olympic Commitee has no influence on who can go to the Olympics.

it is questionable whether anything like teleological relativity exists at all. Here an important difference beween direct and indirect who-questions is clearly evident: While in the former case something like teleological relativity always exists, this is often not the case with the latter. The reason for this difference lies simply in the different pragmatic functions for which direct and indirect who-questions are uttered. If we therefore want to analyse direct questions in terms of indirect ones, then we must exclude this aspect (of teleological relativity) in any case from a semantic analysis.

On the basis of the above-mentioned *syntactic* difficulties, I would, however, make the demand that pragmatic aspects such as teleological relativity should *generally* not be included in the semantic analysis of questions, but should rather be treated on a *pragmatic level of their own*. The problem with truth-conditions in sentences such as (27), indicated by Boër/Lycan, seems to me to be explicable in a similar fashion to what Katz (1980) has suggested with respect to supposed correspondence ambiguities (which similarly influence truth-conditions)[31]; consider

(60) Two workers dig a hole.

versus

(61) Two workers carry a five hundredweight heavy block of stone.

and

(62) Two languages are spoken by everyone in the room.

versus

(63) Sixty-three languages are spoken by everyone in the room. (at the linguistic conference).

The suggestion is that these are cases of highly pragmatic affairs which probably would not have any place at all in a semantic analysis, but which rather demand their own pragmatic explanations.[32]

Let us make a provisional summary: If questions have anything to do with the elimination of knowledge-desiderata, then answers are to be seen as those linguistic responses which potentially eliminate such a knowledge-desideratum. In order to be able to characterize the concept of an answer, therefore, in a manner relating to the nature of questions, it must be clarified when the questioner knows that something in particular (namely that which he asked about) is the case. In section (i) it was shown that a Hintikka/Åqvist analysis of "knowing who" does not satisfy this demand in so far that it does not take into account those aspects such as the so-called "teleological relativity" of "knowing who" which are indispensable as a basis for a practicable answer concept. As shown in section (ii), attempts to incorporate aspects of this teleological relativity into the *semantics* of questions are confronted with dilemmas that suggest a different methodological strategy. I thus conclude that the analysis of an answer concept that attempts to take into account the nature of questions must refer to the aspect—to be modified as will be shown—of teleological relativity. This reference to teleological relativity, however, must be eliminated from question semantics and carried out on the level of a question *pragmatics*. From this point of view, I will attempt in what follows to explicate the concept of a pragmatically significant answer.

(iii) Pragmatically significant answers

In their analysis of the teleological relativity of "knowing who" Boër/Lycan referred only to purposes or projects—independent of whose purposes or projects these were. If we want to use this analysis for the investigation of answers, we have to notice that even though questions indicate knowledge-desiderata, the answers need not necessarily eliminate those desiderata in the sense that the questioner then *knows* the particular information after the answer has been given; often it is already sufficient for him to have some basis for an assumption, supposition, hypothesis etc. The amount of knowledge that will be sufficient for him in each case depends upon what purposes he has and upon what he already knows. The analysis of answers must not concentrate exclusively on purposes and projects, but also on *whose* purposes and projects these are and in what epistemic situation the given persons find themselves. Since the analysis of questions not only deals with *absolute* knowledge, but also with beliefs, suppositions, hypotheses etc., it will also have to be able to express *degrees of knowledge*.

A further modification of Boër/Lycan's concept arises from the following consideration. While in the analysis of truth-conditions for "knowing who" the decisive question is when the potential regress of "Who is ..."-questions *must finally* stop, in the analysis of answers it seems decisive to know why, in a concrete situation, the potential regress of "Who is ..."-questions stops *de facto*. i.e. what conditions must be met in order that this regress *can* stop. What is interesting in the question-answer sequence

(64) Who is the author of "Philosophical Investigations"?
(65) Wittgenstein.

seems to me, then, not why the questioner in (64) *can* potentially ask further "But who is Wittgenstein?", but rather why he potentially does *not need* to ask further. It is clear that this depends on the degree of informativity that the answer has *for the questioner,* and this, in turn, naturally depends on what the questioner already knows, i.e. his epistemic situation. The analysis of the concept of a pragmatically significant answer will then have to refer to a concept of the informativeness of answers which is explicated dependent upon the knowledge situation of the questioner.

In order to achieve an intuitive understanding of pragmatically significant answers, let us consider the following examples:

On November 1, 1978 A wants to reserve a seat on a train to Berlin and is asked by the ticket agent

(66) For what day, Sir?

Consider the answers

(67) For October 15, 1978
(68) For December 6, 2001.

Or: A asks a pedestrian on a sunny afternoon

(69) Can you tell me the time, please?

Answer:

(70) It's 2 o'clock in the morning.

Or: A is asked by a pedestrian on the Kurfürstendamm

(71) Where is the Gedächtniskirche?

Answer:

(72) In Berlin.

Even though the answers in each case are informative in the "objective" sense along the lines Keenan/Hull defined the concept of informativeness,[33] it is, however, decisive here that they are not informative *in a sense relevant to the questioner.* (70) is *too obviously false* to the questioner, (67) would involve an *absurd* action, (72) is probably *already known* to the questioner in the given situation, and the data contained in (68) is *useless* for the purposes of the question in the given action context.

Shall we say that (66), (69), and (71) are linguistically inexact question formulations that only specify unsatisfactorily the question domain and which, accordingly, *for the analysis of questions* should be replaced by more exact formulations, i.e. so-called explicit versions of questions? Now, doubtlessly, vague formulations are often selected in asking questions, but in the given situations they are unambiguously understandable; but it is equally doubtless that not all of these formulations allow the substitution of an "explicit version". The "precise" version of (66), something like

(66′) On what day not in the past and not after the probable date of your death would you like to travel?

sounds absurd.

I conclude, therefore, that in the examples (66) to (72) it is not the questions that are defective, but that the answers can be characterized by the general shortcoming that they are unusable for the satisfaction of the interests which are bound up with these questions. It follows from that that a pragmatically significant answer must be informative in a subjective sense, taking into account the knowledge situation of the questioner, and it must be useful to the questioner relative to the purpose of his question.[34] Now we will consider informativeness.

The point is to explicate a concept of the informativeness of answers that has reference to the change in the subjective beliefs of the questioner resulting from answers. A concept of informativeness that satisfies this requirement must, therefore, refer to the knowledge situation of the questioner at the time of questioning as well as to the knowledge situation of the questioner at the time of answering. The problem is *how* the reference to these knowledge situations should be represented.

The knowledge situation of a person X at time t can be regarded as the set of beliefs X holds at t. But since all these beliefs are naturally not of equal strength on all subjects, the foregoing must be made more specific in so far as the knowledge situation must be characterized by the degree of belief X has at t with respect to the sentences of his language, or, by the degree to which he believes that the states of affairs expressed by the sentences in his language exist.

Since the degree of partial belief that X holds with respect to the sentences of his language L can be identified with the *subjective probability* of the existence for him of certain states of affairs expressed by these sentences, the knowledge situation of a person X at time t can be represented by a probability function $P_{X,t}$.[35] Since it has been demonstrated in probability theory that such a subjectivistic programme involving the measurement of the seemingly vague concept of degree of belief can be realised with recourse to an analysis of rationalbetting behaviour[36], $P_{X,t}$ can be interpreted as a function with the propositions expressible in L as arguments and the degree of X's belief with respect to the truth of such a proposition as the corresponding value. The fact that the function $P_{X,t}$would be very difficult to specify concretely does not invalidate the suggestion that we represent the knowledge situation of X by $P_{X,t}$ any more than the fact that an intension function is very difficult do specify concretely invalidates the suggestion that we represent the intension of an expression by an intension function.

Since $P_{X,t}$ is a probability measure it is subject to the structural specifications stated in the axioms of probability theory. The requirement that $P_{X,t}$ be defined on a set algebra[37] is fulfilled by the assumption that the set of *propositions* expressible in L constitutes the domain of $P_{X,t}$.[38]

Let *M* be the set of propositions expressible in the language L spoken by the questioner X. Let function $P_{X,t}$ defined on *M* represent the knowledge situation of X at time t of questioning and assign the degree of belief held by X (i.e. the degree to which X believes A is true) to every $A \in M$.[39]

Let the questioner's state of belief existing after an answer B at time t' be represented by the probability function $P_{X,t'}$ (also defined on *M*). If the principle of credulity (73) as follows

(73) The questioner believes what the answerer says to be true.

applies, which we presuppose, then the following is valid: $P_{X,t'}(B)=1$. Since $B \in M$ we can define:

(74) An answer B is informative if $P_{X,t}(B) \neq 1$.

Since under $P_{X,t}$ tautologies, as well as all the propositions already known to X, have the probability value 1, the fact that the corresponding sentences cannot be counted as informative answers is accommodated.

Consider, then, such examples as answer B:

(70) It's 2 o'clock in the morning.

answered on a sunny afternoon in response to the question

(69) Can you tell me the time, please?

Following (74), B counts as an informative answer since $P_{X,t}(B)$ is certainly not equal 1. But this is highly implausible due to the *obvious falsity of B to the questioner*. The problem lies in presupposing (73)—X's (the questioner's) credulity. In the case of (70) the questioner's credulity is being overburdened; rather than believing the answerer he will *doubt the answerer's competence* or will assume that the answerer is joking etc. Since the idealization (73) is to be retained on methodological grounds, examples such as (70) require the following revision of (74):

(75) An answer B is informative if $O < P_{X,t}(B) < 1$.

The fact mentioned at the beginning of this section that the questioner need not always be placed in the position of *knowing* something new through answers can easily be accounted for by allowing a smaller value than 1 for $P_{X,t'}(B)$ and by demanding in (75) that $P_{X,t}(B) < P_{X,t'}(B)$. The degree of informativeness of an answer B can then be determined as the difference between $P_{X,t}(B)$ and $P_{X,t'}(B)$. For the sake of simplicity in the following description I continue to assume that $P_{X,t'}(B)=1$.

With this kind of informativeness concept the following kinds of answers are to be regarded as non-informative:

(a) Answers that tell the questioner something he already knows (cf. example (72)).
(b) Answers that are semantically non-informative such as tautologies

and analytically true sentences (a special case of (a); cf. example (2)).

(c) Answers for which the a priori probability $P_{X,t}$ is equal to zero i.e. answers which are obviously false to the questioner (cf. example (70)).

If we start from the assumption that questions offer alternatives among which the answerer has to decide, two important problems arise:

Problem (1): What determines the range over which the offer of these alternatives extends? As the examples in the foregoing sections illustrated, the range is obviously narrower than the set of structurally possible answers. The relevant question can, therefore, be formulated as follows. According to what pragmatic considerations can a subset of the set of structurally possible answers be isolated such that its elements represent the alternatives offered by a particular question?

Problem (2): What are the criteria against which the answerer makes his decision?

Beginning with problem (1), let us consider the following example:

(76) Where is Lutter & Wegner?

Situation (S1): I am having a conversation with friends in Munich about taverns. A joins us and realizes that Lutter & Wegner is a tavern and he asks question (76). He receives the answer (77)

(77) In Berlin

Situation (S2): As an out-of-towner in Berlin I get into a taxi and tell the driver "Lutter & Wegner". In response the taxi driver asks question (76); he receives the answer (78)

(78) Schlüterstraße 55.

Situation (S3): At the Wittenbergplatz in Berlin a pedestrain asks question (76), he receives the answer (79)

(79) Take the Underground to the stop Bahnhof Uhlandstraße and then ask again.

Situation (S4): On the corner of Kantstraße and Leibnizstraße in Berlin, a pedestrain asks question (76), he receives the following answer (80)

(80) Go straight ahead, take the first left turn as far as the second traffic light and then it's right there.

Situation (S5): From a point where one can see Lutter & Wegner a pedestrain asks question (76). The answer combined with a gesture is

(81) Over there.

In none of the above situations (S1)—(S5) does the given answer in any one situation belong to the range of alternatives available for any of the other situations. Should one say that the question (76) in the situations (S1)—(S5) has a different meaning in each case? So, for example, in (S1):

(76′) In what city is Lutter & Wegner?

In (S2):

(76″) In what street is Lutter & Wegner?

In (S3):

(76‴) How can I get to Lutter & Wegner?

I think that this explanation based on the vagueness of the question is inappropriate, because, at least in the situations (S3)—(S5), the question would have the same meaning, and still a small change in the situation as, for example, from (S4) to (S5) would have such a *decisive* effect on the range of answer alternatives that (81) would be significant in (S5) but not in (S4). This means that in the situations (S2) to (S5) the questioner wants to get to Lutter & Wegner and he asks his question for that purpose, and although the *same question* is asked in each of these situations, the ranges of significant answers are different because only certain answers are *helpful* to the questioner in each particular situation. That means that answers must have a *value* or *utility* for the questioner relative to the given situation, and the extent of the range of alternatives offered by a question depends on what is useful to the questioner with respect to the desires underlying his question.

The fact illustrated by the above examples is that an action-desideratum is connected with questions which is not exhaustively described by lack of information, and this motivates the assumption that a *question purpose* Z_Q, recoverable from the question situation, is connected with every question Q. This question purpose, however, is not only the obtaining of information, rather it is the question purpose which determines what kind of information is relevant for the questioner. But since this question purpose determines the restriction of structurally possible answers, the answers can be examined from the point of view of fulfilling this purpose.

This means that possible answers can be compared on the basis of their value for questioner X with respect to a particular question purpose Z_Q. Corresponding to this value a simple preference order can be established among the set of structurally possible answers.

For reasons of simplicity the fact that answers must be judged on their utility for a certain question purpose may be represented by a *function* W_{X,t,Z_Q} that assigns to every structurally possible answer Q the *subjective value*[40] this answer has at time t for the questioner X with respect to a question purpose Z_Q (connected with the question Q). This function is defined on propositions and corresponds to the utility function in decision theory.[41] The fact that the data determining this function is only available in a comparative form does not invalidate the presentation as function any more than not knowing the concrete specification of probability or intension functions invalidates their respective presentation as functions.

We may therefore start from the assumption that W_{X,t,Z_Q} constitutes an idealized reconstruction of the fact that questions have a question purpose and answers must be judged according to their subjective value for the questioner with respect to the fulfillment of this purpose. Based on these considerations we can define

(82) An answer B to the question Q posed by A at time t for the purpose Z_Q is pragmatically significant if it has a positive subjective value W_{X,t,Z_Q}.

Since the subjective value function is defined on propositions in most models of decision theory, in the case of (82) this function would have the propositions expressed by the answers as arguments. But then (82) would—as far as the pragmatic significance of answers is concerned—lead to strange results as illustrated by the following examples:

(83) Do I have cancer?—Yes.
(84) Who will be executed tomorrow?—You.
(85) What kind of wages do I get here?—Low wages.
(86) Who is Marion's lover?—Your husband.

This problem would be avoided if (82) is revised as follows

(87) An answer B to the question Q posed by X at time t for the purpose Z_Q is pragmatically significant if at least one of the alternatives (offered in the question) that has a positive subjective value W_{X,t,Z_Q} is either included or excluded (i.e. if either this alternative or its negation can be inferred).

From the answer "You" to question (84) follows, for example, the negation of the useful alternative "You will not be executed tomorrow".

(87) describes the fact that pragmatically significant answers must have a positive subjective value for the questioner. But since the latter is certainly only the case when answers are also informative, the concept of a pragmatically significant answer must refer to their subjective value *as well as* to their informativeness. It is precisely this double dependence, this interlocking of informativeness and subjective value, that the foregoing examples were intended to illustrate. We therefore must define

(88) An answer B to the question Q posed by X at time t with the purpose Z_Q is pragmatically significant if it has a positive subjective value W_{X,t,Z_Q} and is also informative.

In our idealized quantitative way of speaking the dependence of the pragmatic significance of an answer on its subjective value *and* its informativeness is expressed by the product of these two components. The pragmatic significance of a given answer B at t′ to a question Q posed by X at t (with t and t′ being subject to the corresponding time condition) with the purpose Z ($PS_{X,t',Z_Q}(B)$) can, therefore, be determined as follows:

(89) $PS_{X,t',Z_Q}(B)=W_{X,t,Z_Q}(B) \cdot [1-P_{X,t}(B)]$.

Answers B which are non-informative because $P_{X,t}(B)=1$ are in accordance with (89) not pragmatically significant. For answers C which on the basis of $P_{X,t}(C)=0$ are non-informative (cf. example (70)), the value for W_{X,t,Z_Q} can plausibly be determined as $W_{X,t,Z_Q}(C)=0$. With (89), however, we once again face the implausibility that was illustrated in the examples (83)—(86). In order to avoid this, we must make the following differentiation.

As has already been discussed, propositions constitute the arguments of the subjective value function; in this case these would be the propositions expressed by answers. The above implausibility proceeds from the fact that the pragmatic significance of an answer would be dependent on what subjective value the proposition expressed by the answer has for the questioner. But the subjective value of an answer has less to do with the proposition communicated to the questioner than with the fact that the proposition has been communicated to him. The propositions expressed by the answers "yes" and "no", respectively, are, in the case of question (83), without doubt, of very different subjective value to the questioner, although they probably have the same degree of informativeness, but this should be irrelevant to the consideration of the pragmatic significance of the answer. We therefore have to distinguish between the *subjective value of the communicated proposition* and the *subjective value of communicating this proposition* and the latter is relevant for determining the pragmatic significance of an answer.

We must therefore take into consideration a distinction that has so far been ignored in our discussion: the distinction between the propositions *that it is being answered that p is the case* and *that p is the case.* In the following, answer actions as in the first kind of proposition will be represented by capitals "A", "B", ...; the proposition expressed in an answer B will be represented by a lower case "b" as in the following formula that replaces (89) accordingly:

(90) $PS_{X,t',Z_Q}(B)=W_{X,t,Z_Q}(B) \cdot [1-P_{X,t}(b)]$

(iv) Pragmatic postulates for answers

The second problem formulated in the foregoing section consisted of asking what considerations should constitute the basis for the answerer's decision among the alternatives made available by the question. Proceeding from what we have said so far, we can make two relevant assumptions:

(a) The answerer should give a true answer—unless there are important reasons not to.[42]
(b) The answerer should give a pragmatically significant answer.

In the argument that follows I intend to show how assumption (b) can be expressed and clarified with the aid of the apparatus we have so far adopted from decision theory. i.e. the probability function $P_{X,t}$ and the utility function W_{X,t,Z_Q}. This argument is based on the presupposition that the answerer is, *in principle, willing to cooperate.*

When a person is confronted with a question, his choice among the alternatives offered by the question will, in part, depend on what assumptions he makes about the state of knowledge of the questioner. When the answerer gives answer (77) in response to question (76) in situation (S1), his answer depends, in part, on his assumptions about the questioner's knowledge about Berlin. What the answerer considers the purpose of a question to be in a particular situation also depends on his assumptions about the state of knowledge of the questioner. Whether or not the answerer understands that the purpose of the question

(91) Where is the Eiffel Tower?

posed to him in Paris, is that the questioner wants to get to the Eiffel Tower, will, in part, depend on whether the answerer believes that the questioner knows that he himself is in Paris and that the Eiffel Tower is also in Paris, etc.

Apart from his assumptions about the state of knowledge of the questioner and his assumptions about the purpose of the question conditioned by the first assumptions, the answerer's response will additionally depend on what value the answerer thinks his possible answer has for the questioner, given these assumptions. Given the presupposition that the answerer is willing, in principle, to cooperate, he will decide on an answer having a positive value for the questioner *according to his own (the answerer's) evaluation.*

In the following I first demonstrate how rational behaviour in reponse to an impending decision between alternative actions under consideration is described by decision theory. By analogy with this kind of description I then want to reconstruct the way in which a rational and well-meaning answerer will make his choice. Although my comments are based primarily on Jeffrey's (1965) holistic theory which uses only propositions, I want to sketch out my basic ideas by pointing out some distinctions not displayed in this theory. If we consider the alternative actions $A_1, \ldots, A_n$ considered by a person X, between which X has to make a choice, these actions would have certain results dependent on the occurrence of certain circumstances. Let these *m* circumstances $C_1, \ldots; C_m$ be an exhaustive disjunction of all the circumstances regarded as possible by X, then the possible results available for X to consider can be arranged in an *outcome matrix* $(K_{ij})_{\substack{i \in \{1,\ldots,n\} \\ j \in \{1,\ldots,m\}}}$.

If we now apply the utility function from decision theory, the possible results R_{ij} can be evaluated subjectively in a *utility matrix,* i.e. each of the n x m possible results $R_{11}, \ldots, R_{nm}$ is assigned a value (real number) that represents the utility of R_{ij} for the acting subject. In the case of decisions under risk it is presupposed that the acting subject is in a position to determine the probability of the occurrence of the *m* circumstances. In a *probability matrix*[43] the circumstances are thus assigned their subjective probabilities, i.e. the degree to which the acting subject believes in their occurrence is assigned in such a way that every result of the particular actions which depends on the circumstances is assigned that value which indicates the probability of the occurrence of the particular circumstance as seen by the acting subject.

If we now assume that the subject who has to make a choice between the actions A_i knows enough about the situation in which the decision has to be made, that he is in a position to draw up the three matrices mentioned, he can evaluate the actions under consideration as follows: Let us assume that the line of the utility matrix corresponding to the action A_i is

(92) $W_{i1}, W_{i2}, \ldots, W_{im}$

and the corresponding line of the probability matrix is

(93) $P_{i1}, P_{i2}, \ldots, P_{im}$

then the subject making his choice can "calculate" the *expected utility* of the actions A_i as

(94) $$E(A_i) = \sum_{j=1}^{m} W_{ij}P_{ij}.$$

The expected utility calculated for each of the *n* actions under consideration then provides the foundation for a decision criterion in accordance with Bayes' rule[44] which states: Choose the action among the possible actions the expected utility of which is the greatest.

Let us now turn again to the answers. In order to be able to formulate a decision criterion based on (b) for the choice among the alternatives made available by a question, I start from the assumption that the answerer is in a situation such that he can make a *decision under certainty,* i.e. I start from the assumption that the answerer believes that he knows what the state of knowledge of the questioner is at the time of asking, that he believes that he knows the purpose of the question, that he has reliable sense of what subjective value the answering possibilities under consideration have for the questioner in this situation, and—in accordance with (73)—that he assumes the credulity of the questioner.

Following (a) the answerer Y should only give answers that he believes are true. Let the set of answers which he thinks are true be $M=\{A_1, \ldots, A_n\}$. $M'=\{a_1, \ldots, a_n\}$ be the set of propositions expressed by these answers. Y's assumptions about the state of knowledge of the questioner, relevant to the question situation, can, then, in accordance with the discussion in section (iii), be represented as a function $P^Y_{X,t}$ on M' that indicates to what extent the questioner is convinced, in Y's opinion, of the existence of corresponding states of affairs at the time of questioning. However, the function can only accomplish this if it is guaranteed that it really becomes a probability measure. We must therefore postulate that the function $P^Y_{X,t}$ be extendible to a probability measure, i.e. that it can be extended to, at least, the set algebra generated by M'.[45]

Let W^Y_{X,t,Z_Q} be a function defined on M that represents the value the answers $A_1, \ldots, A_n$ have for X in Y's opinion in view of the question purpose Z_Q as assumed by Y.

In the given situation where Y can make his decision under certainty, Y can compare and weight the answers which he thinks are true according to their pragmatic significance for X. In our idealised quantitative way of speaking the reasoning process Y has to go through, i.e. the "calculating" of the pragmatic significance connected with particular A_i in Y's opinion, can be represented as

$$(95)\quad PS^{Y}_{X,t',Z_Q}(A_i) = W^{Y}_{X,t,Z_Q}(a_i) \cdot [1 - P^{Y}_{X,t}(a_i)]$$

As a decision criterion for choosing among the particular answers, the following pragmatic postulate can be formulated which constitutes a clarification of (b):

(P1) Choose among the answers which you think are true that one for which the assumed (by you) pragmatic significance is greatest.

But the situation in which the answerer has to make his decision for one of the alternatives made available by the question is not always such that the answerer has firm beliefs about the knowledge situation of the questioner, about the question purpose, about the value of possible answers for Y etc., i.e. the answerer's situation is not always such that he can make a decision under certainty. In conclusion I want, therefore, to reconstruct briefly what the situation of the answerer is like if he does not have the firm beliefs mentioned above, if he is in a situation in which he has to make a *decision under risk*.

Again I presuppose that the answerer is, in principle, willing to cooperate and that he assumes the credulity of the questioner. In the situation assumed here the answerer Y is uncertain which one of a series of possible assumptions about the state of knowledge of the questioner applies, and he is also uncertain which one of a series of possible hypotheses about the subjective values of answers has to be entertained.[46] We must therefore assign a degree of probability to these assumptions and hypotheses themselves, which indicates *to what degree* Y is convinced of their correctness. In this situation where Y has to choose among different A_i, he can only assign a pragmatic significance to the particular answers *relative to the degree* to which he thinks his assumptions about the state of knowledge and value situation of the questioner are correct. i.e. he can only reason about what pragmatic significance *is to be expected* for the particular answers.

Now one has to consider

$\mathfrak{W}$ = the set of all probability functions $P_{X,t}$
on $\{a_1, \ldots, a_n\}$ as thought possible by Y[47]

and

$\mathfrak{M}$ = the set of all subjective value functions W_{X,t,Z_Q}
on $\{A_1, \ldots, A_n\}$ as thought possible by Y.

Let P^Y be the probability measure defined on $\mathfrak{W} \times \mathfrak{M}$ that represents what (subjective) probability Y assigns to the existence of particular probability functions $P_{X,t}$ (states of knowledge of X) and value functions W_{X,t,Z_Q} (subjective values of the answers for X).

On the analogy of the determination of the expected utility in decision theory, *Y's expected pragmatic significance* (EPS) of the answers he thinks are true can be determined as follows (as the weighted arithmetic mean of particular $PS(A_i)$ with the probabilities for W and P as weights):

(96) $$EPS^{Y}_{X,t',Z_Q}(A_i) = \sum_{\substack{P_{X,t} \in \mathfrak{W} \\ W_{X,t,Z_Q} \in \mathfrak{M}}} [W_{X,t,Z_Q}(A_i) \cdot (1 - P_{X,t}(a_i))] \cdot P^{Y}(W_{X,t,Z_Q}, P_{X,t})$$

On the analogy of Bayes' rule, a pragmatic postulate for answers in situations in which someone has to make his decision under risk can be formulated as follows:

(P2) Choose among the answers which you think are true that one for which the expected (by you) pragmatic significance is greatest.

Freie Universität Berlin
Fachbereich Germanistik

Notes

[1] I am grateful to Wolfgang Spohn for many helpful discussions of various issues treated in this paper.

[1] Cf. Åqvist (1975), chapter vi.

[2] Hintikka (1962), p. 142 ff and Hintikka (1969a), p. 96 ff.

[3] Cf. Quine (1960) and Quine (1966).

[4] Cf. e.g. Hintikka (1969) and particularly Hintikka (1975a).

[5] This consequence is not avoided by Hintikka's correcting his statements in Hintikka (1962) to those in Hintikka (1975a), p. 52, where he points out that in the case of quantification into epistemic contexts the bound variables are not supposed to range over the set of acquaintances of the epistemic subject but over the set of individuals descriptively individuated by the subject.
[6] Cf. Boër/Lycan (1975), sections iv and vii.
[7] Link (1976), p. 23.
[8] Cf. Kaplan (1971), p. 138.
[9] Kaplan (1971), p. 135—136.
[10] As is also stated justifiedly by Boër/Lycan (1975).
[11] From this point of view Kaplan's analysis provides certainly no necessary condition for S to know who D is.
[12] I only take into account the final version; cf. Boër/Lycan (1975), p. 338.
[13] According to Boër/Lycan "ß" ranges over expressions of S's "language of thought". With this demand the authors try to avoid the S's ability to know something being linked to a competence in a particular natural language.
[14] The apparent opacity of "knowing who" is explained away by Boër/Lycan (p. 319 f.) as follows:
a) Often replacements of "N" in "S knows who N is" are not coreferring singular terms but definite descriptions (or proper names) *used attributively* (and referential opacity is simply a case of syntactic ambiguity).
b) In cases where the replacements of "N" are referential singular terms, the apparent opacity is often the result of a parameter shift, i.e. two different values of the teleological parameter are being appealed to and this is the reason for a change of the truth-value upon substitution.
If neither a) nor b) applies, the position of "N" supports substitution.
[15] Boër/Lycan (1975), p. 328.
[16] In most cases this category puts constraints on the sort of uniquely individuating facts which can fulfill the particular function.
[17] I ignore the case where C(P) fails to delimit any set of C(P)-determinables, e.g. if one wants to know which blond someone is. One obtains this information if one finds out that he is the blond with the property G, where G here is *any given* property which he is the only blond to have.
[18] The only exception is S. Boër (1978), which I will discuss later.
[19] Although Wunderlich (1976) calls Åqvist's analysis pragmatic, this judgement seems to be based more on Åqvist's concept of logical formalization than on pragmatic aspects of his question theory.
[20] On this criticism see also Boër (1978), p. 311.
[21] As Boër (1978) shows, this does not only apply to epistemic constructions like "know who" but also to "tell who", "agree on who", "control who" etc.
[22] Karttunen (1977), p. 22.
[23] Boër (1978), p. 317.
[24] As e.g. in Karttunen, where this leads to a duplication of the verbs which allow the embedding of that-clauses as well as wh-clauses.
[25] Boër's motivation for this analysis results from the assumption that the mentioned factivity is not a property of question-embedding verbs—as was assumed by Karttunen; in "debate", "decide", "agree", for example, it does not exist. If, however, this factivity is ascribed to the special semantics of the indirect question sentences themselves, it should

then be explained why this factivity does *not* exist in certain of these question sentences. The explanation provided by Boër for such a "nullification" of the inherent factitivy (cf. p. 326 ff.) I do not find very convincing for various reasons.

26 A context family generated by a context property η^* is the set of context properties η for which it is true that $w \in \eta(a)$ only if $w \in \eta^*(a)$ (where *a* is a surface token).

27 I.e. $w \in \eta^*(a)$ iff the utterer of *a* professes *K* insofar at least as *a* is concerned.

28 Cf. Boër (1978), p. 331.

29 Note that D_0 is now the set of *open* propositions.

30 That $n \leqslant 2$ is required here is connected with a special feature of the semantic rule for *who*^{q} which I will not discuss here.

31 Cf. Katz (1980), p. 13 and 26 ff.

32 In my opinion this also applies for the so-called bijective reading of multiple wh-questions for which Higginbotham/May look for a *semantic* solution, apparently without success. Such a reading is much less probable in cases like
(a) Which man has kissed which woman?
than, for example, in
(b) Which man has married which woman?
and this also has pragmatic reasons.

33 Cf. Keenan/Hull (1973).

34 For the following analysis of pragmatically significant answers I naturally presuppose that the concept of a syntactically correct and semantically true answer has been clarified.

35 I am naturally not referring to the normative interpretation of probability but rather to the empirical-descriptive interpretation.

36 Cf. Stegmüller (1973), vol. iv, part ii, sect. 5 and 6, as well as appendices ii and iii, where it is shown that the subjective probability concept can be specified with mathematical precision, insofar as one is prepared to accept certain basic idealizations in the form of rationality criteria.

37 In order to avoid unnecessary complications, in the following we always proceed from the finite case for which it is not required that the domain of $P_{X,t}$ is a σ-algebra.

38 Concerning the interpretation of propositions as sets, see Carnap (1971). A presentation of the Carnapian reconstruction of propositions as set-theoretical entities can be found in Stegmüller (1973), p. 446 ff. and Spohn (1978), p. 90 ff.

39 The time index t refers here and in what follows not only to a time point t but to the situation determined by this time point.

40 Following Spohn (1978), p. 36, I prefer the concept "subjective value" to the concept "utility" incorporated into decision theory.

41 I.e. it is subject to the so-called desirability axiom that relates the concept of subjective value with the probability concept (cf. Jeffrey (1965), chapter 5.5, Stegmüller (1973), p. 395 f.) as well as to stipulations concerning the norming of this function (cf. Jeffrey (1965), chapter 6.2, Stegmüller (1973), p. 327 f.).

42 On the grounds of foreseeable injurious effects on the questioner it can, in certain cases, be irresponsible "to tell him the truth".

43 I only consider the case of a probability matrix where the probabilities are independent of the actions under consideration.

44 A presentation of the Bayesian principle can be found, among other places, in Jeffrey (1965), chapter 1, Stegmüller (1973), p. 297; details about controversies arising from this principle are given by Spohn (1978), p. 39.

45 The set algebra generated by M‘ (on *M*) is the smallest set algebra (on *M*) that contains

M′ as a subset. This requirement is unproblematic. It demands only that this function satisfy the Kolmogoroff axioms, such that, for example, the number 2 cannot be assigned to any argument, and that the degree of belief assigned to propositions that contain elements from M′ depends on the values of these elements, etc.

46 This includes Y's uncertainty about the purpose Z_Q that must be assumed for the question.

47 For these functions it must be valid that they can be extended to a probability measure.

References

Åqvist, L., A new approach to the logical theory of interrogatives. Tübingen 1975 (1. edition 1965).

Åqvist, L., "Revised foundations for imperative-epistemic and interrogative logic". Theoria 1, 33-73, 1971.

Belnap, N.D., An analysis of questions: Preliminary report. Santa Monica. 1963.

Belnap, N./Bennet, M., Questions in Montague Grammar. University of Pittsburgh, mimeo 1977.

Blau, U., Glauben und Wissen. Diss. München. 1969.

Boër, S.E., ""Who" and "whether": Towards a theory of indirect question clauses". Linguistics and Philosophy 2, 307-345. 1978.

Boër, S.E./Lycan, W.G., "Knowing who". Philosophical Studies 28, 299-344. 1975.

Carnap, R./Stegmüller, W., Induktive Logik und Wahrscheinlichkeit. Wien. 1958.

Carnap, R., "A basic system of inductive logic". part I. In: R. Carnap/ R.C.Jeffrey (eds.), Studies in inductive logic and probability. vol. I. Berkeley 1971.

Conrad, R., Studien zur Syntax und Semantik von Frage und Antwort. studia grammatica XIX. Berlin. 1978

Cresswell, M., Logics and languages. London. 1973.

Gazdar, G., Pragmatics. New York. 1979.

Hamblin, C.L., "Questions in Montague English", Foundations of Language 10, 41-53. 1973.

Higginbotham, J./May, R. "Questions, quantifiers and crossing". The Linguistic Review 1, 41—80. 1981.

Hintikka, J., Knowledge and belief. Ithaca. 1962.

Hintikka, J., Models for modalities. Dordrecht. 1969.

Hintikka. J., "Semantics for propositional attitudes". In: Hintikka (1969), 87-111. 1969a.

Hintikka, J., The intentions of intentionality and other new models for models for modalities. Dordrecht. 1975.

Hintikka, J., "Objects of knowledge and belief: Acquaintances and public figures". in: Hintikka (1975). 43-58. 1975a.

Hintikka, J., "Answers to questions". In: Hintikka (1975), 137-158. 1975b.

Hintikka, J., "Knowledge, belief, and logical consequence". In: Hintikka (1975), 179-191. 1975c.

Hintikka, J., ''Questions about questions''. In: M.K. Munitz/P.K. Unger (eds.), Semantics and Philosophy. New York. 1974.

Jeffrey, R.C., The logic of decision. New York 1965.

Kaplan, D., ''Quantifying in''. In: L.Linsky (ed.), Reference and modality. Oxford, 112-144. 1971.

Karttunen, L., ''Syntax and semantics of questions''. Linguistics and Philosophy 1, 3-44. 1977.

Katz, J.J., ''Chomsky on meaning''. Language 56, 1-41. 1980.

Keenan, E.L./Hull, R.D., ''The logical presuppositions of questions and answers''. In: J. Petöfi/D. Franck (eds.) Präsuppositionen in Philosophie und Linguistik. Frankfurt , 441-466. 1973.

Link, G., Intensionale Semantik. München. 1976.

Montague, R., ''The proper treatment of quantification in ordinary English''. In: R. Thomason (ed.), Formal Philosophy. Selected papers of Richard Montague. New Haven, 247-270. 1976.

Quine, W.v.O., Word and object. Cambridge, Mass. 1960.

Quine, W.v.O., ''Quantifiers and propositional attitudes''. In: W.v.O. Quine, The ways of paradox. New York, 183-194. 1966.

Savage, L.J., The foundations of statistics. New York. 1954.

Spohn, W., Grundlagen der Entscheidungstheorie. Kronberg. 1978.

Stegmüller, W., Probleme und Resultate der Wissenschaftstheorie und Analytischen Philosphie. vol. IV. Personelle und Statistische Wahrscheinlichkeit. Berlin/Heidelberg-/New York. 1973.

Wunderlich, D., ''Fragesätze und Fragen''. In: D: Wunderlich, Studien zur Sprechakttheorie. Frankfurt, 181-250. 1976.

Eva Hajičová

On Some Aspects of Presuppositions of Questions

1. The notion of presupposition still belongs to one of the widely discussed notions in the present-day linguistic writings. We tried to show elsewhere (Hajičová, 1971; 1974) that the difficulties concerning the test of negation that is used as an operational criterion for the determination of presuppositions are closely connected with the position of the relevant element of the sentence either in the topic, or in the focus of the sentence. (1) is a presupposition of (2), because it is entailed both by (2) and by (3); (3) can be followed by (4) rather than by (5). The bearer of the intonation centre in all our examples is denoted by capitals.

(1) We WON.
(2) Our victory was caused by JOHN.
(3) Our victory wasn't caused by JOHN.
(4) ...He tried hard but it was Fred, who took over all the initiative, was the best player of the team and helped most of all to get back the Cup.
(5) ... This time, unfortunately, we lost the game

However, (6) may have both (4) and (5) as its continuations, i.e. it does not entail (1).

(6) John didn't cause our VICTORY.

In (2) and in its negative counterpart (3) the NP in guestion (**our victory**) is in the topic part of the sentence (we speak about our victory, and we assert that it was caused by John). In (6), on the other hand, the NP **our victory** is in the focus part of the sentence and there is only a potential possibility under negation of what was entailed by the affirmative sentence.

These considerations led us to distinguish three kinds of entailment that can be specified in the following way:

(i) **meaning proper** (assertion): A is a (part of the) meaning proper of B, if B entails A and not-B entails not-A;[1]

Ferenc Kiefer (ed.), Questions and Answers, 85–96.

(ii) **presupposition**: A is a presupposition of B, if B entails A and not-B entails A;

(iii) **allegation** : A is an allegation of B, if B entails A and not-B entails neither A nor not-A.

Recent discussions have shown the necessity to differentiate the phenomena that have been subsumed under the notion of presupposition in a more detailed manner. It seems that the introduction of the notion of allegation is useful for a solution of some of the problems tackled in those discussions (see Hajičová, in prep.).

2. To specify what is a presupposition of a question (or, to be more precise, of an interrogative sentence) is even a more difficult problem because the test of negation cannot be used directly for this purpose. Let us first discuss from this point of view some aspects of wh-questions.

An intergrated formal analysis taking into account both logical and linguistic aspects of wh-questions was given by Keenan and Hull (1973), who define presupositions of questions as logical consequences of every pair consisting of the given question and one of its logical answers. According to their definition an L-sentence (i.e. roughly a logical form of a sentence) S ''is a logical presupposition of a question Q just in case, for every answer A to Q, S is a logical consequence of the pair (Q,A)'', where A is the phrase which with other approaches would be considered the (non-omissible) focus of the answer.

With such a specification of a presupposition of a question based on the logical answers to the question it is not quite clear whether a negative pronoun might be considered a logical answer to a wh-question: If one supposes that ''nobody'' is a possible answer to (7), then—using the above mentioned framework—we see that (8) is not presupposed by the given question, since (8) is not a logical consequence of the pair (Who came? Nobody.); only if one assumes a priori that ''nobody'' does not belong to appropriate answers to the given question, then (8) is presupposed by the question.

(7) Who came?
(8) Somebody came.

The view that (8) is a presupposition of (7) is shared by may of those who discuss this problem (see Katz and Postal, 1964; Karttunen, 1978; Bolinger, 1978a, 1978b; Hintikka, 1978, but cf. below).

A more differentiated view is held by Kiefer (1977); he makes a distinction between a **presupposition** of a question (which must be shared by the answer) and a **background assumption** (which may but need not be shared by the answer). He exemplifies this distinction on (9) to (11).

(9) Who has studied water pollution?
(10) There is no water pollution.
(11) Nobody.

(10) is a negation of (one of) the presupposition(s) of the question (9 (one can speak here about ''presupposition failure'': the response might have started with the words ''You're mistaken, there is no water pollution'').[2] On the other hand, (11) only indicates that the hearer does not share the background assumption of the speaker (''somebody has studied water pollution'').[3]

Joshi (in his lecture in Prague, 1979) proposed to make an interesting distinction between presuppositions and presumptions of a question: P is a **presupposition** of Q, if for all direct answers A_i of Q, $A_i \rightarrow P$ and $-A_i \rightarrow P$. P is a **presumption** of Q, if for all direct answers A_i except one, say A_j, $A_i \rightarrow P$, $-A_i \rightarrow P$, $i \neq j$. This is to say that in case P is a presupposition of Q, then one cannot answer Q by a negative pronoun (see (12) and (13)).

(12) When did John take CSE 110?
(13) John took CSE 110. (= presupposition)

If, on the other hand, P is just a presumption of Q, such an answer is possible (see (14) to (16)).

(14) Which faculty members teach CSE?
(15) Faculty members teach CSE. (= presumption)
(16) Noone.

In the latter case Joshi adds the questioner may add ''if any'', which admits the negative answer (16).

We tried to show (Hajičová, 1976), that the intuitive acceptability of a negative answer such as (19) to wh-questions depends on the way in which the question is pronounced: if the intonation centre is on the wh-element (as in (18)), the (19) is highly inappropriate, and almost breaks down the dialogue (the speaker might have add ''You're mistaken, noone came late''), while if the intonation centre is at the end of the question (as in (17)), such an answer is quite acceptable.[4]

(17) Who came to the MEETING?
(18) WHO came to the meeting? = WHO was it who came to the meeting?
(19) Nobody.

With (18) one expects to be given a non-empty list of persons who attended the meeting, which is not the case with (17).

If these intuitions are true, then again the presuppositions of questions must be studied in close connection with the topic/focus articulation of questions. The intonation centre on the wh-element shows that the rest of the question belongs to the topic part; if the intonation centre lies on the last element of the question, then (at least) this element belongs to the focus (see Hajičová, 1976, for the topic/focus distinction in questions).

It should be mentioned in this connection that Bolinger's (1978b) analysis of the wh-element in wh-questions is based on very similar considerations; if the wh-element is in the final position, then only the wh-element is assumed to be in the comment (focus), the whole rest of the question belonging to the topic (20) (a).

(20) (a) You gave the book to WHOM?
(b) WHOM did you give the book to?

In this particular paper,[5] Bolinger does not take into consideration the possibility of the front position of the wh-word and of the shift of the intonation centre on it, thus marking it also as the comment (focus) (cf. (20) (b)).

When examining the way how the distinction between presupposition and presumption (as defined by Joshi) is determined by the structure of the interrogative sentence, one easily finds that the difference between the placement of the intonation centre on the wh-element and on some other element of the question is only one of the relevant factors: While this criterion is sufficient for such examples as (21) or (22) (where a negative answer is acceptable only for the (a) variants, so that (c) is a presumption of (a) and a presupposition of (b)), in other examples, such as (23), (c) belongs to the presuppositions of both (a) and (b).

(21) (a) Who came LATE?
(b) WHO came late?
(c) Someone came late.

(22) (a) What did you buy for him for a Christmas PRESENT?
(b) WHAT did you buy for him for a Christmas present?
(c) You bought him something for a Christmas present.

(23) (a) Why did you came LATE?
(b) WHY did you come late?
(c) I came late for some reason.

These considerations led us first to a preliminary hypothesis that this distinction is connected with that between inner participants (inner cases) and free modifications (adjuncts).[6] It soon turned out, however, that the facts are not so simple. There are examples in which an interrogative sentence with a wh-element in the syntactic position of a free modification is connected with the presupposition (c) only in its (b) variant; this is the case in Joshi's example (14) above, as well as in (24), and probably also (25). On the other hand, there are examples of interrogative sentences which include a wh-element in the position of an inner participant, but are connected with a respective presupposition in both variants (cf. (26), where (c) is a presupposition of both (a) and (b)).

(24) (a) How many people DIED?
(b) HOW MANY people died?
(c) Some people died.

(25) (a) When did you visit ITALY?
(b) WHEN did you visit Italy?
(c) You visited Italy at some time.

(26) (a) To whom did Mary give the BOOK?
(b) To WHOM did Mary give the book?
(c) Mary gave the book to someone.

Also (27) quoted by Bierwisch in the discussion at the conference on question-answering at Visegrad, May 1980, behaves similarly as (26) above, i.e. the answer ''Nobody'' is inappropriate; it is connected with a presupposition failure.

(27) Who took my COFFEE?

The position of the intonation centre is connected (as we have already remarked) with the topic/focus articulation of the sentence; if the bearer of the intonation centre is the wh-element, all other elements of the interrogative sentence belong to the topic of the sentence. It is quite natural that, if the verb is included in the topic, the event (action) identified by such a verb is assumed to be ''given'' and the answer to the question by a negative pronoun renders a presupposition failure, as in (21) (b) above. However, even this is not a fully reliable criterion: compare (28), in which all elements except the attribute **French** belong to the topic, and yet a negative answer (b) is fully appropriate.

(28) (a) Where is there a FRENCH film on?
(b) I'm sorry, there is no French film on this week.

Also other examples have been found where the situation is not quite clear: as for **how many** , an explanation offers itself that in interrogative sentences standing close to mathematical formulations (see e.g. (29)) also the variant (b) may have the negative pronoun as an appropriate answer.

(29) (a) How many points with the mentioned properties lie inside the triangle as specified ABOVE?
(b) HOW MANY points with the mentioned properties lie inside the triangle as specified above?

The above discussion indicates that a further empirical investigation of some larger corpus is necessary, because also some contextual features seem to be at stake here, which have not yet been systematically studied.

Joshi made an analogy between his concept of a presumption (mentioned above) and the notion of allegation of a declarative sentence. I am convinced that his analogy is corroborated by the following argument:

If the interrogative sentence is understood as a request having the form of a declarative sentence, then e.g. (30) differs from (31) just in topic/focus articulation; the question word is the only element of the focus of (31), so that ''somebody's coming late'' is included in the topic (it is not in the scope of the negation) and it belongs to the presuppositions of (31). In (30) ''coming late'' belongs to the focus of the question and is connected with an allegation: (32) may be followed by (33) as well as by (34).

(30) I request you to tell me who came LATE.
(31) I request you to tell me WHO came late. (= ...WHO it was who came late)
(32) I don't request you to tell me who came LATE.
(33) I know all were there in time.
(34) I know that John did.

However, as we have remarked, why-questions (and perhaps others) seem never to allow for an answer with a negative pronoun, i.e. they are connected with presuppositions even if the ''inducer'' of the presupposition belongs to their focus: in this they behave similarly as sentences with factive verbs and (simple) proper nouns.

It should be emphasized that we do not claim that presuppositions and ''inclusion in the topic'' are the same phenomenon; the inclusion in the topic of the sentence is only one of the factors that lead to presuppositions, the other being the syntactic structure of the sentence (factive verbs with their complements), proper names, questioned modifications such as **why** , and perhaps others. Thus inside a topic, there may be elements with ''multiple'' or ''strengthened'' presuppositions, cf. e.g. (35) and (36).

(35) Why did John marry JOAN?
(36) Why did JOHN marry Joan? (= Why it was JOHN who married Joan?)

In (35) the presupposition that Mary is married is based on the fact that (35) is a why-question, while in (36) the placement of the intonation centre on John (as well as the cleft construction in the equivalent structure) ''strengthens'' the said presupposition, since in (36) the fact of Joan being married is stated in the topic of the question (as ''given'' and recoverable information).

In this connection, Hintikka's (1978) modification of his original proposal for a formal treatment of questions is worth mentioning. He distinguished within a question two ingredients, namely the optative (or imperative) operator and the desideratum; the presupposition of a question then equals to the desideratum of the question minus its initial epistemic operators. Thus (37) would entail that the speaker wants it to be made true that (38), which arguably implies (39). As Hintikka (1978, p. 286, ex.25 to 27) says, this would lead to a mistaken implication: ''part of the force of the question would be to try to marry Mary off''. Therefore he modifies the optative operator and changes the original formula into (40).

(37) Who is Mary married to?
(38) (Ex) K_I Mary is married to x
(39) (Ex) Mary is married to x
(40) Assuming that (Ex) F(x) bring it about that (Ex) $K_I F_{(x)}$

The motivation of the change seems to be clear:[7] the consequences of its acceptance are somewhat dubious. What happens if the assumption (evidently of the questioner) is not fulfilled (i.e. there does not exist any x such that F(x))? Tichý (1978) would say that such a question ''does not arise'', but it does arise, as is exemplified by (37).

3. Passing to the yes/no questions, we can take Kiefer's (1980) considerations as the point of departure. He uses again the notion of background assumptions (a proposition that is formed by substituting a Pro-element such as **somebody, sometime** etc. for the focused element in the question) and for that purpose he distinguishes a focused part of the question (italics in (41)). If there is such a focused part present in a question, then the speaker takes the background assumption for granted and asks, in fact, for a more specific modification.

(41) Is John leaving for Stockholm *TOMORROW*?
(42) WHEN is John leaving for Stockholm?

Thus (41) should be interpreted by the hearer as (42): if the hearer answers by a simple **No** , then the answer is not complete from the point of view of the questioner.

On the other hand, if (in Kiefer's terms) there is no focused element in the question (as in (43)), then the speaker wants to know whether his assumption is right or wrong:

(43) IS John leaving for Stockholm tomorrow?

In this case, the answer **No** is a complete answer.

I want to add just two remarks. First, it is true that with a question such as (41) the negative answer **No** may mean that the speaker admits that John is leaving for Stockholm, but that it is not tomorrow, while in (43)—with the intonation centre on the verb—this cannot be the case. In our approach to topic/focus articulation every sentence (including interrogative sentences) has a focus. In (41), the focus is the time adverbial **tomorrow**; in (43) only the verb belongs to the focus. In case the verb belongs to the topic, the action (event) identifed by the verb is assumed as "given" and a negative answer to the question has in the scope of negation only the focused part of the sentence (he leaves for Stockholm, (but) not tomorrow). If the verb belongs to the focus of the question, as in (43), the action identified by the verb is negated by the negative answer (he does not leave for Stockholm).

Also other examples show that yes/no questions are sensitive to topic/focus articulation in the same manner as declarative sentences are, and that in yes/no questions the type of presuppositions connected with the inclusion of an element into the topic of the sentence is also present. If the speaker asks (44), then in one of the readings of the question only Stockholm belongs to the focus, i.e. (44) in this reading is connected with the presupposition that John is leaving tomorrow for some place.

(44) Is John leaving for STOCKHOLM tomorrow?

The hearer can state that this presupposition is not fulfilled (as e.g. in (45)).

(45) Oh, you are mistaken, John is not leaving tomorrow.

A mere **No** denies that it is Stockholm for which John is leaving tomorrow, and accepts that John is leaving somewhere tomorrow.

The "markedness" Kiefer ascribes to some of his examples is not surprising if we accept that there exists a systemic ordering of participants of verbs given by the character of the participants and observed in the focus part of the sentence; every sentence the participants in which are not ordered in accordance with this systemic ordering has some feature of markedness in Kiefer's sense. Thus (46)—his (37) (b)—has the order direction—means (manner), which is not in accordance with the systemic order of there participants (**I'm going by train to STOCKHOLM** rather than **I'm going to Stockholm by TRAIN** is a most natural answer to **What are you doing TOMORROW?**). In such a case the phrase **by train** is (as Kiefer says) almost exclusively determined as the focus of the question (**to Stockholm** belongs to the topic).

(46) Are you going to Stockholm by TRAIN?

The same holds true, when the intonation centre is placed on an element in some other position than the final one: this has the consequence that all modifications (participants) following the bearer of the intonation centre are in the topic. Our explanation of the ''marked character'' of (47)—Kiefer's example (38)—consists in the fact that the marked intonation of (47) is combined with a marked word order, differring from the systemic ordering.

(47) Are you going to STOCKHOLM by train?

The non-marked counterpart of (47) is (48), with the order means—direction.

(48) Are you going by train to STOCKHOLM?

Here, it is not quite clear where the boundary between topic and focus lies: not only the verb, but also the phrase **by train** can belong to the topic (if it is contextually bound, see Sgall and Hajičová, 1977) as well as to the focus (if is is non-bound). This ambiguity may be understood as one of the reasons for using the marked counterpart (47) instead of the non-marked one (48).

This example illustrates the interplay of word order, intonation, communicative dynamism and contextual boundness in yes/no questions and suggests a possibility how to account for this interplay by means of a framework which has been found to give valuable results for declarative sentences.

Charles University
Institute of Numerical Mathematics

Notes

[1] Our understanding of not-X (see Hajičová, 1973) is not identical with 'the logicians' formulation ''It is not true that...'', since we are convinced that this formulation disguises the linguistic structuring of negative sentence, esp. the distinction between sentences with and without a topic (categorial and thetic judgements).

[2] Sometimes this phenomenon is explained in terms of cohesion: the dialogue breaks down at that moment (see Kiefer, 1977).

[3] When making a distinction between speaker's and hearer's assumptions one should bear in mind that the speaker always formulates his utterance according to his assumptions about the speaker's assumptions.

[4] Our approach seems to be corroborated by Stechow's (1980) account of the difference between **Who likes HANS-ROBERT?** (p. 87, ex. 176A) and **WHO did call?** (p. 78, ex. 143). According to Stechow, his 176A can be appropriately answered by **NOONE likes Hans-Robert** and it is not connected with an assumption that someone likes Hans-Robert, whereas his 143 has a 'topic' ''Someone called''.

[5] However, in other writings on this subject, Bolinger duly works with intonation as one of the most important factors determining the semantic structure of the sentence, see esp. Bolinger (1972).

[6]For the distinction between inner and free modification, see Panevová (1974; 1978).

[7]See our discussion of (21) (a) above.

References

Bolinger D. (1972), Accent is Predictable (if you're a mindreader). Language 48, 633-644.

Bolinger D. (1978a), Yes-No Questions are not Alternative Questions, in Hiż (1978), 87-105.

Bolinger D. (1978b), Asking More than One Thing at a Time, in: Hiż (1978), 107-150.

Hajičová E. (1971), Some Remarks on Presuppositions, presented at the Int. Conf. on Computational Linguistics, Debrecen 1971; printed in Prague Bulletin of Math. Ling. 17, 1972, 11-23.

Hajičová E. (1973), Negation and Topic vs. Comment, Philologica Pragiensia 16, 81-93.

Hajičová E. (1974), Meaning, Presupposition and Allegation, Philologica Pragensia 17, 18-25.

Hajičová E. (1976), Question and Answer in Linguistics and in Man—Machine Communication, SMIL, 30-46.

Hajičová E. (in prep.), Presupposition and Allegation Revisited, prepared for Journal of Pragmatics.

Hintikka J. (1978), Answers to Questions, in Hiż (1978), 279-300.

Hiż H. (1978), ed., Questions. D. Reidel Publ. Co., Dordrecht, Holland.

Karttunen L. (1978), Syntax and Semantics of Questions, in: Hiż (1978) 165-210.

Katz J.J. and P.M. Postal (1964), An Integrated Theory of Linguistic Descriptions. Cambridge, Mass.

Keenan E.L. and R.D. Hull (1973), The Logical Presuppositions of Questions and Answers, in: Petöfi and Franck (1973), 441-466.
Kiefer F. (1977), Some Semantic and Pragmatic Properties of Wh-Questions and the Corresponding Answers, SMIL (Journal of Linguistic Calculus) No. 3, 42-71.
Kiefer F. (1980), Yes-No Questions as Wh-Questions, in: Searle, Kiefer and Bierwisch (1980), 97-119.
Panevová J. (1974), On Verbal Frames in Functional Generative Description, Part I, Prague Bulletin of Mathematical Linguistics 22, 3-40; Part II, PBML 23, 1975, 17-52.
Panevová J. (1978), Inner Participants and Free Adverbials, in: Prague Studies in Mathematical Linguistics 6, 227-254.
Petöfi J.S. and D. Franck (1973), eds., Präsuppositionen in Philosophie und Linguistik, Frankfurt a/M.
Searle J.R., Kiefer F. and M. Bierwisch (1980), eds., Speech Act Theory and Pragmatics, D. Reidel Publ. Co. Dordrecht, Holland.
Sgall P. and E. Hajičová (1977), Focus on Focus, Part I, Prague Bulletin of Mathematical Linguistics 28, 5-54; Part II, PBML 29, 1978, 23-41.
Stechow von A. (1980), Notes on Topic and Focus of Interrogatives and Indicatives, Sonderforschungsbereich 99 Linguistik, Univ. Konstanz.
Tichý P. (1978), Questions, Answers, and Logic, American Philosophical Quarterly 15, 275-284.

Roland R. Hausser

The Syntax and Semantics of English Mood

0. Introductory remarks

What is a 'meaning' of a natural language expression, and how is it encoded in the natural surface structure? The literature on formal semantics has provided various answers to this question. Consider the following four principles:

(i) The meaning of a complex expression is a function of the meaning of its basic constituents and their mode of composition.
(ii) The meaning of a logical operator is specified in terms of its meta-language definition.
(iii) The meaning of a constant is defined in terms of the model-theoretic object(s) it denotes.
(iv) The meaning of a declarative sentence (proposition) consists in the truth-conditions of the sentence.

Principle (i) is our version of the so-called Fregean principle. (ii) reflects the so-called T-condition of Tarski (1935, 1944). (iii) is inherent in the model-theoretic approach as persued, for example, by Montague (1974). And (iv) has been formulated in this particular way by Davidson (1967).

Each of the four principles captures a valid aspect and is justified in its own context, but none suffices as a complete formal treatment of meaning. Rather, the four principles complement each other in various degrees, and formal analyses of meaning in natural language differ in their emphasis and interpretation of each of the principles. Before we turn to the main task of this paper, namely the formal analysis of the syntax and semantics of 25 English sentences (of different syntactic moods and different internal constructions), let us briefly indicate the particular status of the above principles in our overall theory.

The traditional purpose of formal logic is to characterize valid inferences. From that point of view, natural languages seem highly irregular and structurally misleading, especially since the standard

Ferenc Kiefer (ed.), Questions and Answers, 97–158.

framework of referential semantics does not provide for a distinction between *literal meaning* and the *use* of literal meaning by a speaker. Thus the validity of principle (i) for *natural* languages is regarded as highly doubtful in the literature. Methods to bring out the underlying or real logical structure of natural language include 'regimentation' (Quine 1960) and transformations.

It is thus a notable feature of the syntactico-semantic analyses of our 25 sample sentences that they fulfill the Fregean principle as stated in (i) in a strict sense, namely as applying to the linguistic surface. Our analyses are "surface compositional" in the sense that the surface syntax is based solely on the constituent words and a mood marker. These constituents are combined on the basis of only *one* rule, namely category combination (category canceling). Following Montague (1974), we characterize the meaning of analyzed surface structures via translation into model-theoretically interpretable formulas of intensional logic. These translations are surface compositional in the sense that they consist only of the word and mood marker translations which are combined by means of only one rule, functional application. Functional application is the semantic counterpart of category combination.

It is only natural that this strict way of applying principle (i) in our analysis of naturallanguage expressions will have consequences on the status of the other principles in our overall framework. Principle (ii), however, applies in full in our theory (on the level of the auxiliary language of intensional logic). It has been said with regards to Tarski's T-condition that it transposes the problem of formally characterizing meaning to a higher level. However, if we accept set theory as a basic formal language which is mathematically well defined and universally learnable, then the definition of logical operators in the meta-language of set theory does indeed provide for a well founded formal characterization of the meaning of these operators. Further support for the validity of principle (ii) in the analysis of meaning is the fact that these meta-language definitions may be operationalized and have been widely tested in this form. The T-condition underlying (ii) is implicitly generalized to a D-condition in our system in the sense that the meta-language definitions characterize *D*enotations of all types and not only *T*ruth-values.

Regarding principle (iii), questions arise as to the nature of the model theoretic objects denoted. According to the main stream view in model theory, the formal model is regarded as a representation of reality. Thus the meanings of constants are treated as model theoretic objects (or sets thereof) which are real. This view, which is motivated by the desire to apply valid inference systems to actual scientific theories, leads to a number of serious problems in the definition of formal meanings. Following Hausser (1979c), where these problems are discussed in detail, we treat intensions rather than extensions as the primary type of denotation of natural language expressions and treat the model structure as a representation of a speakers lexical intuition rather than a representation of reality. These considerations are formally reflected in the use of a strictly intensional logic, i.e. a logic where the recursion of the syntactic and semantic rules is defined uniformly on the intensional level.[1] This strictly intensional logic has the additional advantage of a much simpler notation than Montague's logic defined in PTQ, which is intensional only in the sense that it contains an intensional operator but is otherwise extensional in the sense that extensions are treated as the primary type of denotation.

The abstract model theoretic treatment of formal meanings in our system, while motivated on its own grounds, provides the semantic foundations for our surface compositional approach to the analysis of natural surface structures. The relation between formal meanings and reality is constituted by the *use* of expressions relative to a context, and is discussed here in section 6. Due to the strictly intensional definition of our formal translation language and the reinterpretation of the model structure, principle (ii) and (iii) turn out to be simply variants of the same principle in our framework: operators and constants are alike in that they uniformly denote *functions* the domain and range of which is defined over abstract model sets.

We turn finally to principle (iv), which is probably the most widely accepted definition of meaning within referential semantics. As far as declarative sentences are concerned, (iv) is fully accommodated in our approach. We do not agree with those proposals, however, which derive non-declaratives from declaratives or propositions in order to integrate non-declaratives into the framework of "truth-conditional semantics".[2] There is no reason to treat truth-values (or rather truth-functions) as somehow the only meaningful type of denotation of complete surface expression. Rather, (iv) is applicable only in the case of declaratives, while the denotation of non-declaratives (which intuitively do not denote truth values) will be defined on the basis of a strict application of principle (i), i.e. as the compositional result of the particular kind of surface structure characteristic of the respective mood.

After discussing the distinction between literal meaning and speaker meaning, moods and speech acts, semantics and pragmatics in section 1, we turn in section 2 to a description of our overall system of syntactico-semantic analysis. The 25 sample sentences are analyzed in the sections 3, 4, and 5 in 'canonical form'. Each canonical analysis specifies the surface serialization (vertical order of the basic surface constituents) and the logical serialization (horizontal order of the constituent translations) simultaneously in form of an *orthogonal tree,* a concept introduced in section 2.4. An orthogonal tree also specifies the sub-categories of the basic constituents (i.e. the words and a mood marker) and their standard translation into intensional logic. A canonical analysis is completed with a lambda-reduced meaning^1-formula. The meaning^1-formula of a canonical analysis must be provably equivalent with the respective translated surface formula, whereby the latter results from combining the constituent translations according to the functor/argument structure specified by the orthogonal tree (using functional application as the only rule).

Since the syntactico-semantic analyses themselves should convince, the reader might first like to take a look at the orthogonal tree structures of our 25 sample sentences presented in the sections 3, 4, and 5, and turn afterwards to the background information contained in the section 1, 2, and 6. Section 6 concludes the general discussion of the nature of meaning by describing how canonical analyses are assumed to function in a general framework of communication. In line with earlier work (Hausser 1979b, 1979c, 1980a, 1981), the concept of a speaker simulation device (SID) is presented, on the basis of which the notions of *context* and *pragmatic interpretation* (of a literal meaning relative to a context) are provided with an intuitive interpretation in formal terms.

1. Moods and speech acts

1.1 *Moods*

This paper presents a grammatical treatment of the major syntactic moods of English. Thus we will be dealing with expressions in the *declarative, imperative,* and *interrogative* mood. Syntactic moods must be distinguished from verbal moods like indicative, subjunctive (conjunctive), optative, etc. Syntactic mood is understood here in the sense of 'macro-syntactic construction'.

The following examples will be analyzed:

Declarative

(1) John goes home.
(2) John reads a book.
(3) Mary knows a story.
(4) Mary knows that John walks.
(5) Mary knows whether John walks.
(6) Mary knows who walks.
(7) Mary wonders who walks.
(8) Mary tries a cooky.
(9) Mary tries to walk.
(10) John persuades Mary to walk.
(11) John promises Mary to walk.

Imperative

(12) Go home!

Interrogative

(13) Who goes home?
(14) Where does John go?
(15) Who loves whom?
(16) Who does Bill say that Mary loves?
(17) Does John go home?
(18) Does John love Mary or Suzy? (Yes.)
(19) Does John love Mary or Suzy? (Suzy.)
(20) Does John love Mary or Bill Suzy?

Responsive

(21) John.
(22) Home.
(23) John Mary.
(24) No.
(25) Yes.

The *responsive* is a new mood,[3] but its definition is straigthforward enough and is in agreement with our concept of mood as a mode of surface syntactic construction. We are interested in responsives in connection with the analysis of interrogatives. For the sake of simplicity, the tensed mood-expressions of the above examples are in the present tense, which sometimes results in a certain awkwardness to be taken into consideration.

1.2 *Speech acts*

Of an entirely different theoretical nature than moods are speech acts, such as *statements, questions, commands, answers,* etc. Speech acts involve "a speaker, a hearer, and an utterance by the speaker".[4] Natural language expressions of certain moods are *used* in certain speech acts. Traditionally, moods and speech acts are correlated in the following way:

(26)

mood	speech act
declarative	statement
imperative	request
interrogative	question
responsive	answer

Contrary to the assumptions of most of the literature on "questions, answers", and related topics it is a fact of nature that moods and speech acts are not in a one to one correlation.[5] Two (or more) expressions of different moods may be used for the same kind of speech act. And one expression of one certain mood may be used for two (or more) different speech acts. Consider (27) as a case where two different expressions may be used for the same speech act:

(27.1) I ask you who goes home. (declarative)
(27.2) Who goes home? (interrogative)

Unfortunately, expressions like (27.1) are usually called "indirect questions", which introduces a fourfold terminological confusion: that between speech act (question) and mood (interrogative), and that whether the intended referent of "question" is supposed to be the whole declarative sentence (27.1) or only the complement. In the literature, the term "indirect question" has been used in all four interpretation. That (27.1) is indeed a declarative may be seen from its syntactic paradigm.

(28) I ask you who goes home.
I asked you who goes home.
. . .

I ask him who goes home.
I asked him who goes home.
. . .
He asks you who goes home.
He asked you who goes home.[6]
. . .

To complete the proof that moods and speech acts are not in a one to one correspondence it remains to show the converse, namely an example of an expression with an obvious literal meaning (mood: interrogative) used in two different kinds of speech acts.

(29.1) *Question:*
John visits Bill in the hospital, where Bill is treated for some impairment of his motor function. John says to Bill: "Can you pass the salt?"

(29.2) *Request:*
John and Bill are at the dinner table. John says to Bill: "Can you pass the salt?".

Examples demonstrating the point in question may be easily multiplied. Interrogatives may also be used to convey information ("Did you know that John eats bat wings?", "How do you like being on night shift tomorrow?", etc.) and it is only a matter of ingenuity to find different speech act examples for all the different moods.

1.3 *Syntax, Semantics, and Pragmatics*
Syntactic moods are a structural property of natural language expressions. Their study belongs to the domain of syntax and semantics. Semantics describes the compositionally encoded literal meaning of expressions. Speechacts, on the other hand, are constituted by the phenomenon of using expressions in meaningful ways under varying contextual circumstances. The study of speech acts includes the domain of pragmatics as well as semantics. Semantics and pragmatics jointly contribute to the speakers intuitive notion of "meaning".

In the following, we distinguish between two different types of meaning, namely *meaning*^{1} and *meaning*^{2}. Meaning^1 is defined as the *literal meaning* of natural language expressions. Meaning^2, on the other hand, is the so-called *speaker meaning,* consisting of the use of the *form and meaning*[1] of a surface expression in a certain context with a certain speaker intention (compare Grice (1957) and Ziff (1967)). The relation between syntax, semantics, and pragmatics in our system is expressed by the following formula:[7]

(30)

syntax
⋮
use of $\left\{\begin{array}{c}\textbf{form}\\ |\\ \textbf{meaning}^{1}\end{array}\right\}$ **relative to a context=meaning**^{2}
⋮
pragmatics *semantics* *speech act theory*

The notions of *use* and *context* will be explained in a more formal sense in section 6.

Assuming our structural definition of *mood* in 1.1 and 1.2 above, the point of (30) is that the syntactico-semantic treatment of mood must be restricted to the analysis of *form* (i.e. surface syntax) and *meaning*[1] (i.e. literal meaning). By assuming that the model-theoretically analyzed literal meanings are encoded in the natural language surfaces in a strictly compositional way, we obtain a clear standard for the border between semantics and pragmatics.

2. The syntactico-semantic framework of analysis

2.1 *The surface/meaning-mapping in Montague grammar*

Our goal is to analyse English expressions of different moods solely in terms of the constituent words and a mood-marker, whereby the words are used in their standard lexical analysis motivated from their role in the declarative mood. The mood-markers translate into standard formulas of intensional logic[8] consisting of variables, lambda-operators, context-variables, and the usual logical operators, but containing no constants (performative clause) or non-standard operator like (x?) (illocutionary force indicators).

To establish a common denominator of discussion, let us consider a syntactico-semantic analysis of an English declarative in a style close to Montague's PTQ.

(31)

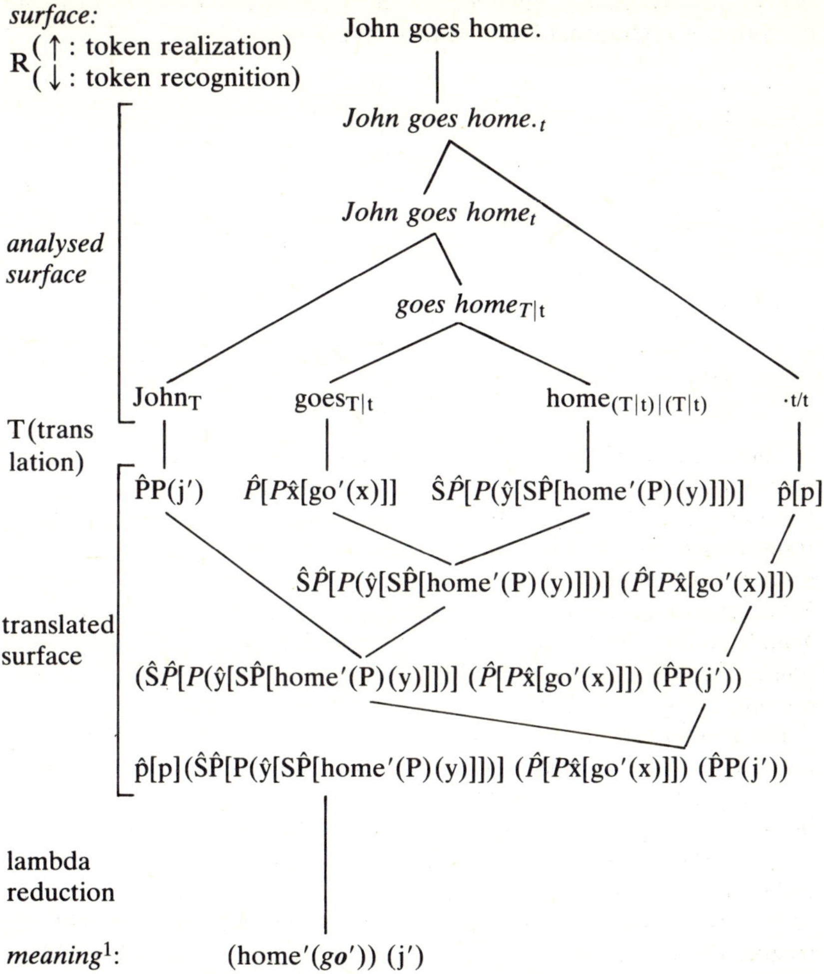

The variables and constants used in (31) are of the following types (stated in terms of the corresponding category for simplicity, c.f. section 2.3).

The categorially analysed surface in (31) uses only one rule, namely category canceling (35) (cf. section 2.3), while the translated surface makes use only of functional application, which is the semantic rule interpreting category canceling. All other syntactico-semantic properties of the words are encoded in the translation of the words into formulas of intentional logic (lexical translations).

(32) *Variables*	*Category*
p, q	t
x, y	e
P, Q	$e\|t$
P, Q	$(e\|t)\|t=T$
S	$((e\|t)\|t)\|t=T\|t$

Constants	*Category*
j′	e
go′	$e\|t$
home′	$(e\|t)\|(e\|t)$

The word translations in (31) are of a higher type structure, built up with variables and lambdas around constants, which are of the lowest possible type. The reason for having these higher type structures in the translated surface is linguistic in nature. The higher type structures are used to accommodate certain linguistic generalizations of English. Montague, for example, raised the translation of a proper name like **John** from the traditional category e to category **$(e|t)|t$** in order to treat names like **John** (translation: PP(j′)) and quantified noun phrases like **a man** (translation: $\hat{P}$Vx[man′(x)∧P(x)]) surface syntactically alike.

For similar reasons the category of **goes** is raised in (31) from $e|t$ to $((e|t)|t)|t$. We follow Bartsch & Vennemann (1972) and others who have argued that the verb is the functor and the subject the argument, both on the logical and the surface level. Montague's alternative way in PTQ (though not UG), of defining intransitive verbs as $e|t$-phrases rather than $T|t(=((e|t)|t)|t)$ phrases, and transitive verbs as $T|(e|t)$ rather then $T|(T|t)$ phrases, leads to problems in connection with the treatment of quantifier scope, relative clauses (**man who kissed Mary** versus **man whom Mary kissed**), a uniform treatment of collective versus distributive plural[9] and other phenomena. These difficulties are avoided by raising the category of **goes** to $T|t$ in the manner indicated in (33.2) below.

The category of the adverb **home** is raised from **a $(e|t)|(e|t)$**-constant to a $(T|t)|(T|t)$ word translation. This is a consequence of treating intransitive verbs on the surface **as $T|t$**-phrase, since adverbs are modifiers on the intransitive verb. The higher type structures of the word translations evaporate in the course of *lambda-conversion* (cf. (34) below).

Since in our surface compositional system syncategorematic operations are prohibited, all syntactico-semantic properties of a sentence are systematically derived from properties of the constituent words. Thus the analysis of words is a major concern of our grammatical approach. For reasons of space we cannot go here into the details of our lexical theory (cf. Hausser 1981, 1982b (chapter 4)), but shall have to make due with the following brief remarks.

Montague's "lexicon" in PTQ lists only surface words in so-called sets of basic expressions B_A (where A is a category). These words are then translated by means of rules listed together with the combinatorial translation rules. Alternatively, let us assume a lexical structure where surface words are listed as fully analyzed *molecules* derived from roots by lexical derivation rules. Molecules are regarded as the basic constituents of the surface syntax. They consist of (i) the surface form of the word, (ii) the sub-category, which specifies the surface combinatorial properties of the molecule, i.e. the syntactic properties of the word, and (iii) the analyzed translation which specifies the semantic properties of the word and corresponds in type to the subcategory.[10] An example of a molecule is given in (33.0):

(33.0) $goes_{T|t}$
$\hat{P}[P\hat{x}[go'(x)]]$

go' of category e|t in the translation is called a *root.* In order to capture syntactic and semantic generalizations in the area of word analysis we derive molecules from roots via lexical derivation rules. Consider (33), where the lexical derivation of the molecules used in (31) from the respective roots is indicated schematically.[11]
The notion of a molecule is similar to that of a *lexeme* (Lyons 1967, Matthews 1974) in that a molecule specifies a word morphologically (surface form), syntactically (sub-category), and semantically (translation). However, while different inflectional forms like *go, goes, want,* etc., are regarded as different forms of the same lexeme, they constitute different molecules. Furthermore, we distinguish the following types of molecules:

(a) concrete surface molecules, e.g. $\begin{array}{c}\textbf{went}_{T\uparrow t}\\ | \\ \hat{P}[\mathrm{H}P\hat{x}[\mathrm{go}'(x)]]\end{array}$

(b) mood-marker molecules, e.g. $\begin{array}{c}\cdot t\uparrow t\\ | \\ \hat{p}[p]\end{array}$

(c) Ø-surface molecules, e.g. $\begin{array}{c}\boldsymbol{\emptyset}_{T}\\ | \\ \hat{P}[P(x)]\end{array}$

(33.1) *root* *molecule*

$$\mathrm{j}' \longrightarrow \begin{array}{c}\textbf{John}_{(e|t)|t(=T)}\\ | \\ \hat{P}P(\mathrm{j}')\end{array}$$

(33.2) *root* *molecule*

$$\mathrm{go}' \longrightarrow \begin{array}{c}\textbf{goes}_{T\uparrow t}\\ | \\ \hat{P}[P\hat{x}[\mathrm{go}'(x)]]\end{array}$$

(33.3) *root* *molecule*

$$\mathrm{home}' \longrightarrow \begin{array}{c}\textbf{home}_{(T\uparrow t)\uparrow(T\uparrow t)}\\ | \\ \hat{S}\hat{P}[P\hat{y}[S\hat{P}[(\mathrm{home}[P))(y)]]]\end{array}$$

(33.4) *root* *molecule*

$$\emptyset \longrightarrow \begin{array}{c}\cdot t\uparrow t\\ | \\ \hat{p}(p)\end{array}$$

The definition of a well-formed molecule has to fulfill the following criteria:

(34.1) The type of the translation formula must correspond to the subcategory of the surface.

(34.2) In the translation of complex surface expressions, the lambda structures of the molecule translations must systematically reduce to simple, first-order like formulas.

Both conditions are satisfied in (31) (as based on (33)). The proof that lambda reduction from the translated surface to the meaning[1]-formula in (31) is well-defined, rendering the translated surface formula *logically equivalent* to the meaning[1]-formula is given in (34).

(34) *Lambda reduction:*

$$\hat{p}[p](\hat{\mathrm{S}}\hat{P}[P\hat{y}[\mathrm{S}\hat{\mathrm{P}}[\mathrm{home}'(\mathrm{P})(y)]]](\hat{P}[P\hat{x}[\mathrm{go}'(x)]])(\hat{\mathrm{P}}\mathrm{P}(j')))$$

$$\hat{\mathrm{S}}\hat{P}[P\hat{y}[\mathrm{S}\hat{\mathrm{P}}[\mathrm{home}'(\mathrm{P})(y)]]]\ (\hat{P}[P\hat{x}[\mathrm{go}'(x)]])\ (\hat{\mathrm{P}}\mathrm{P}(j'))$$

$$\hat{P}[P\hat{y}[(\hat{P}[\hat{P}\hat{x}[\mathrm{go}'(x)]])\ [\hat{\mathrm{P}}[\mathrm{home}'(\mathrm{P})(y)]]]]\ (\hat{\mathrm{P}}\mathrm{P}(j'))$$

$$\hat{\mathrm{P}}\mathrm{P}(j')\ (\hat{y}[(\hat{P}[P\hat{x}[\mathrm{go}'(x)]])\ [\hat{\mathrm{P}}[\mathrm{home}'(\mathrm{P})\ (y)]])$$

$$\hat{\mathrm{P}}\mathrm{P}(j')\ (\hat{y}[(\hat{\mathrm{P}}[\mathrm{home}'(\mathrm{P})\ (y)])\ (\hat{x}[\mathrm{go}'(x)])])$$

$$\hat{\mathrm{P}}\mathrm{P}(j')\ (\hat{y}[((\mathrm{home}'(\hat{x}[\mathrm{go}'(x)]))\ (y)]) \qquad \hat{x}[\mathrm{go}'(x)]=\mathrm{go}'$$

$$\hat{\mathrm{P}}\mathrm{P}(j')\ (\hat{y}[((\mathrm{home}'(\mathrm{go}'))\ (y))]$$

$$(\hat{y}[((\mathrm{home}'(\mathrm{go}'))\ (y)])\ (j')$$

$$(\mathrm{home}'(\mathrm{go}'))\ (j')$$

Lambda-reduction is part of the surface/meaning[1]-mapping illustrated in (31) above.

2.2 *Surface compositionality*

The idea behind the surface compositionality constraint (SCC)[12] is the Fregean principle, which we state as follows:

(38) The meaning of a complex expression is a function of the meaning of its parts and their mode of composition.

The SCC applies this principle to the *surface* of natural language expressions, taking words as the basic parts of the syntax. It follows that syncategorematic introduction of morphemes or words must be excluded from the surface syntactic composition. This applies both to Montague's syncategorematic treatment of quantifiers, connectives, etc. in PTQ and transformational treatments as proposed by Lewis (1972), Cooper (1975), and others. Such transformational operations must be excluded because they obscure the composition of meaning in the natural surface on the basis of the constituent words in their standard combinatorics and translations.

(31) is surface compositional in the sense that the translation formula consists solely of word- and mood-marker translations, which are composed on the basis of only one rule, namely standard category canceling as defined in Ajdukiewizcz (1938) or Montague (1974). The surface compositionality constraint is conceived as a constraint on the surface/meaning mappings exemplified in (31). It is intended to insure preservation of meaning. The idea is: the more the translated surface mirrors the structure of the analysed surface, the less can the literal meaning encoded in the translated surface deviate from the surface meaning. Thus the translated surface is regarded as a *transformer* which is structurally equivalent to the analyzed surface (where structural equivalence is defined by the SCC) and denotationally equivalent to the $meaning^1$-formula. The logical equivalence between the translated surface and the $meaning^1$-formula is provable in terms of lambda-reduction. Lambda-reduction is the only transformation-like operation in our system. It is a semantically well-defined operation.

The higher type structures of the word-translations designed to mirror the categorial structure of the analysed surface (in accordance with the SCC) may seem acrobatic at times, but their purpose is well-motivated. The use of these higher type structures simply constitutes the application of a well-defined formalism to the full extent of its descriptive power. What may look like a complicated derivation in (31) and (34) is nevertheless a completely algorithmic process, which is simple in the sense that it uses only two recursive rule schemata to get from the surface to the $meaning^1$-formula, namely (1) category canceling in combination with functional application and (2) lambda-conversion. That the translation of surface words consists of complex formulas should be seen not as a complication but an advancement into the field of word semantics.

The principle of surface compositionality is relevant for our semantic analysis of mood because it defines the border between semantics and pragmatics in a clear and obvious way. The literal meaning of surface expressions is defined over their categorial functor/argument structure and the translation of their constituent words, nothing more and nothing less. Even idiomatic expressions like "John kicked the bucket" are analyzed compositionally in our system. The expression is not semantically ambiguous between a literal and an idiomatic reading, where the idiomatic reading is regarded as semantically equivalent to "John died." Rather, the relation between "John kicked the bucket." and "John died." is treated as a purely pragmatic one, as equivalence (to a certain extent) of *use.*

2.3 Serialization in categorial grammar

An important assumption of surface compositional analysis is that the surface syntax consists solely of the functor/argument relations which are determined by the specific combinatorial properties of the constituent words. The combinatorial properties are encoded in the recursively defined categories and sub-categories of the words. Thus the use of combinatorially transparent categories like t, e, $e|t$, etc. instead of the familiar phrase structure categories S, NP, VP, etc. is essential for our approach, since the latter PS-categories are combinatorially opaque, non-recursive primitive symbols. With categorial categories, the syntax needs only one rule (or rather rule schema), namely category canceling:

(35) $A_{\alpha/\beta} \cdot B_{\beta} = AB_{\alpha}$

According to rule (35), which stems from Leśniewski (1929) and Ajdukiewicz (1935), the functor always precedes the argument. A system based on this rule alone therefore cannot accommodate natural language serialization, where functions may both precede and follow their arguments. Bar-Hillel (1953), however, defines a notation providing for both types of serialization of functor and argument.

(36.1) $A_{\frac{\alpha}{\overleftarrow{\beta}}} \cdot B_{\beta} = BA\alpha.$ (36.2) $A_{\frac{\alpha}{\overrightarrow{\beta}}} \cdot B_{\beta} = AB_{\alpha}$

Geach (1972), furthermore, discusses alternative canceling rules of the following kind:

(37.1) $A_{\alpha/\beta} \cdot B_{\beta/\gamma} = AB_{\alpha\gamma}$ (37.2) $A_{(\alpha/\beta)/\gamma} \cdot B_{\beta} = AB_{\alpha\gamma}$

Geach's presentation is obstructed by an almost illegible notation and the absence of semantic definitions for the canceling rules (37). It will be shown below, however, that straightforward definitions can be provided for the rules (37) in a higher order type logic with lambda calculus. Furthermore, a combination of the subcategories inherent in (36) and the canceling rules (35) and (37) results in a mathematically well-defined categorial super system that accommodates all possible serializations of natural language, including discontinuous elements.

The first task in defining our syntax is to specify the sub-categorial system of molecules, since these sub-categories uniquely specify the combinatorial properties of expressions in our system. The sub-categorial system is based on a system of *categories,* which are defined in (38) below:

(38) Def. 1 *The categories of ORTAX*[13]

(i)	e ε CAT
(ii)	t ε CAT
(iii)	If A, B ε CAT, then (A|B) ε CAT.
(iv)	Nothing is in CAT, except as specified in (i—iii) above.

This definition is like Montague's (PTQ), except that a complex category is written as A|B rather than Montague's B/A. Thus in our system categories (e.g. e|t) and types (e.g. ⟨s,⟨⟨s, e⟩, t⟩⟩ use the same Domain/Range serialization in the notation, namely D|R.

(39) Def. 2 *The sub-categories of ORTAX*

(i)	If A ε CAT, then $\overset{m}{A}$ ε SCAT, where m≥0.
	Convention: If m=0, then $\overset{0}{A}$=A.
(ii)	If $A\overset{m}{\vert}B$ ε SCAT, then also $A \overset{m}{\downarrow} B$, $A \overset{m}{\uparrow} B$, $\underline{A} \overset{m}{\downarrow} B$, $\underline{A} \overset{m}{\uparrow} B$, $\underline{\underline{A}} \overset{m}{\downarrow} B$, $\underline{\underline{A}} \overset{m}{\uparrow} B$, ε SCAT.
(iii)	Nothing is in SCAT, except as specified in (i—ii) above.

The first part of this definition, i.e. (i), is a generalization of Montague's double slash method (e.g. A/B versus A//B) for doubling the categories of a given domain/range structure. The index is superior in that it allows denumerably many sub-categories of a given category, including e and t. This multiplication of sub-categories will have numerous applications, such as the distinction between different cases, number, and other surface markings which control the surface composition beyond the frame of the functor/argument structure. (A similar proposal to this effect was made in Kiyong Lee (1982).) The second part of the definition, i.e. (ii), is in some respects a variation of Bar Hillel's categories R ← D and R → D, except that we use a horizontal D ↑ R and D ↓ R notation. The diacritics '–' and '=' exhibited by some of the sub-categories control the surface-serialization of so-called discontinuous elemnts, a phenomenon Bar-Hillel could find no solution for in a pure (i.e. context-free) categorial grammar.

It remains to specify the rules which combine molecules like those illustrated in (33) according to their sub-category into orthogonal trees.

(40) Def. 3 *The rules of ORTAX*

ST0. $M_Z \subset P_Z$, for every $Z \in$ SCAT.

ST1.1 If $\alpha \in P_{A\uparrow B}$ and $\beta \in P_A$, then $F_1(\alpha, \beta) \in P_B$ and

$$\beta_A$$

$$F_1(\alpha, \beta) = \alpha_{A\uparrow B}$$

$$\alpha^\circ\ (\beta^\circ)$$

where α° and β° are the unanalyzed translations of α and β, respectively.

ST1.2 If $\alpha \in P_{A\downarrow B}$ and $\beta \in P_A$, then $F_2(\alpha, \beta) \in P_B$ and

$$F_2(\alpha, \beta) = \alpha_{A\downarrow B}$$

$$\beta_A$$

$$\alpha^\circ\ (\beta^\circ)$$

ST2.1 If $\alpha \in P_{\underline{\underline{A}}\uparrow B}$ and $\beta \in P_{C\uparrow A}$, then $F_3(\alpha, \beta) \in P_{C:\uparrow B}$, and

$$\beta_{C\uparrow A}$$

$$F_3(\alpha, \beta) = \alpha_{\underline{\underline{A}}\uparrow B}$$

$$\hat{x}_C(\alpha^\circ\ (\beta^\circ(x_C)))$$

where x_C is a variable of type $\langle s, f(C)\rangle$.

ST2.2 If $\alpha \varepsilon P_{\underline{\underline{A}}\uparrow B}$ and $\beta \varepsilon P_{C\downarrow A}$, then $F_4(\alpha, \beta) \varepsilon P_{C:\downarrow B}$, and

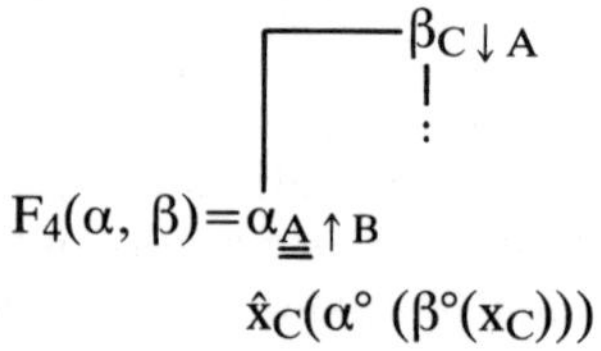

ST2.3 If $\alpha \varepsilon P_{\underline{\underline{A}}\uparrow B}$ and $\beta \varepsilon P_{\underline{C}\downarrow A}$, then $F_5(\alpha, \beta) \varepsilon P_{C:\downarrow B}$, and

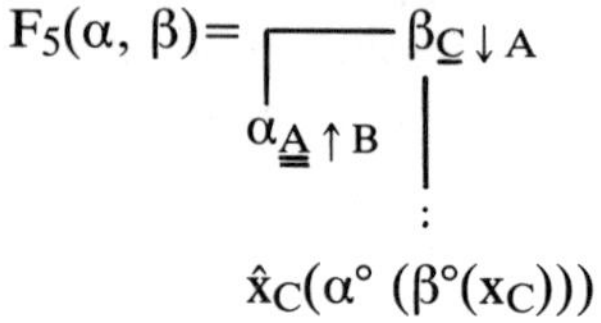

ST2.4 If $\alpha \varepsilon P_{\underline{\underline{A}}\downarrow B}$ and $\beta \varepsilon P_{C\downarrow A}$, then $F_6(\alpha, \beta) \varepsilon P_{C:\downarrow B}$, and

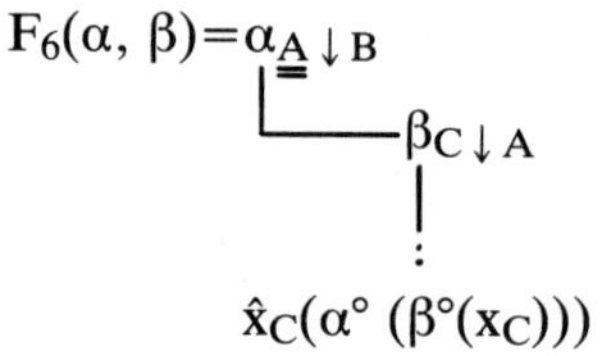

ST2.5 If $\alpha \varepsilon P_{\underline{\underline{A}}\downarrow B}$ and $\beta \varepsilon P_{C\uparrow A}$, then $F_7(\alpha, \beta) \varepsilon P_{C:\uparrow B}$, and

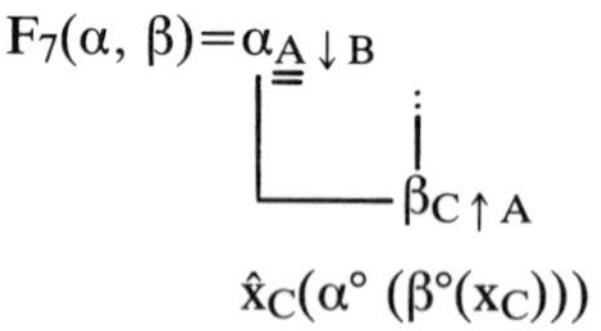

ST2.6 If $\alpha \varepsilon P_{\underline{\underline{A}}\downarrow B}$ and $\beta \varepsilon P_{\underline{C}\uparrow A}$, then $F_8(\alpha, \beta) \varepsilon P_{C:\uparrow B}$, and

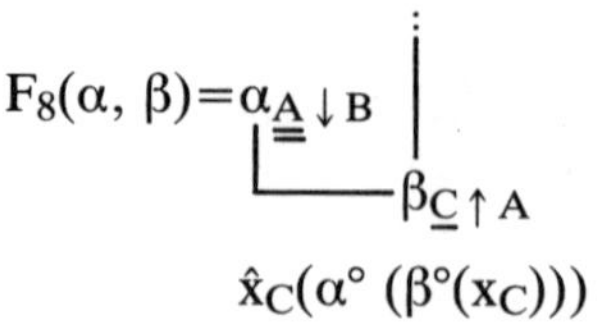

ST3. If $\zeta \,\varepsilon\, P_{C:\uparrow B}$ or $P_{C:\downarrow B}$ and $\gamma \,\varepsilon\, P_C$, then $F_9(\zeta, \gamma) \,\varepsilon\, P_B$ and

$$F_9(\zeta, \gamma) = \zeta{:}\!\!-\!\!-\!\!-\gamma$$

$$\zeta^\circ\,(\gamma^\circ)$$

The rules ST 1—3 specify (i) the categories of the two input expressions, (ii) the category of the output expression, (iii) the resulting local orthogonal tree, and (iv) the associated logical structure. The rules of definition 3 (cf. (40) above) are called ST.-rules because they combine the purposes of Montague's S- and Montague's T-rules (compare PTQ).

2.4 *Orthogonal tree structures*

In this section we illustrate the concept of *orthogonal trees,* a new type of tree structure, in terms of which our 25 sample sentences will be analyzed below. Orthogonal trees are systematically generated by the rules ST0.—ST3. defined in (40) of section 2.3. Consider the derivation of example (41).

(41) John reads a book.

The derivation of an orthogonal tree is executed in three stages. The first is the derivation of an indexed bracketing, as exemplified in (41.1):

(41.1) $F_1(\cdot_{t\uparrow t},\, F_1(F_2(\text{reads}_{T\downarrow(T\uparrow t)},\, F_2(\text{a}_{CN\downarrow T},\, \text{book}_{CN})),\, \text{John}_T))$

The second stage is to 'unfold' the orthogonal tree by applying all orthogonal F-operations of the indexed bracketing. This is done in a step by step manner:

(41.2)

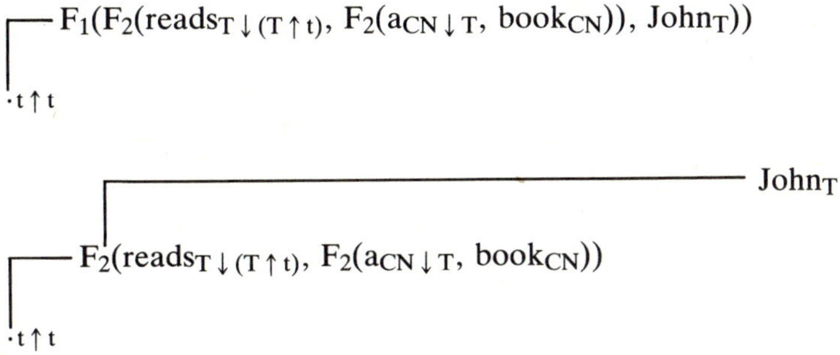

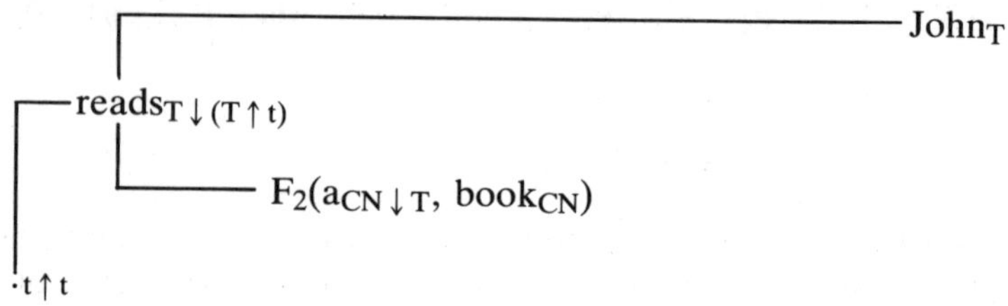

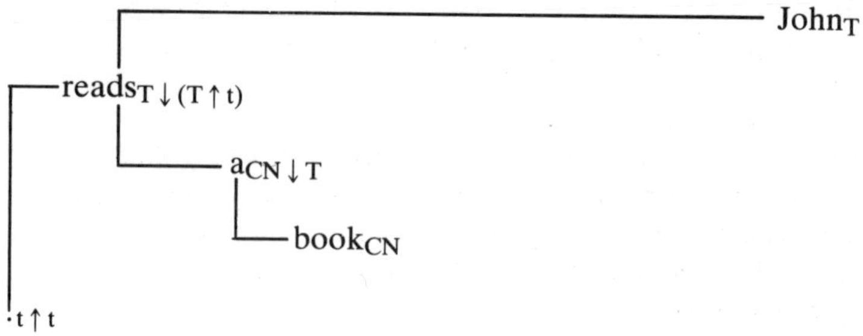

The third stage is to supply for each of the above steps the corresponding translation as indicated inthe respective rule. In the case of the example analyzed in (41.1) and (41.2) the resulting logical form is that of (41.3):

(41.3) .°((reads°(a°(book°))) (John°))

The information contained in (41.1), (41.2), and (41.3) may be summarized in the standard form of a so-called canonical analysis, given in (41.4):

(41.4) John

reads

a

book

.

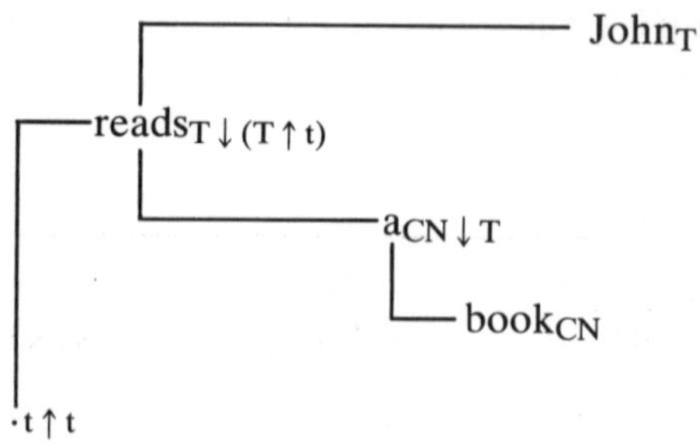

.°(reads°(a°(book°))) (John°))

The vertically encoded surface serialization may be read of in the column on the left. The horizontally encoded logical order is utilized for obtaining the translation formula. Horizontally, the words are in a one to one correspondence with their translations in the translation formula. As desired, the translation formula consists of nothing but word translations and the moodmarker translation. We distinguish two levels of translation, the unanalyzed translation (e.g. John°) and the analyzed translation (e.g. $\hat{P}P(j')$). The analyzed translation systematically lambda reduces to the meaning[1] formula specified in (34).

As another example consider the canonical analysis in (42) which is a modification of the type of analysis shown in (31) above. In (42), (31) is reanalyzed in terms of an orthogonal tree structure.

(42)

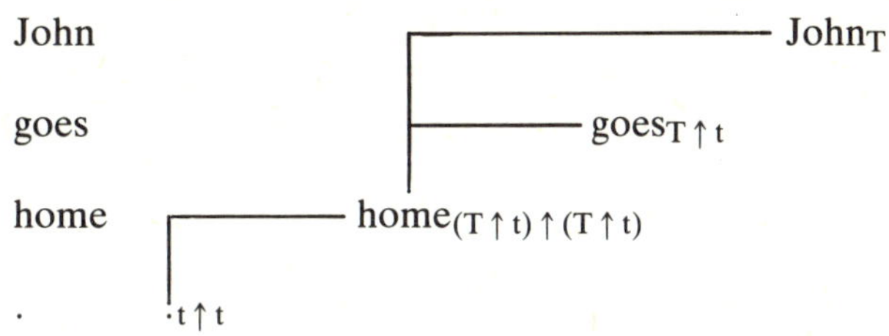

$\hat{p}[p]\ \hat{S}\hat{P}[P\hat{y}[S\hat{P}[\text{home}'(P)\ (y)]]]\ \hat{P}[P\hat{p}[\text{go}'(x)]]\ \hat{P}P(j')$

meaning[1]: (home′(go′)) (j′)

The orthogonal tree structures used in (41) and (42) have the following advantages over traditional categorial trees as used in (31):

(43.1) Orthogonal trees explicitly exhibit the functor/argument structure in the surface tree. Compare for example the traditional categorial trees (a, b) with the orthogonal versions (c, d):

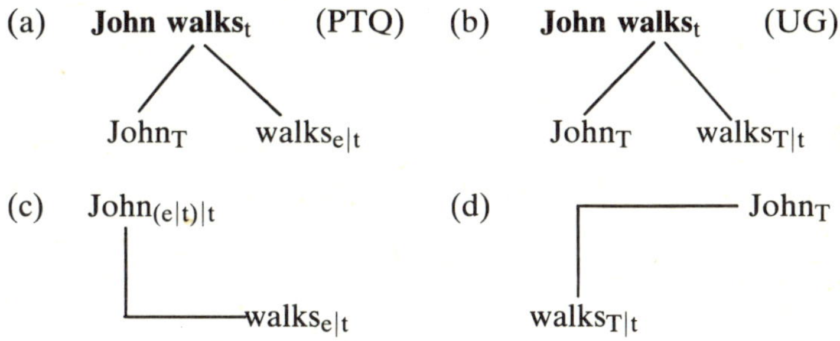

(43.2) Only one orthogonal tree is needed to characterize the composition both in the analysed surface and the translated surface. The surface serialization can be found by vertical projection while the logical serialization can be found by horizontal projection of the tree constituents.

(43.3) Each word and each category symbol appear only once in an orthogonal tree.

Since the logical and the surface order are effectively separated in orthogonal tree structures, so-called discontinous elements can be standardly represented. As an example consider:[14]

(44) John looked the word up.

Assuming that **looked** and **up** are sub-categorized as $\textbf{looked}_{\mathbf{IAV}\downarrow(T\uparrow t)}$ and $\textbf{up}_{T\uparrow IAV}$, we may form the following indexed bracketing on the basis of definition 3.

(44.1) $F_1(._{t\uparrow t}, F_1(F_9(F_7(\text{looked}_{\mathbf{IAV}\downarrow(T\uparrow t)}, \text{up}_{T\uparrow IAV}), F_2(\text{the}_{CN\downarrow T}, \text{word}_{CN}), \text{John}_T))$

Next we unfold the corresponding orthogonal tree by applying all the orthogonal F-operations specified in (44.1).

(44.2)

ST1.1 —— $F_1(F_9(F_7(\text{looked, up}), F_2(\text{the, word})), \text{John})_t$

$\cdot_{t\uparrow t}$

$.^\circ\ (F_1(F_9(F_7(\text{looked, up}), F_2(\text{the, word})), \text{John})^\circ$

ST1.1 —— John_T

—— $F_9(F_7(\text{looked, up}), F_2(\text{the, word}))_{T\uparrow t}$

$\cdot_{t\uparrow t}$

$.^\circ\ ((F_9(F_7(\text{looked, up}), F_2(\text{the, word}))^\circ\ (\text{John}^\circ))$

ST3.

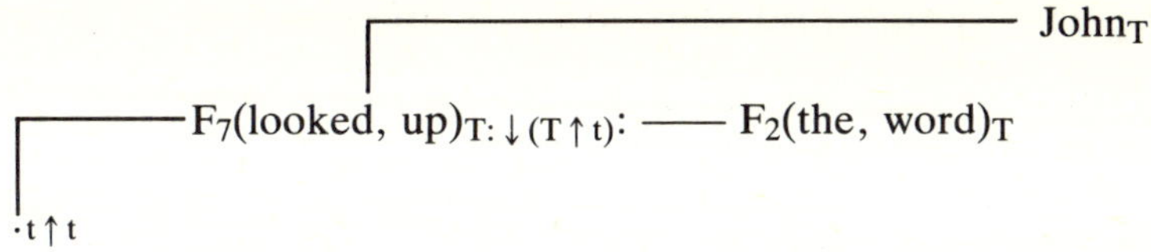

$.^\circ\ ((F_7(\text{looked, up})\ {}^\circ\ (F_2(\text{the, word})^\circ)\ (\text{John}^\circ))$

ST2.4.

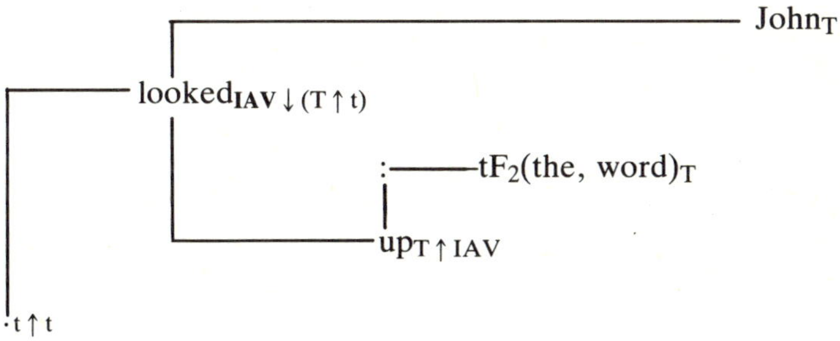

$.^\circ\ ((\hat{P}_T(\text{looked}^\circ(\text{up}^\circ(P_T)))\ (F_2(\text{the, word})^\circ)\ (\text{John}^\circ))$

ST1.2.

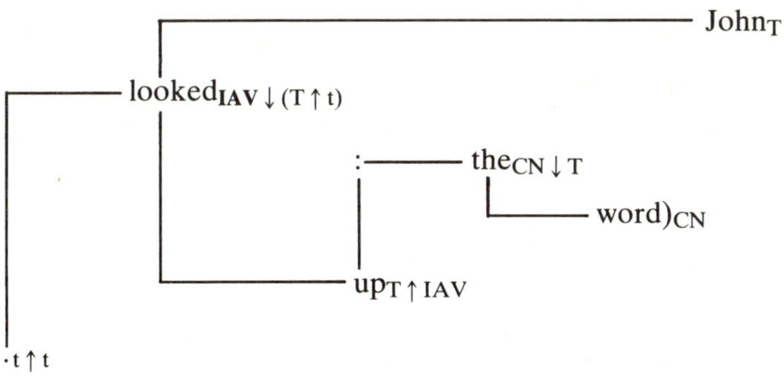

$.^\circ\ ((\hat{P}_T(\text{looked}^\circ(\text{up}^\circ(P_T))\ (\text{the}^\circ(\text{word}^\circ))))\ (\text{John}^\circ))$

Orthogonal trees are the most perspicuous as well as parsimonious mode of presentation I could find. Orthogonal tree structures formalize the concept of words as the basic elements of composition inherent in the surface compositional approach and they provide something like a conversion key for reparsing a logical serialization into a surface order and vice versa.

3. The syntax and semantics of imperatives

Instead of reducing non-declaratives to propositions (declaratives) in order to benefit from the link up with "truth", we treat truth-values in the sense of categorial grammar, namely as one of two basic categories and infinitely many recursively derived categories. Mathematically speaking, there is no reason to treat the denotation of a t-expression as something more special than the denotation of an e- or e|t-expression. The type ⟨s, t⟩ is used to semantically characterize declaratives (propositions). So why shouldn't some other type be used to semantically characterize other moods like imperative or interrogative? Propositions may occur independently or as part of a larger structure. Why shouldn't the same hold for expressions of other types?

Once we allow all categories (and corresponding types) as potential types of possible denotation for natural language expressions, it is only a question of motivating which type of possible denotation should be chosen for which type of expression of English. In earlier work[15] it was proposed to translate imperatives into properties of individual concepts, which corresponds to the type ⟨s, ⟨⟨s, e⟩, t⟩⟩ and the category e|t. This property is taken to be the one which the speaker requests the hearer to acquire. The following canonical analysis of the imperative "Go home!" consists of a T|t-phrase **go home** and the mood-marker **!** of category (T|t)|(e|t), which contains a restriction to the hearer in its translation.

(45)

Go $\qquad go_{T\uparrow t}$

home $\qquad home_{(T\uparrow t)\uparrow(T\uparrow t)}$

! $\qquad !_{(T\uparrow t)\uparrow(e|t)}$

translation formula:

$$\hat{S}\hat{x}[\ulcorner^2(x)_\wedge S(\hat{P}P(x))]\;\hat{S}\hat{P}[P(\hat{y}[S\hat{P}[home'(P)(y)]])]\;\hat{P}[P\hat{x}[go'(x)]]$$

meaning^1: $\quad \hat{x}[\ulcorner^2(x)_\wedge home'(go')(x)]$

The variables and constants used in (45) are of the types specified in (32) above. The context-variable $\ulcorner^2$, furthermore, corresponds to the category e|t and represents the property of being "second person" or adressee. The meaning of $\ulcorner^2$ is formulated in terms of its reconstruction condition, which relates the context-variable to the addressee provided by the formal context.[16] The lexical derivation and translation of **go** is like that of **goes** in (33.2), the translation of **home** is that of (33.3), and the translation of the imperative mood-marker is given in (33.5):

(33.5) *root* *molecule*

$$\hat{x}[\Gamma^2(x) \wedge P(x)] \longrightarrow \; !_{(T|t)|(e|t)} \;\; \hat{S}\hat{x}[\Gamma^2(x) \wedge S(\hat{P}P(x))]$$

Mood-markers characterize moods by inducing a characteristic surface syntax and a characteristic type of possible denotation. While the "."-marker (cf. 33.4) translates vacuously into $\hat{p}[p]$, it still fulfills a surface syntactic function in that it *closes* the orthogonal tree structure:

(46) John
kisses
Mary
.

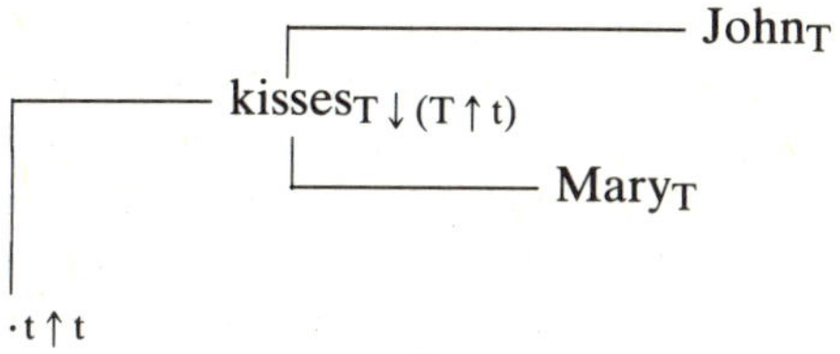

The !-operator likewise closes orthogonal tree structures, thus generating an imperative. It also induces the category e|t for the complete expression, which differs from the category T|t of the argument expression. Furthermore, the !-operator provides the contextual restriction to the adressee.

Meaning properties of imperatives that go beyond our semantic characterization as properties of adressees (i.e. that property which the hearer wants the adressee to attain) are treated in the pragmatics. Traditional intuitions regarding the *use* of imperatives are formulated in the following pragmatic *fulfillment condition*:

(47) If the speaker utters A! (where A is an intransitive verb phrase of appropriate tense and person) towards a hearer h at time j in order to make a command, then this utterance is a fulfilled command if and only if there is a time j′, j′>j, such that $\vee x[x=h \wedge A(x)]$ is true at j′.

Our semantic characterization of the imperative does not contain any illocutionary force indicators, performative clauses, or mood-operators.

Syntactic mood constitutes only one of various factors determining the use potential of an expression. Thus the pragmatic fulfillment condition (47) does not predict that imperatives are used solely for the speech act of commands.

Our use of mood-markers like (33.4) and (33.5) is reminiscent of Ballmer's (1975, 1978) *punctuation signs.* On the other hand, Ballmer discusses mainly different "."-translations, which he uses to serialize and to logically structure various forms of declaratives. Interpunctations for non-declaratives are discussed only marginally and then translated by means of non-standard operators like (x?) or (x!) which are interpreted as "illocutionary force indicators". In our system, on the other hand, declaratives are structured over their constituent categories, while the "." of standard declaratives translates as the identity function. Mood-markers with complex translations like (33.5) come into play mainly in connection with the analysis of moods other than standard declaratives, as illustrated by our analysis of imperatives in (45).

Our analysis of the imperative satisfies all syntactic, semantic, and pragmatic desiderata discussed in earlier sections. Syntactically, it is strictly surface compositional, using the words in their standard categories and translations,resulting in a semantic representation which is a completely standard formula of intensional logic. The meaning^1-formula does not contain any illocutionary force indicators, performative clauses, or mood-operators, which have never been provided with logically satisfactory definitions. The type and formal meaning assigned to imperatives, furthermore, is intuitively plausible. Pragmatically, the analysis is appropriate insofar as untenable connections between mood and speech acts are avoided. (cf. (47)).

4. Interrogatives and responsives

4.1 *General considerations*

We turn now to the analysis of *interrogatives* and *responsives.* As in the case of the imperative, we characterize interrogatives and responsives solely in terms of (i) their constituent words in their standard form and translation and (ii) a mood marker that compositionally combines with the constituent(s) of the expression to result in a complete expression, which translates into a well-defined formula of standard intensional logic. Further desiderata are (iii) to capture the phenomenon of syntactico-semantic *compatibility* between certain interrogatives and certain responsives, and to account formally for the fact that responsives are *context-dependent* expressions.

Consider the following examples:

	Interrogative		*Responsive*
(48.1.1)	Does John go home?	(48.1.2)	Yes.
(48.2.1)	Where does John go?	(48.2.2)	Home.
(48.3.1)	Who goes home?	(48.3.2)	John.

These examples show that the category of the constituent of the responsive must agree with the category of the Wh-word of the interrogative. The categories of the Wh-words and the responsive constituents are $t|t$ in (48.1) (where the Wh-constituent in morphologically empty, c.f. section 4.4)), $(T|t)|(T|t)$ in (48.2) (**where, home**), and T (**who, John**) in (48.3). Due to this categorial correlation, each of the above responsives is compatible only with one of the above interrogatives. For example, "John." is not a responsive compatible with the interrogative "Where does John go?", because the category of **John** does not agree with the category of the Wh-word **where.**

An additional compatibility-criterion are *sub-categories.* In the case of English Wh-adverbs the following sub-categories must be distinguished: **where**^{p} (place), **where**^{d} (direction), **when** (time), **why** (cause or reason), and **how** (manner). The expressions in (48.4), for example, are not compatible:

(48.4.1) Where does John go? (48.4.2) Slowly.

Even though the Wh-word in the interrogative (**where**) is of the same category as the constituent of the responsive (**slowly**), namely $(T|t)|(T|t)$, the two expressions in question are of different subcategories (*direction* versus *manner*).

While responsives are usually used as answers, they are not the only type of expression that may be used to answer a question. Taking a particular interrogative, e.g. (49), the following kinds of pragmatically compatible answer-expressions may be distinguished.

	Question		*Answer*	
(49)	Who came?	(49.1)	John.	T-responsive
		(49.2)	John did.	T+do-responsive
		(49.3)	John came.	declarative
		(49.4)	John, because of Mary.	explicatory T-responsive
		(49.5)	John did, because of Mary.	explicatory T+do responsive
		(49.6)	John came, because of Mary.	explicatory declarative

The declaratives (49.3) and (49.6) have a truth-value independent of the question they are used to answer (if they are used as answers). Responsives, on the other hand, depend in their truth-value on the interrogative relative to which they are interpreted. Consider for example (50):

(50.1) Who goes home?
(50.2) Who doesn't go home? (50.3) John.

The responsive (50.3) is an elliptical expression which cannot be interpreted unless related to a compatible interrogative, which will determine its truth-value.

On the whole, we have to distinguish between the structurally defined compatibility between interrogatives and responsives, and the pragmatic compatibility between questions and answers. For complete declaratives used as answers there is no structural compatibility relation with the respective interrogative, as shown in (51):

(51.1) Who went home?
(51.2) Where did John go? (51.3) John went home.

Furthermore, the pragmatic relation between a declarative used as an answer and an interrogative used as a question can be quite *indirect,* as shown in (52):

(52.1) Where is John? (52.2) Mr. Smith usually takes a nap in the afternoon.

In the following let us leave pragmatic questions aside and concentrate on the structural correlations between certain interrogatives, responsives and declaratives.

4.2 *The formal ingredients of analysis*

Interrogatives, responsives, and declaratives are structurally related as follows:

(53.1) *interrogative:* (53.2) *responsive:*

Who goes home? John.

(53.3) *declarative:*

John goes home.

How can we accommodate these facts formally? Following Ajdukiewicz (1929), let us translate the Wh-word by a *variable* of proper type. The translation of (53.1) will thus consist in part of the formula (54):

(54) [(home′(go′)) (x)]

But one doesn't like unbound variables in the logical representation of a complete expression like an interrogative. For this reason, presumably, Ajdukiewicz (1929) adds a so-called "interrogative operator" of the form (x?) in front of the open formula (54) to bind the otherwise unbound Wh-variable:

(55.1) (x?) [(home′(go′)) (x)]

The (x?)-operator is paraphrased as *For what x,* so that formula (55.1) is paraphrased as (55.2):

(55.2) For what x, goes home?

However, in absence of a type theoretic analysis of the operator (x?) it is not clear of what type the formula (55.1) is supposed to be. Furthermore, in absence of a semantic definition of (x?) it remains in the dark whether (55.1) is supposed to characterize a speech act or a mood. Alternatively, we use the lambda-operator instead of the (x?)-operator to (i) bind the Wh-variable and (ii) characterize interrogatives semantically in terms of the resulting characteristic type of possible denotation. Thus instead of (55.1) we characterize (53.1) as in (56):

(56) $\hat{x}[(\text{home}'(\text{go}'))\ (x)]$

According to the definitions of lambda-calculus, (56) is of the type corresponding to $e|t$. We say in general that interrogatives denote sets (or rather properties) of their Wh-variable denotation.

We turn now to the analysis of the responsive (53.2). The translation of expression (53.2) will consist in part of its constitutent translation, i.e. $\hat{P}P(j')$, which corresponds to the category $(e|t)|t$. The whole responsive, on the other hand, is (i) of category t and (ii) context-dependent. These facts are formally accommodated in that we use a *context-variable*[17] $\ulcorner_{e|t}$ which combines with the constituent translation to render a t-expression:

(57) **John.**$_t$

$\hat{P}P(j')\ (\ulcorner_{e|t})$ $\quad$ $(=\ulcorner_{e|t}(j'))$

In order to interpret a context-dependent expression like a responsive or an imperative, the context-variable(s) must first be contextually reconstructed. The context-variable in responsives is reconstructed relative to a compatible interrogative. That is, the context-variable is replaced by an interrogative expression (provided by the formal context, cf. section 6), which is of the same type as the context-variable.

The formal correlation between the interrogative (53.1) the responsive (53.2) and the declarative (53.3) may now be formally characterized as follows:

(58) **Who goes home?**$_{e|t}$ $\qquad$ **John.**$_t$

$\hat{x}[(\text{home}'(\text{go}'))\ (x)]$ $\longrightarrow$ $\ulcorner_{e|t}(j'_e)$

result of contextual reconstruction:
$\hat{x}[(\text{home}'(\text{go}'))\ (x)]\ (j')$

Lambda-reduction:
$[(\text{home}'(\text{go}'))\ (j')]$

Thus the contextual reconstruction of the responsive (53.2) relative to the compatible interrogative (53.1) results in a formula equivalent to the translation of the declarative (53.3). We account for the elliptical nature of responsives by contextually reconstructing them into complete declaratives.

The indicated analysis of interrogatives and responsives provides a simple and obvious syntactico-semantic account of the following phenomena:

(59.1) the compatibility between interrogatives and responsives
(59.2) the relation between interrogatives and declaratives
(59.3) the relation between responsives and declaratives
(59.4) the semantics of interrogatives by providing plausible formal meanings
(59.5) the context-dependency of responsives.

Since the category of the Wh-words and the constituent of a compatible responsive must agree, we may say that interrogatives denote sets of their compatible responsive *constituent-denotation,* which is equivalent so say that interrogatives denote sets of their wh-denotations. In this sense we have captured the intuition (Stahl (1969), Hamblin (1973)) that "questions" denote their "answers".

4.3 *Non-restricted interrogatives*

In the case of the imperative, we dealt with a rather uncomplicate mood: the constituent consists simply of a standardly derived T|t phrase, to which the mood-marker applies. In the case of interrogatives, on the other hand, we find a systematic variety of structures. This is due to the category variation of the Wh-words and corresponding responsive constituents. We distinguish the following types of interrogatives in English.

(60) *non-restricted interrogatives*

(60.1) T-interrogative:
Who goes home?$_{e|t}$ John.

(60.2) (T|t)|(T|t)-interrogative:
Where does John go?$_{((e|t)|(e|t))|t}$ Home.

(60.3) multiple interrogative:
Who loves whom?$_{e|(e|t)}$ John Mary.

(60.4) embedded T-interrogatives:
Who did John say that Mary loves?$_{e|t}$ Bill.

(61) *restricted interrogatives*
(61.1) t|t-interrogative:
Does John go home?$_{t|(t|t)}$ — No.
(61.2) t|t-interrogative with disjunction:
Does John love Mary or Suzy?$_{t|(t|t)}$ — Yes.
(61.3) T-disjunctive interrogative:
Does John love Mary or Suzy?$_{e|t}$ — Mary.
(61.4) Multiple disjunctive interrogative:
Does John love Mary or Bill Suzy?$_{e|(e|t)}$ — John Mary.

The distinction between non-restricted and restricted interrogatives is both a syntactic and a semantic one. Non-restricted interrogatives have an overt Wh-word (like *who*), which is translated by means of a variable ranging over all denotations of its type. That is, non-restricted interrogatives contain variables with non-restricted range (though these variables will still be sorted). In restricted interrogatives, on the other hand, there is a *Wh-disjunction* instead of an overt Wh-word. As the responsives in (61) show, there are different categories of responsive constituents. Therefore, different categories of Wh-disjunctions must be assumed in the analysis of restricted interrogatives. In (61.1) and (61.2) the Wh-disjunction is morphologically empty. In the Wh-disjunction in (61.3) and (61.4), on the other hand, the range of the Wh-variable contained in the translation of the Wh-disjunction is restricted by explicit enumeration.

There are probably more kinds and sub-kinds of non-restricted and restricted interrogatives in English, but the above set may serve as a representative sample to test

(i) the semantic theory of interrogatives and responsives outlined in section 4.1 and 4.2,
(ii) the feasability of 'mass-producing' canonical analyses of the expressions (1—25) based on orthogonal tree structures.

In the present section the non-restricted interrogatives (60) are analysed, while the following section presents the canonical analyses of the restricted interrogatives (61). Comments on specific features of the analyses will be given as we go along.

(60.1.1) *T-interrogative:*

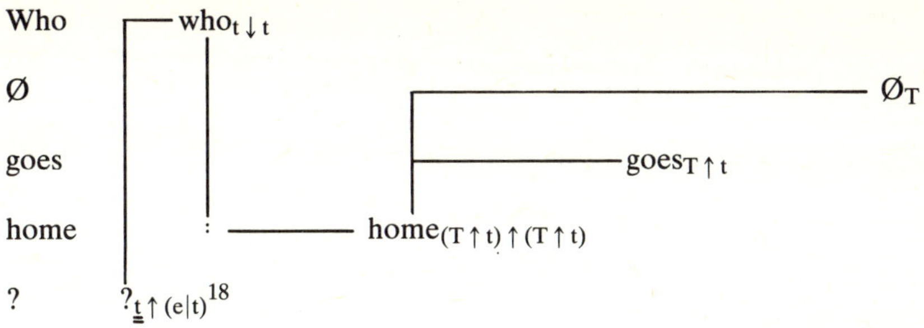

$$\hat{p}_z\hat{z}[p_z]\ \ \hat{p}_x[\hat{x}[p_x](z)]\ \ \hat{S}\hat{P}[P\hat{y}[S\hat{P}[\text{home}'(P)\ (y)]]]\ \ \hat{P}[P\hat{z}[\text{go}'(z)]]\ \ \hat{P}P(x)$$

Lambda reduction:

$$\hat{p}_z\hat{z}[p_z]\ (\hat{p}_x[\hat{x}[p_x](z)]\ ((\hat{S}\hat{P}[P\hat{y}[S\hat{P}[\text{home}'(P)\ (y)]]]\ (\hat{P}[P\hat{z}[\text{go}'(z)]]))\ (\hat{P}P(x)))$$

$$\hat{p}_z\hat{z}[p_z]\ (\hat{p}_x[\hat{x}[p_x](z)]\ (\hat{P}[P\hat{y}[(\hat{P}[P\hat{z}[\text{go}'(z)]])\ [\hat{P}[\text{home}'(P)\ (y)]]]])\ (\hat{P}P(x))))$$

$$\hat{p}_z\hat{z}[p_z]\ (\hat{p}_x[\hat{x}[p_x](z)]\ (\hat{P}P(x)\ (\hat{y}[(\hat{P}[P\hat{z}[\text{go}'(z)]])\ [\hat{P}[\text{home}'(P)\ (y)]]])))$$

$$\hat{p}_z\hat{z}[p_z]\ (\hat{p}_x[\hat{x}[p_x](z)]\ (\hat{P}P(x)\ (\hat{y}[(\hat{P}[\text{home}'(P)\ (y)]\ (\hat{z}[\text{go}'(z)])])))$$

$$\hat{p}_z\hat{z}[p_z]\ (\hat{p}_x[\hat{x}[p_x](z)]\ (\hat{P}P(x)\ (\hat{y}[((\text{home}'(\hat{z}[\text{go}'(z)]))\ (y)])))\qquad \hat{z}[\text{go}'(z)]=\text{go}'$$

$$\hat{p}_z\hat{z}[p_z]\ (\hat{p}_x[\hat{x}[p_x](z)]\ (\hat{P}P(x)\ (\hat{y}[((\text{home}'(\text{go}'))\ (y)])))$$

$$\hat{p}_z\hat{z}[p_z]\ (\hat{p}_x[\hat{x}[p_x](z)]\ (\hat{y}[((\text{home}'(\text{go}'))\ (y)])\ (x))$$

$$\hat{p}_z\hat{z}[p_z]\ (\hat{p}_x[\hat{x}[p_x](z)]\ ((\text{home}'(\text{go}'))\ (x)))$$

$$\hat{p}_z\hat{z}[p_z]\ (\hat{x}[(\text{home}'(\text{go}'))\ (x)]\ (z))$$

$$\hat{p}_z\hat{z}[p_z]\ ([(\text{home}'(\text{go}'))\ (z)])$$

$$\hat{z}[(\text{home}'(\text{go}'))\ (z)]$$

meaning[1]: $\hat{z}[(\text{home}'(\text{go}'))\ (z)]$

(60.1.2) *T-responsive:*

John ——— $John_T$

. $\cdot T \uparrow t$

$\hat{P}[P(\Gamma_{e|t})]$ $\hat{P}P(j')$

meaning[1]: $\Gamma_{e|t}(j')$

contextual reconstruction of (60.1.2) relative (60.1.1) renders:

(home′(go′)) (j′)

The variable p_x in the ?-translation ranges over propositions denoted by formulas open in x. The Wh-word **who** is translated as $\hat{P}P(x)$ (and not as P, as in Hausser (1978a)), resulting in the overall category $e|t$ (and not $T|t$) in (60.1.1). This change is motivated by the desire to assign the lowest possible category to the various moods.

Since imperatives are likewise of category $e|t$, **who**-interrogatives and imperatives have the same type of possible denotation. This type overlap is not problematic since we characterize mood as a mode of macrosyntactic construction, which is explicitly defined in the mood-marker translation. While the type associated with each mood must be semantically and pragmatically plausible, it is only one factor characterizing a certain mood, resulting from the overall syntactico-semantic composition of complete expressions. Imperatives and **who**-interrogatives still differ sufficiently in that imperatives are context-dependent and denote adressee properties, while **who**-interrogatives are not context-dependent and denote sets of Wh-denotations.

The variable 'a' corresponds to category $(e|t)|(e|t)$, the variable 'A' corresponds to category $(T|t)|(T|t)$. 'A' and 'a' are sorted to range over denotations of *place*-adverbials. All other variables are as defined in (32).

(60.2.1) and (60.2.2) illustrate again our strategy of having the meaning[1]-formulas of the lowest possible type structure, while accommodating surface syntactic generalizations by using lexical translations with levated type structures. The proof of the pertinent lambda-reductions in (60.2) and the following examples is analogous to (60.1.1).

Note that the "."-translation in (60.2.2) differs from that in (60.1.2).

(60.2.1) *(T|t)|(T|t)-interrogative:*

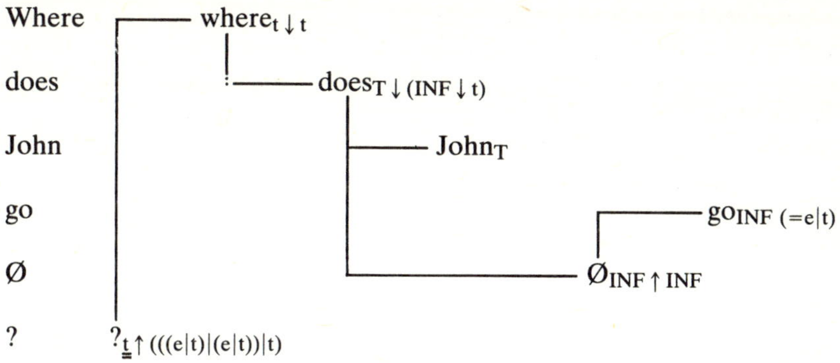

$\underline{\hat{p}_a \hat{a}[\hat{p}_a]}$ $\underline{\hat{p}_a[\hat{a}[p_a](a)]}$ $\underline{\hat{P}\hat{P}(P(P)]}$ $\underline{\hat{P}P(j')}$ $\underline{\hat{P}[a(P)]}$ $\underline{go'}$

meaning[1]: $\hat{a}[a(go')\ (j')]$

(60.2.2) *(T|t)|(T|t)-responsive:*

$\hat{A}[\Gamma_{((e|t)|(e|t))|t}(\hat{Q}\hat{x}[A([\hat{P}P(Q)]\ (\hat{P}P(x))])]\ \hat{S}\hat{P}[P\hat{y}[S\hat{P}$
$[home'(P)\ (y)]]]$

meaning[1]: $\Gamma_{((e|t)|(e|t))|t}(home')$

contextual reconstruction of (60.2.2) relative (60.2.1) renders:

[(home′(go′)) (j′)]

This is necessary to accommodate the category difference of the respective constituents and to insure that the context-variables agree in type with the respective classes of compatible interrogatives. The **?** in (60.2) differs from that in (60.1) in the variable subscripts (p_x versus p_a).

The T—T responsive (60.3.2) does not seem to be used in English. Instead one has to use a complete declarative like "John kisses Mary."

In German, on the other hand, responsives like (60.3.2) are standardly acceptable as answers to multiple interrogatives. There are, however, interesting restrictions on the order of constituents in such responsives, which does not always exactly reflect the order of Wh-words in the related multiple interrogative.[19] Note that there are also T—(T|t)|(T|t)-interrogatives such as "*Who* went *where*?". By applying the standard rules of our analysis, quite complex multiple interrogatives may be constructed, though hardly used, like "*Who* gave *what* to *whom where when why*?".

(60.3.1) *multiple interrogative:*

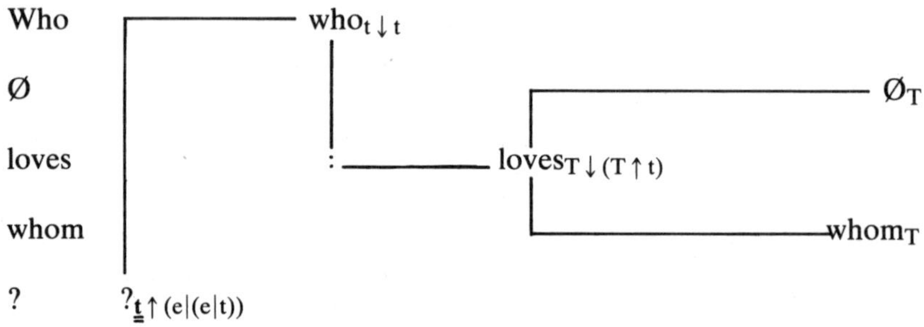

$\hat{p}_{xy}\hat{x}\hat{y}[p_{xy}]\ \hat{p}_x[\hat{x}[p_x](x)]\ \hat{P}_1\hat{P}_2[\hat{P}_2\hat{x}[\hat{P}_1\hat{y}[love'(x, y)]]]\ \hat{P}P(y)\quad \hat{P}P(x)$

(60.3.2) *T—T-responsive:*

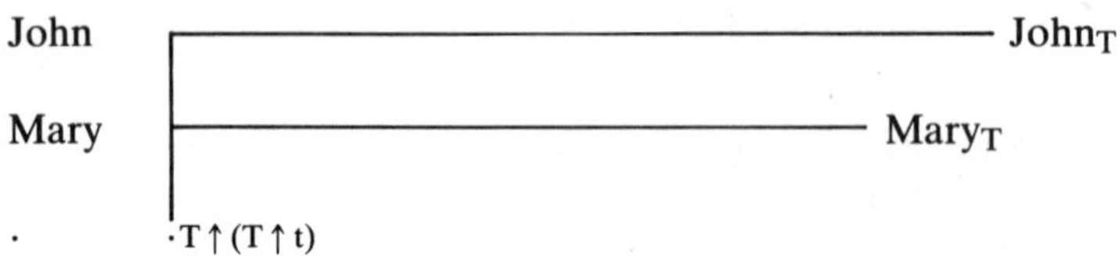

$\hat{P}_1\hat{P}_2[\hat{P}_2\hat{x}[\hat{P}_1\hat{y}(\Gamma_{e|(e|t)}(x, y))]]\hat{P}P(m')\ \hat{P}P(j')$

meaning^1: $[\Gamma_{e|(e|t)}(j', m')]$

contextual reconstruction of (60.3.2) relative (60.3.1) renders: $[love'(j', m')]$

(60.4.1) *embedded T-interrogative:*

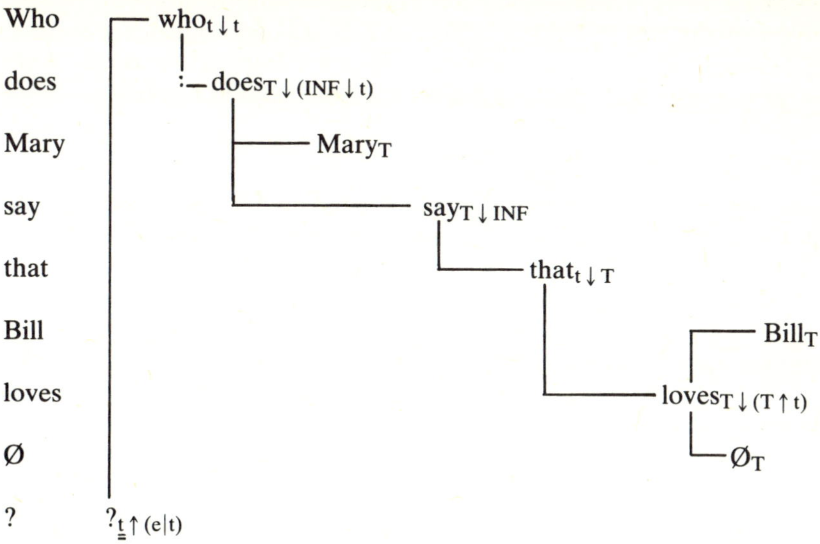

$\hat{p}_y\hat{y}[p_y]\hat{p}_z[\hat{z}[p_z](y)]$ $\hat{P}\hat{P}[P(P)]$ $\hat{P}P(m')$
$\hat{P}\hat{x}[P\hat{z}[say'(x, z)]]$ $\hat{p}\hat{P}\mathrm{V}x[P(x)=p]$
$\hat{P}_1\hat{P}_2[P_2\hat{x}[P_1\hat{y}[love'(x, y)]]]$ $\hat{P}P(z)$ $\hat{P}P(b)$

meaning[1]: $\hat{y}[say'(m', \hat{P}\mathrm{V}x[P(x)=love'(b', y)])]$

(60.4.2) *T-responsive:* See (60.1.2)

contextul reconstruction of (60.4.2) relative (60.4.1) renders:

$say'(m', \hat{P}\mathrm{V}x[P(x)=love'(b', j')])$

(60.4.1) contains a compositional treatment of the complementizer *that*$_{t|T}$. This construction will be discussed in more detail in section 5.

Our analysis of non-restricted interrogatives extends straight-forwardly to Wh-quantifiers like **which**$_{CN|T}$ and **what**$_{CN|T}$. A Wh-quantifier is translated as $\hat{Q}\hat{P}[\mathrm{V}x\varepsilon[Q(x)_\wedge\Gamma_0(x)]^1\ P(x)_\wedge x=y]$. in other words, a sentence like **Which girl walks.** is translated equivalent to **Who is the girl that walks.** This assimilation of the Wh-quantifier **which** to the Wh-term **who** applies mutatis mutandis to **what**$_T$ and **what**$_{CN|T}$. The treatment of the definite article presumed here is developed in Hausser (1974b, 1976a). Furthermore, our analysis of interrogatives is compatible with the analysis of presuppositions based on P-inducers proposed in Hausser (1973, 1976a). The notion of a P-induced presupposition applies uniformly to declaratives and non-declaratives alike.

4.4 *Restricted interrogatives*

Like non-restricted interrogatives, restricted interrogatives are built up by means of a mood-marker '?' translating as $\hat{p}_{\alpha}\check{\alpha}[p_{\alpha}]$ and a Wh-element. The Wh-variable in restricted interrogatives is part of the so-called Wh-disjunction. Consider for example (61.3):

(61.3.1) Does John love Mary or Suzy? (61.3.2) Mary.

The Wh-disjunction **Mary or Suzy** is analyzed as follows:

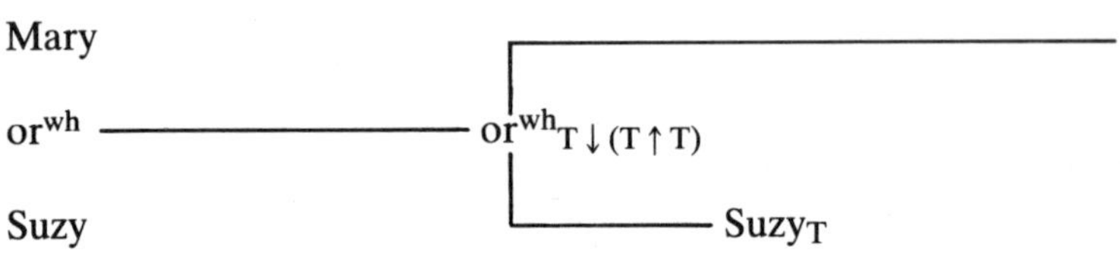

$$\underline{\hat{P}_3\hat{P}_2\hat{P}[P(x)\wedge\hat{Q}Q(x)=\hat{P}[P_2(P)\vee P_3(P)]]}\quad \underline{\hat{P}P(s')}\quad \underline{\hat{P}P(m')}$$

reduction: $\hat{P}[P(x)\wedge\hat{Q}Q(x)=\hat{P}[P(m')\vee P(s')]]$

The regular T|(T|T)-**or** translation appears as the underlined part of the reduced formula. We assume that **or**$^{\mathbf{wh}}$ is lexically derived in various categories and corresponding lambda-structures in the translation, just as the regular **or.**

In the case of the so-called yes/no-interrogatives the Wh-disjunction "yes or no?" is usually left off. One says "Does John walk?" rather than "Does John walk, yes or no?". In these cases we assume a morphologically empty Wh-disjunction called **Ø-or**$^{\mathbf{wh}}$ translating like **yes or**$^{\mathbf{wh}}$ **no.** The concept of morphologically empty surface constituents is needed also to account for cases like the plural of the indefinite article in English ($\mathbf{Ø}_{CN|T}\mathbf{girls}_{CN}$) and other cases where a paradigm contains a 'hole'.

Morphologically empty surface constituents do not affect the decidability of our surface compositional categorial grammar[20] as long as the *recursion* of Ø-words (i.e. the application of a Ø-functor to a Ø- or Ø(A)-argument) is excluded by a constraint on the lexicon.

(61.1.1) *t|t-interrogatives*

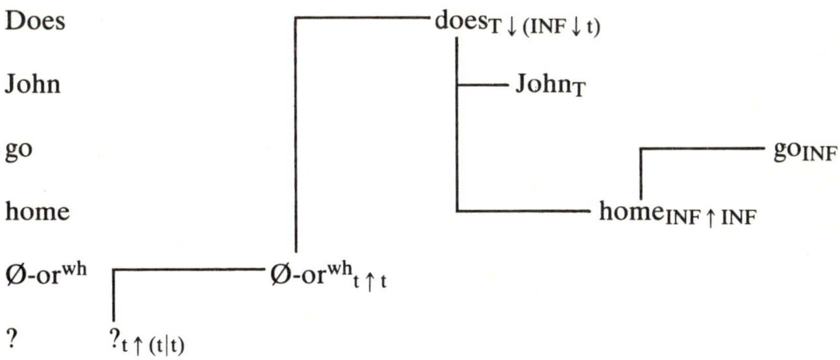

$\hat{p}_r r[p_r]\ \hat{q}[r(q)\wedge((r=\hat{p}(p))\vee(r=\hat{p}(\sim p)])]\ \hat{P}\hat{P}[P(P)]\ \hat{P}P(j')\ \hat{P}[home'(P)]\ go'$

meaning[1]: $\hat{r}[r[(home'(go'))\ (j')]\wedge((r=\hat{p}(p)\vee(r=\hat{p}(\sim p)))]$

(61.1.2) *t|t-responsive:*

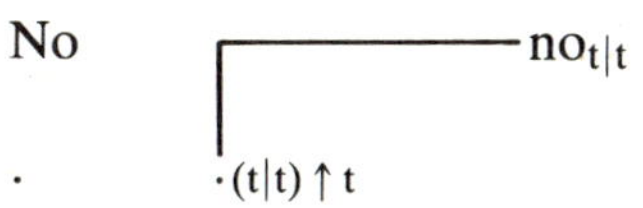

$\hat{r}[\Gamma_{t|(t|t)}(r)]\ \hat{p}[\sim p]$

meaning[1]: $\Gamma_{t|(t|t)}(\hat{p}[\sim])$

contextual reconstruction of (61.1.2) relative (61.1.1):

$\sim(home'(go'))\ (j')\wedge((\hat{p}(\sim p)=\hat{p}(p))\vee(\hat{p}(\sim p)=\hat{p}(\sim p))$
$=\sim home'(go'))\ (j')$

(61.2.1) *t|t-interrogatives with conjunction:*

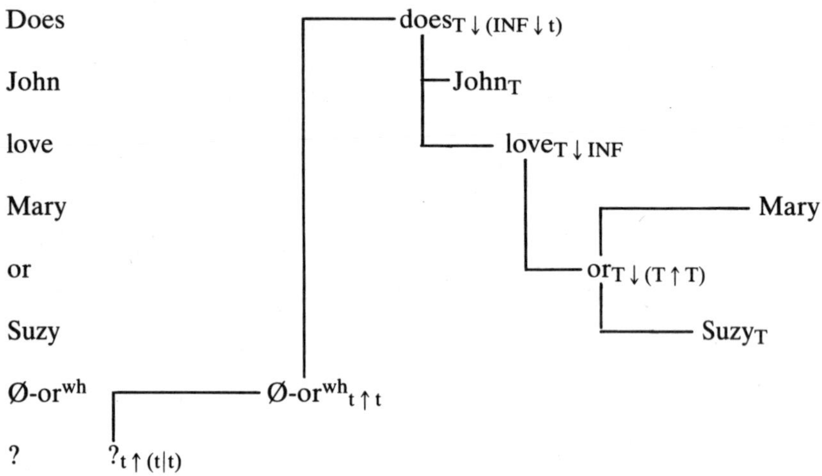

$\hat{p}_r\hat{r}[p_r]\ \hat{q}[r(q) \wedge ((r=\hat{p}(p)) \vee (r=\hat{p}(\sim p)))$
$\hat{P}\hat{P}[P(P)]\ \hat{P}P(j')\ \hat{P}\hat{x}[P\hat{y}[love'(x, y)]]$
$\hat{P}_3\hat{P}_2\hat{P}[P_2(P) \vee P_3(P)]\ \hat{P}P(s')\ \hat{P}P(m')$

meaning$_1$: $\hat{r}[r[love'(j', m') \vee love'(j', s')] \wedge ((r=\hat{p}(p)) \vee (r=\hat{p}(\sim p))]$

(61.2.2) *t|t-responsive:* See (61.1.2)

contextual reconstruction of (61.1.2) relative (61.2.1):

$\sim(love'(j', m') \vee love'(j', s')) \wedge ((\hat{p}(\sim p)=\hat{p}(p)) \vee (\hat{p}(\sim p)=\hat{p}(\sim p))$
$=\sim(love'(j', m') \vee love'(j', s'))$

(61.3.1) *disjunctive T-interrogative:*

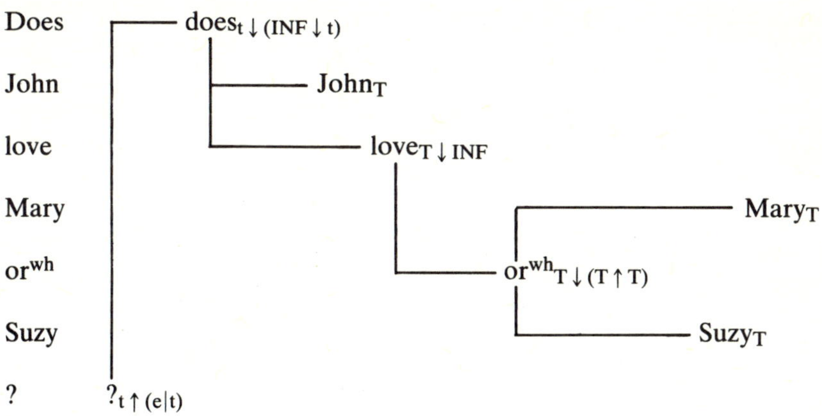

$\hat{p}_x\hat{x}[p_x]$ $\hat{P}\hat{P}[P(P)]$ $\hat{P}P(j')$ $\hat{P}\hat{x}[\hat{P}\hat{y}[love'(x, y)]]$
$\hat{P}_3\hat{P}_2\hat{P}[P(x)\wedge\hat{Q}Q(x)=\hat{P}[\hat{P}_2(P)\vee\hat{P}_3(P)]]$ $\hat{P}P(s')$ $\hat{P}P(m')$
meaning^1: $\hat{x}[love'(j', x)\wedge\hat{Q}Q(x)=\hat{P}[P(m')\vee P(s')]]$

(61.3.2) *T-responsive:*

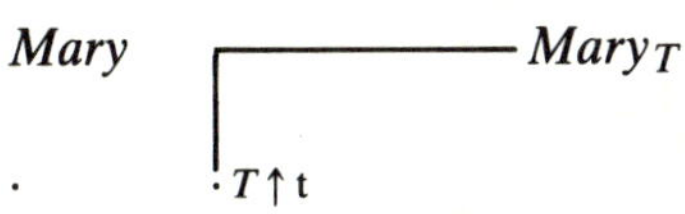

$\hat{P}[P(\ulcorner_{e|t})]$ $\hat{P}P(m')$
meaning^1: $\ulcorner_{e|t}(m')$

contextual reconstruction of (61.3.2) relative (61.3.1):
$[love'(j', m')\wedge\hat{Q}Q(m')=\hat{P}[P(m')\vee P(s')]]$

(61.4.1) *multiple disjunctive interrogative:*

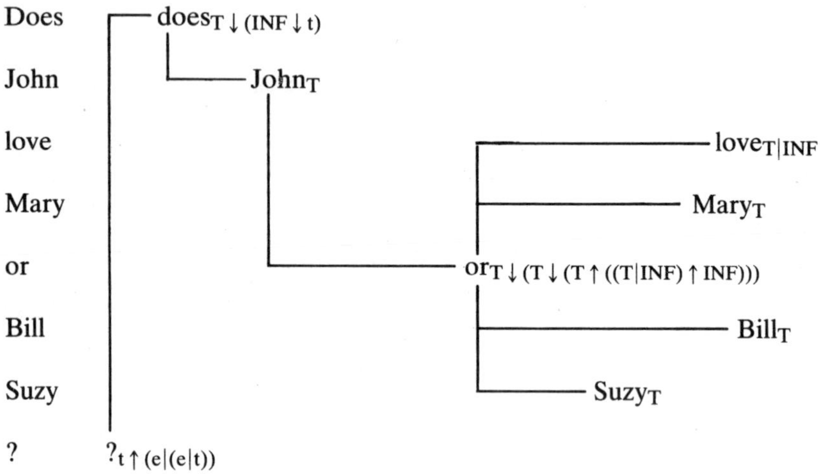

$\hat{\mathrm{p}}_{xy}\hat{x}\hat{y}[\mathrm{p}_{xy}]\ \hat{P}\hat{\mathrm{P}}[P(\mathrm{P})]\ \hat{\mathrm{P}}\mathrm{P}(j')$
$\hat{P}_2\hat{P}_3\hat{P}_1\hat{\mathrm{R}}\hat{\mathrm{x}}\mathrm{V}\mathrm{F}[\mathrm{F}(x, y)=[\mathrm{R}(P_1)\ (\mathrm{x})\vee P_2[\mathrm{R}(P_3)]]]$
$\hat{\mathrm{P}}\mathrm{P}(b')\ \hat{\mathrm{P}}\mathrm{P}(s')\ \hat{\mathrm{P}}\mathrm{P}(m')\ \hat{P}\hat{\mathrm{x}}[\hat{P}\hat{\mathrm{y}}[\mathrm{love}'(\mathrm{x})]]$

(F is a variable corresponding to e|(e|t), R is a variable corresponding to category (T|(e|t)).)

meaning[1]: $\hat{x}\hat{y}\mathrm{V}\mathrm{F}[\mathrm{F}(x, y)=[\mathrm{love}'(j', m')\vee \mathrm{love}'(b', s')]]$

(61.4.2) *T—T-responsive:* See (60.3.2)

contextual reconstruction of (60.3.2) relative (61.4.1) renders:

$[\mathrm{love}'(j', m')=[\mathrm{love}'(j', m')\vee \mathrm{love}'(b', s')]]$

Answering a restricted interrogative with an expression not contained in the open disjunction results in a contradictory reconstruction. This is schematically indicated in (62):

Does John love Mary or Suzy? Sandy.
(John loves X and (X=Mary or X=Suzy)?)

Reconstruction: John loves Sandy and (Sandy=Mary or Sandy=Suzy). This reconstruction is obviously false.

In the case of yes/no-interrogatives, the following expressions

Certainly.
Possibly.
Yes, certainly.
No, that's not likely.

are counted as compatible responsives. We assume that constituents like **certainly,** etc. arise as *modifiers* of **Ø-yes.**

The ambiguity of

or^{wh} → Mary.
↑
Does John love Mary or Suzy?
↓
or → Yes.

is explained in our analysis in terms of the distinction between regular **or** and **or**^{wh} (cf. (61.2.1), (61.3.1)).

Note that a T-responsive like **Mary.** is compatible with a restricted and a non-restricted interrogative (e.g. (61.3.1) and (60.1.1)). The same holds for a T—T-responsive like **John Mary.,** which is compatible with the restricted interrogative (61.4.1) and the non-restricted interrogative (60.3.1). The **or**^{wh} construction in (61.4.1) is similar to the **or**-construction in gapped declaratives.

5. Complement constructions

Our analysis of "questions" would be incomplete if it didn't provide for a treatment of "indirect questions", or rather declaratives with open sentential complements. For systematic reasons we will analyse English complement constructions in general, including closed sentential complements and infinitival complements. We distinguish between the following four subcategories of terms (T-phrases):

T^1: *proper names and quantified noun phrases,* e.g. **Mary, a story.**
(65.1) **Mary**$_T$ **knows a story**$_T$.

T^2: closed sentential complements, e.g. **that John walks**$_T$.
(65.2) **Mary knows that**$_{t\downarrow T}$ **John walks**$_t$**.**

T^3: open sentential complements, e.g. **whether John walks$_T$, who walks$_T$, where John goes$_T$, who loves whom$_T$, whether John loves Mary or Suzy$_T$.**

(65.3) **Mary knows whether$_{t\downarrow T}$ Ø-or$^{wh}{}_{t\downarrow t}$ John walks$_t$.**
(65.4) **Mary knows who$_{t\downarrow T}$ Ø$_T$ walks$_{T\uparrow t}$.**
(65.5) **Mary knows where$_{t\downarrow T}$ John Ø$_{(T\uparrow t)\downarrow(T\uparrow t)}$ goes$_{T\uparrow t}$**
(65.6) **Mary knows who$_{t\downarrow T}$ Ø$_T$ loves$_{T\downarrow(T\uparrow t)}$ whom$_T$.**
(65.7) **Mary knows whether$_{t\downarrow T}$ John loves Mary or^{wh} Suzy$_t$.**

T^4: infinitival complements, e.g. **to walk$_T$**.

(65.8) **John tries to$_{inf\downarrow T}$ walk$_{inf}$.** (where inf=e|t)
(65.9) **John promises Mary to$_{inf\downarrow T}$ walk$_{inf}$.**
(65.10) **John persuades Mary to$_{inf\downarrow T}$ walk$_{inf}$.**

There are transitive verbs like **know,** which take T^1, T^2, and T^3 object terms, but no T^4 object terms. There are verbs like **believe,** which take only T^1 and T^2 object terms (*John believes who walks). **Regret** takes T^1, T^2, and T^4, but no T^3 object terms:

John regrets
(1) the incident.
(2) that Mary leaves.
(3) *who goes home.
(4) to anger Mary.

Restrictions on subcategories of terms (category: (e|t)|t) in object-position are different from those on T-expressions which occur as subjects. But all four subcategories occur as subjects. This is exemplified in

(66.1) *The story* is boring.
(66.2) *That Mary goes home* irritates John.
(66.3) *Whether Mary goes home* cannot be predicted.
(66.4) *To walk* can be fun.

In order to obtain the proper combinations a sub-categorial system for the four types of subject/object-terms has to be incorporated into the analysis of verbs.

As before, we will not be concerned here with the combinatorial details of subject/object terms and certain predicates. The common main category of the four term-types, however, will be accommodated in our semantics by translating terms of all four types uniformly as $\hat{P}[\ldots P \ldots]$-formulas, which correspond to $(e|t)|t$ categories as desired.

T^1: **a story**

(67.1) $\hat{P}\mathrm{V}x[\mathrm{story}'(x) \wedge P(x)]$

T^2: **that John walks**

(67.2) $\hat{P}\mathrm{V}x[P(x)=\mathrm{walk}'(j')]$

T^3: **whether or^{wh} John walks, who Ø walks, where John Ø goes**

	universal	*existential*
(67.3)	$\hat{P}\mathrm{V}x\mathrm{V}r[r(P(x))=r(\mathrm{walk}'(j'))]$	$\hat{P}\mathrm{V}x\mathrm{V}r[r(P(x))=r(\mathrm{walk}'(j'))]$
(67.4)	$\hat{P}\mathrm{V}y[P(y)=\mathrm{walk}'(y)]$	$\hat{P}\mathrm{V}y[P(y)=\mathrm{walk}'(y)]$
(67.5)	$\hat{P}\mathrm{V}x\mathrm{V}a[a(P)(y)=a(\mathrm{walk}')(j')]$	$\hat{P}\mathrm{V}x\mathrm{V}a[a(P)(x)=a(\mathrm{walk}')(j')]$

T^4: **to walk**

(67.6) $\hat{P}[P=\mathrm{walk}']$

T^2, T^3, and T^4 complements correspond to the declarative, interrogative, and imperative moods, respectively. A declarative and a T^2 complement have in common that they both contain a closed t-expression (no free variables). But these t-expressions are themselves arguments, and arguments of different functions. In the case of a declarative, the higher functor is the mood-marker, while in the case of a T^2 *complement* the higher functor is the complementizer **that**$_{t|T}$. In the case of interrogatives and T^3-complements we have the same situation. Here the common argument expression is an open sentence, i.e. a sentence with unbound Wh-variables. An additional task arising with interrogatives and T^3-complements is binding the Wh-variable of the argument expression. The **?**-mood marker binds the Wh-variables with lambdas, thus changing the open sentence into a higher function, while the complementizer quantifies the wh-variable, thus changing the open sentence into a T^3-complement. In the case of complementizer-wh-quantification we must distinguish between existential versus universal quantification (existential versus universal complementizer).[21]

This distinction is motivated as follows. "John *knows* who came to the party." is true if and only if it holds for *all* x that John knows whether x came to the party or not. "John *wonders* who came to the party." on the other hand, is true if there is *at least one* x of which John wonders whether x came to the party or not. The pertinent examples are canonically analysed in (69.4) and (69.5).

Note that verbs taking object terms other than or in addition to T^1 must have the object in opaque position. The reason is that T^2, T^3, and T^4-arguments do not reduce to e-arguments but instead to t or $e|t$ arguments. For example, if we translated **knows** as $\hat{P}_1\hat{P}_0[P_0\hat{x}P_1\hat{y}$ $[\text{know}'(x, y)]]$ (i.e. like **love** in (68.3) with transparent object position) rather than $\hat{P}_1\hat{P}_0[P_0\hat{x}[\text{know}'(x, P_1)]]$, we would get nonsense if **knows** combines with a sentential object like **that John walks** $(\hat{P}\bigvee x[P(x)=\text{walk}'(j')])$. For a canonical analysis see (69.2). For this reason we must restrict T^2, T^3, and T^4-complements to narrow scope, thus preventing them from binding **he**$_n$-type variables.[22]

T^1-terms like **a woman,** on the other hand, must be allowed both wide and narrow scope relative to other quantifiers, negation, and intensional verbs. Consider for example (68):

(68.1) Every man loves a woman.
(68.2) $\bigvee y[\text{woman}'(y) \wedge \bigvee x[\text{man}'(x) \rightarrow \text{love}'(x, y)]]$

The syntactic tool to derive such wide scope quantifier readings in PTQ are the so-called rules of quantification (S14—16, PTQ, p. 252, 262), which Montague uses also for handling anaphoric pronouns.

In our system, a surface compositional version of the quantification-rule is employed solely for controlling quantifier scope, but not for pronouns,which are assimilated into a general treatment of contextdependency.[23] As an example of a wide scope derivation in terms of a canonical analysis consider (68.3):

(68.3)

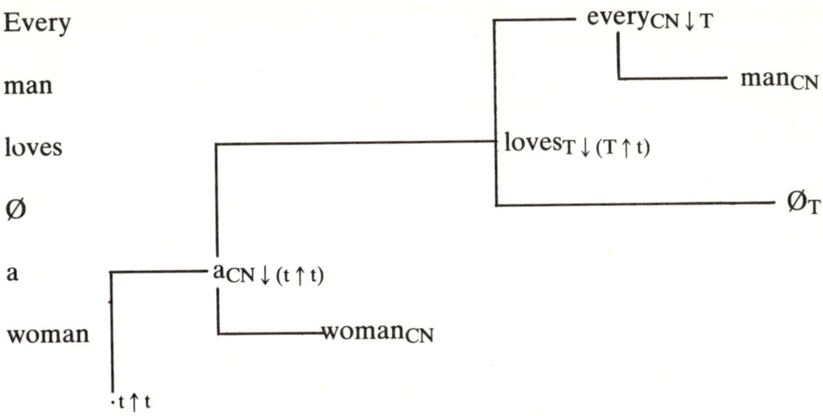

$\underline{\hat{p}[p]}$ $\underline{\hat{Q}\hat{p}_y Vy[Q(y)_\wedge p_y]}$ $\underline{\text{woman}'}$ $\underline{\hat{P}_2\hat{P}_1[P_1\hat{x}[P_2\hat{y}(\text{love}'(x, y))]]}$
$\underline{\hat{Q}\hat{P}Vx[Q(x) \rightarrow P(x)]}$ $\underline{\text{man}'}$ $\underline{\hat{P}P(y)}$

meaning[1]: $Vy[\text{woman}'(y)_\wedge Vx[\text{man}'(x) \rightarrow \text{love}'(x, y)]]$

Like Montague, we use a place holder pronoun in (68.3), which allows to build sentences with (an) unbound variable(s). The open sentence combines with a *wide scope* or t|t-version of a quantified noun phrase. In the following consider the narrow and the wide scope version of **a man.**

narrow scope: $\hat{P}Vx[\text{man}'(x)_\wedge P(x)]_{(e|t)|t}$
wide scope: $\hat{p}_x Vx[\text{man}'(x)_\wedge p_x]_{t|t}$

p_x stands for a variable p ranging over propositions denoted by formulas open in x. We use this notation both for interrogative mood markers (e.g. $\hat{p}_x\hat{x}[p_x]$) and wide scope quntifiers (e.g. $\hat{Q}\hat{p}_x Vx[Q(x)_\wedge p_x]$). For precise definitions of the new lambda-operator $\hat{p}_x$ and the variable p_x see Hausser (1982b), p. 3.54—3.54.

The following canonical analyses (69) illustrate the predicate **know** in combination with T[1] (69.1), T[2] (69.2), and several T[3]-complements (69.3—5). (69.5) illustrates the *existential* complementizer in combination with **wonder** — in contrast to **know** in (69.4). (69.7—9), finally, analyzes the predicates **try, promise,** and **persuade** in combination with T^4-complements. The difference between **persuade** and **promise** is treated as indicated in the following simplified translation:

$$\hat{P}_3\hat{y}\hat{x}[\text{persuade}'(x, y, \hat{P}[P_3(P) \wedge P(y)])]$$
$$\hat{P}_3\hat{y}\hat{x}[\text{promise}'(x, y, \hat{P}[P_3(P) \wedge P(x)])]$$

The semantic difference between **promise to walk** and **persuade to walk** is thus treated in the respective predicate translations—not in the complementizer **to,** in contradistinction to **know, wonder** and T^3-complements.

(69.1)

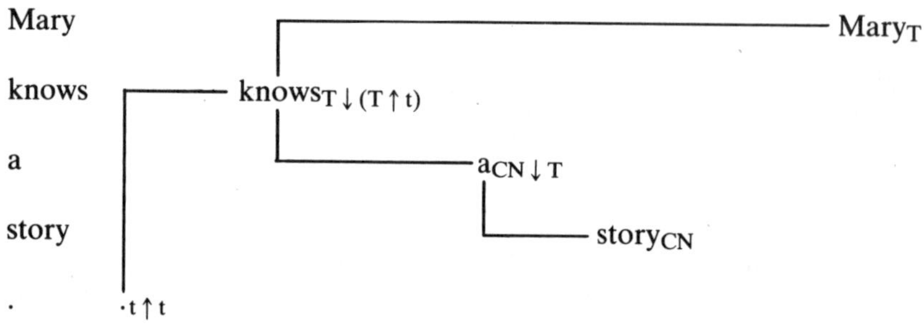

$\underline{\hat{p}[p]}$ $\underline{\hat{P}_1\hat{P}_0[P_0(\hat{x}[\text{know}'(x, P_1)])]}$ $\underline{\hat{Q}\hat{P}\vee x[Q(x) \wedge P(x)]}$ $\underline{\text{story}'}$ $\underline{\hat{P}P(m')}$

meaning[1]: $\text{know}'(m', \hat{P}\vee x[\text{story}'(x) \wedge P(x)])$

(69.2)

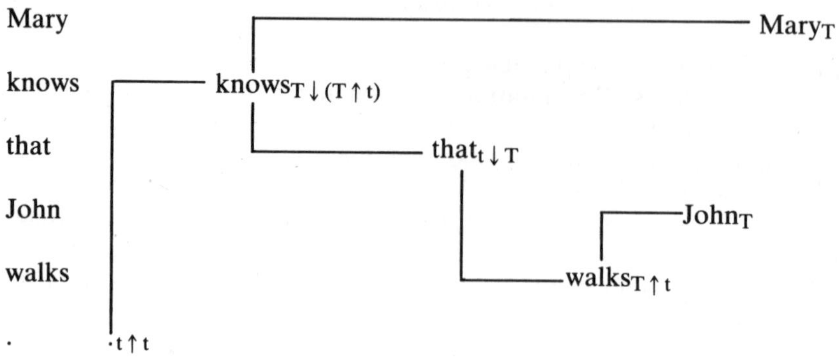

$\underline{\hat{p}(p)}$ $\underline{\hat{P}_1\hat{P}_0[P_0(\hat{x}[\text{know}'(x, P_1)])}$ $\underline{\hat{p}[\hat{P}\bigvee x[P(x)=p]]}$
$\underline{\hat{P}[P\hat{y}[\text{walk}'(y)]]}$ $\underline{\hat{P}P(j')}$ $\underline{\hat{P}P(m')}$

meaning[1]: $\text{know}'(m', \hat{P}\bigvee x[P(x)=\text{walk}'(j')])$

(69.3)

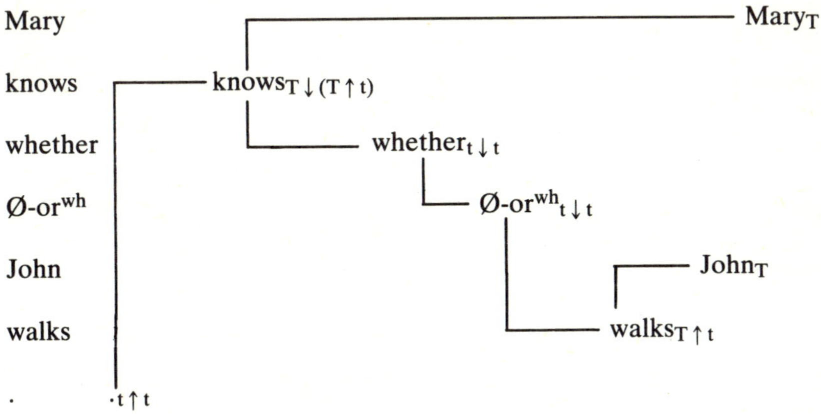

$\underline{\hat{p}(p)}$ $\underline{\hat{P}_1\hat{P}_0[P_0(\hat{x}[\text{know}'(x, P_0)])}$ $\underline{\hat{p}_r\hat{P}\bigvee x\bigwedge r[r(P(x)=p_r]}$
$\underline{\hat{q}[r(q)\wedge((r=\hat{p}(p))\vee(r=\hat{p}(\sim p)))]}$ $\underline{\hat{P}[Py[\text{walk}'(y)]]}$ $\underline{\hat{P}P(j')}$ $\underline{\hat{P}P(m')}$

meaning[1]: $\text{know}'(m', \hat{P}\bigvee x\bigwedge r[r(P(x))=(r[\text{walk}'(j)\wedge((r=p(p)\vee (r=p(\sim p)))])])$
$=\text{know}'(m', \hat{P}\bigvee x\bigwedge r[r(P(x))=(r[\text{walk}'(j)])])$

(69.4)

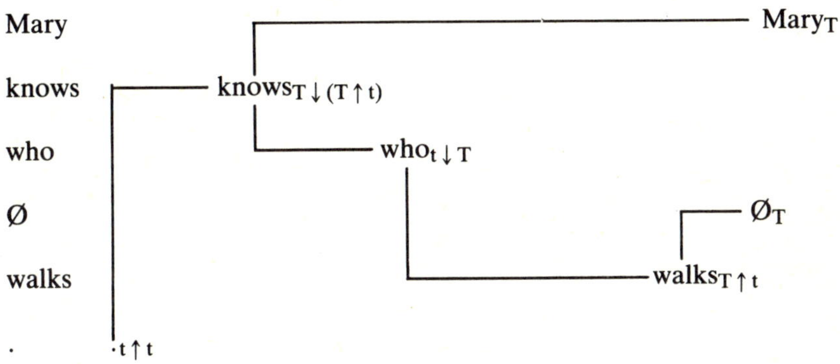

$\underline{\hat{p}[p]}$ $\underline{\hat{P}_1\hat{P}_2[P_2\hat{x}[\text{know}'(x, P_1)]]}$ $\underline{\hat{p}_y\hat{P}\bigwedge y[P(y)=p_y]}$
$\underline{\hat{P}[P\hat{x}[\text{walk}'(x)]]}$ $\underline{\hat{P}P(y)}$ $\underline{\hat{P}P(m')}$

meaning[1]: $\text{know}'(m', \hat{P}\bigwedge y[P(y)=\text{walk}'(y)])$

(69.5)

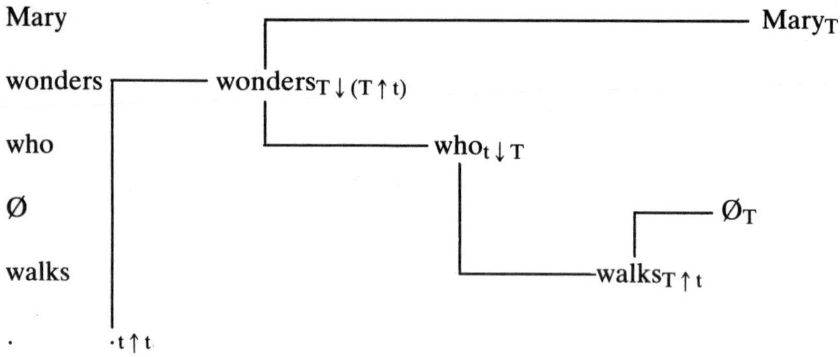

$\underline{\hat{p}[p]}$ $\underline{\hat{P}_1\hat{P}_2[P_2\hat{x}[\text{wonders}'(x, P_1)]]}$ $\underline{\hat{p}_y\hat{P}\bigvee y[P(y)=p_y]}$
$\underline{\hat{P}[P\hat{x}[\text{walk}'(x)]]}$ $\underline{\hat{P}P(y)}$ $\underline{\hat{P}P(m')}$

meaning[1]: $\text{wonder}'(m', \hat{P}\bigvee y[P(y)=\text{walk}'(y)])$

(69.6)

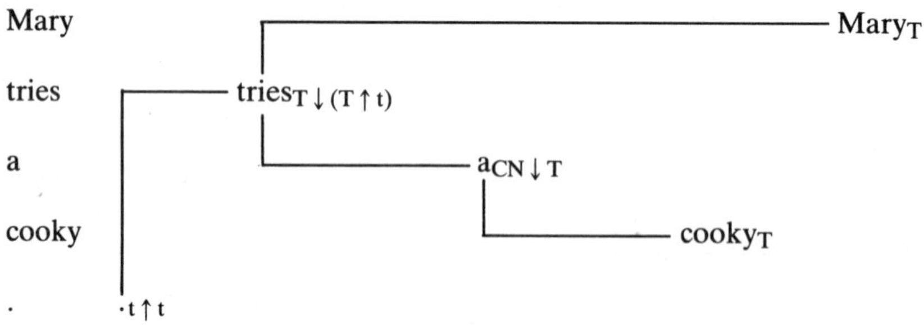

$\underline{\hat{p}(p)}$ $\underline{\hat{P}_1\hat{P}_0[P_0\hat{x}[\text{try}'(x, \hat{P}[P_1(P)\wedge P(x)])]]}$
$\underline{\hat{Q}\hat{P}\bigvee y[Q(y)\wedge P(y)]}$ $\underline{\text{cooky}'}$ $\underline{\hat{P}P(m')}$

meaning[1]: $\text{try}'(m', \hat{P}\bigvee y[[\text{cooky}'(y)\wedge P(y)]\wedge P(m')])$

(69.7)

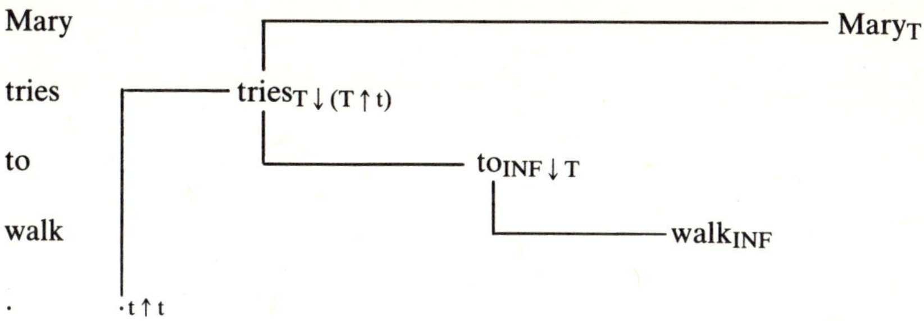

$\underline{\hat{p}(p)}$ $\underline{\hat{P}_1\hat{P}_0[P_0\hat{x}[try'(x, \hat{P}[P_1(P)_\wedge P(x)])}$ $\underline{\hat{Q}\hat{P}[P=Q]}$ $\underline{walk'}$ $\underline{\hat{P}P(m')}$

meaning[1]: $try'(m', \hat{P}[P=walk'_\wedge P(m')])$

(69.8)

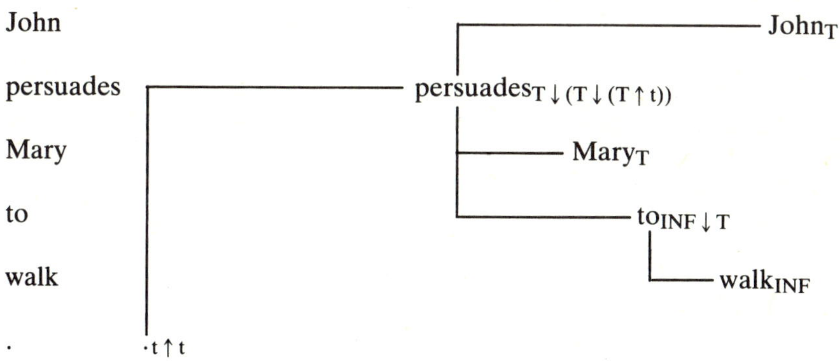

$\underline{\hat{p}[p]}$ $\underline{\hat{P}_2\hat{P}_3\hat{P}_1[P_1\hat{x}[P_2\hat{y}[persuade'(x, y, \hat{P}[P_3(P)_\wedge P(y)])]]]}$
$\underline{\hat{P}P(m')}$ $\underline{\hat{Q}\hat{P}[P=Q]}$ $\underline{walk'}$ $\underline{\hat{P}P(j')}$

meaning[1]: $persuade'(j', m', \hat{P}[[P=walk']_\wedge walk'(m')])$

(69.9)

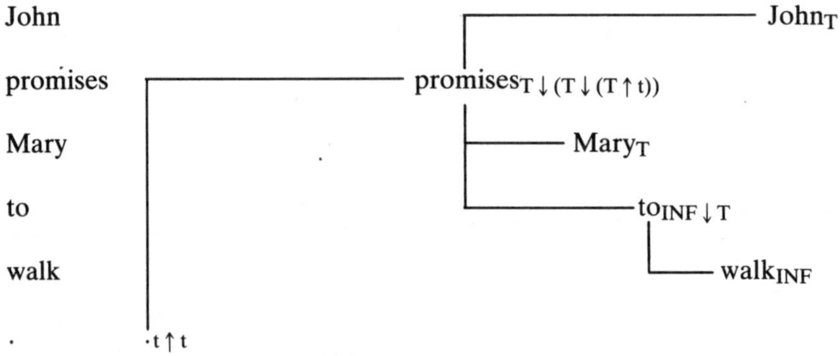

$\underline{\hat{p}[p]}$ $\underline{\hat{P}_2\hat{P}_3\hat{P}_1[P_1\hat{x}[P_2\hat{y}[\text{promise}'(x, y, \hat{P}[P_3(P)_\wedge P(x)])]]]}$
$\underline{\hat{P}P(m')}$ $\underline{\hat{Q}\hat{P}[P=Q]}$ $\underline{\text{walk}'}$ $\underline{\hat{P}P(j')}$

meaning[1]: $\text{promise}'(j', m', \hat{P}[[P=\text{walk}']_\wedge \text{walk}'(j')])$

6. Speaker simulation device (SID)

Now that the 25 sample sentences listed in section 1 have been canonically analysed in the course of the sections 3, 4, and 5 it might be interesting to see how this specific form of syntactico-semantic analysis links up with the rest of the communicative process. At some point one must ask again: In what sense do the logical formulas associated with surface expressions by the formal grammar represent an analysis of the literal meaning (meaning[1]) of these expressions? And what is the relation between canonical analyses and pragmatics?

Our meaning[1]-formulas consist of three types of symbols: operators, variables, and constants.[24] Operators receive their meaning from semantic definitions in a meta-language. The operators of intensional logic, including the lambda, are well investigated tools of logic, which have been put into operational use. We may therefore assume that as far as the definition of the operators is concerned we are on safe ground. Similar arguments may be given for the existence of variables. The motivation for the definitions of operators and variables as symbols with a fixed formal meaning is purely logical, derived from the structure of the overall system. Constants, on the other hand, have a twofold existence. On the one hand, they are logical entities, functions of a domain/range structure determined by the category. On the other hand, constants denote or refer to objects in the model-structure.

If we assume that the model-structure is a purely abstract object-language entity, constants retain a uniform logical character, because "reference" is established by explicit definition. If one assumes, on the other hand, that the model-structure is or includes *reality,* then constants acquire a double nature: besides being logical functions they are assumed to refer to real objects. Despite efforts by Donnellan, Kripke,[25] and others, the nature of this 'real' kind of reference is completely unclear on a systematic level. The question that remains open is how the logical analysis of meaning links up with the pragmatic process of reference.

In agreement with the model-theoretic main stream, Montague assumed that the model-structure is a representation of reality. It has been acknowledged occasionally, however, that this 'standard' model theoretic approach, and Montague grammar in particular, is not suited to handle phenomena of the following kind: (a) word meanings (Dowty 1979, p. 33), (b) pragmatics (Apostel 1971, p. 4), and (c) propositional attitudes (Partee 1978). These problems all have a common source, namely the definition of meaning in the standard model theoretic approach.

In standard model theoretic semantics, meaning is defined as a direct relation between expressions and model theoretic objects, where (a) no distinction between literal meaning and use-aspects is specified (cf. section 1.3), (b) the model structure is interpreted as a representation of reality, and (c) the speaker, if mentioned at all, is treated as part of the model structure. Yet, as L. Apostel (1971) points out correctly, "pragmatics in the sense of Morris has not been obtained" as long as the "concept of a speaker is presupposed and not constructed".

Alternatively to the standard model theoretic approach let us assume that the model-structure is part of the speaker rather than the other way around. Following earlier papers[26] we interpret the system of syntactico-semantic analysis discussed in the previous sections as part of a speaker simulation device (SID). An SID is a theoretical construct designed to simulate communication among speakers. We distinguish SID's in the speaker and hearer mode. We also distinguish between the outside reality and the representation of reality inside the SID (as perceived through the SID's sense organs).

It is assumed that the literal meaning of *tokens* is modeltheoretically characterized in terms of models which would satisfy the meaning[1] formula of the token. The model or models representing a meaning^1 are *synthesized* in a partially defined model structure, called *lexical space.* In the lexical space of an SID the denotation of all constants of the logic (e.g. go′, home′) is specified according to the type of the constants in question. The lexical intuition of the SID is characterized in terms of the set-theoretic overlap, inclusion, or disjointness of the (abstract) extensions of constants of equal type.

It is furthermore assumed that the *context* is a model-theoretic representation of what the SID perceives or remembers in the 'interpretation intervall'. The context-model is synthesized in the same lexical space as the token model. A token is interpreted relative to a context by *matching* the token model with the context model:

(70)

token
| denotation^1
token-model
: reference
context-model
| denotation^2
perception & memory data

The matching relation between the token-model and the context-model includes *reference,* which is treated as a pragmatic concept, in contrast to denotation, which is a semantic concept.

The grammatical schema indicated in (70) is shown as part of an SID in (71). The SID is shown schematically as a speaker, who perceives John walking and articulates this observation by uttering the token "John walks." (or rather a token like it), thus making a true statement. The mapping from the internal token representation to the token-model is algebraically generated by the type of grammar discussed in sections 2, 3, 4, 5. For the definition of the context we may assume the techniques of discourse semantics. The context together with the memory constitutes the sensual and social reality of the SID. We define the context as a system of various parameters the content of which is stated in logical form (e.g. time digits, spacial orientation, activation of movement,

(71)

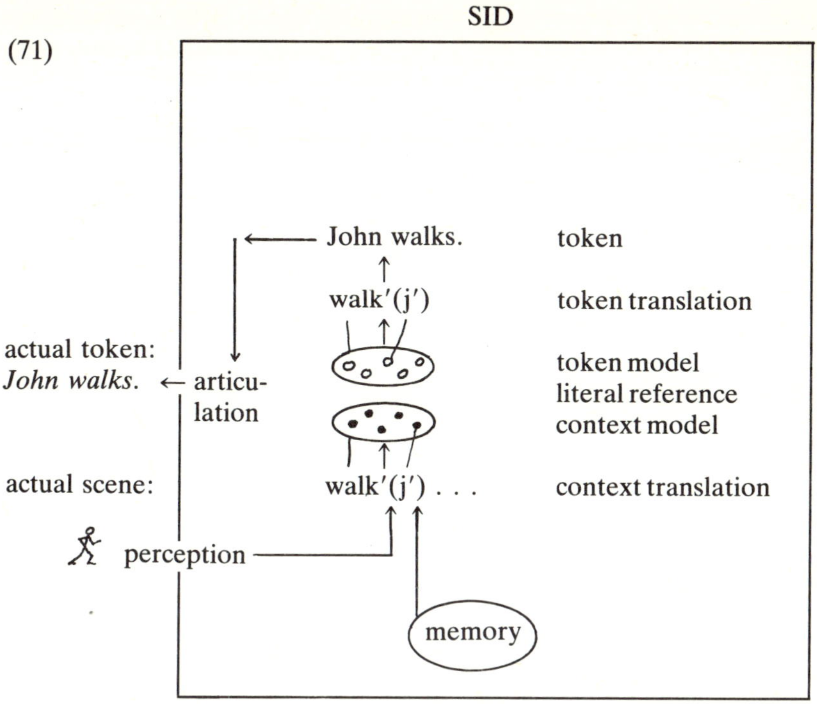

propositional description of what is perceived, reasoned, desired, etc.).[27]

The notion of meaning assumed by the standard model theoretic approach is the relation between the actual token and the actual scene (cf. (71)), whereas in the theory presumed here this mapping is routed through the speaker/hearer, which results in the indicated sub-mappings. The relation between expressions and meanings[1] constitutes only one of these sub-mappings, namely denotation[1]. Meaning[2], on the other hand, is interpreted as the matching of the two models, which in the case of metaphoric, ironic, etc, use will be a matter of highly complex interaction between the two models. In (71) however, the traditional notion of truth (Aristotle, Tarski (1944)) is illustrated. In this case perception is accurate, the relation between the two models is a complete match (or an accurate (partial) copy), and no speech- or perception errors occur. We must distinguish between two notions of truth, a formal notion[28] and a pragmatic notion. The formal notion refers to the 1 in the set of truth-values in model-theory. The pragmatic notion refers to a certain type of language *use,* involving accurate perception, accurate interpretation, etc.

The SID-approach briefly outlined above may be motivated in several ways.[29] The point in the present paper is that it conceptualizes the formula

$$\text{use of meaning}^1 = \text{meaning}^2$$

in a sufficiently precise way to motivate our rather aseptic semantics, based on synthesizing set-theoretic meanings in a lexical space, and the strict application of the Fregean principle in the sense of surface compositionality.

Acknowledgement

The manuscript of this paper was written in October 1980 in Munich, Germany. As the syntactic theory presumed developed into a more standardized form in Hausser (1980c), (1981) and (1982a), the original manuscript of this paper contained some orthogonal analyses which from the present point of view looked rather unorthodox and problematic. I am very much indebted to Claudia Gerstner of the Institut für Deutsche Philologie, Universität München, for undertaking the laborious and often tricky task of adjusting the original version of this paper to the notation and principles of analysis as laid down in the later papers on categorial syntax.

March 19, 1982

Universität München
Institut für Deutsche Philologie

Notes

[1] The strictly intensional logic used here is explicitly defined in Hausser (1978b). Hausser (1979c), furthermore, contains a version of strictly intensional logic with a belief-operator. The idea that natural language expressions should be defined to denote intensions may be found in Tichý (1971), Bressan (1972), and Lewis (1972, 1974). The crucial differences, however, reside in the formal method of implementing this idea. Lewis (1972, 1974), for example, proposes functions from intensions to intensions. These functions, however, are themselves extensions:

Lewis: $$\overbrace{\langle\langle \underline{s, a}\rangle, \langle \underline{s, b}\rangle\rangle}^{\text{extension}}$$
intensions

Hausser: $$\overbrace{\langle s, \langle \underline{\langle s, a\rangle, b}\rangle\rangle}^{\text{intension}}$$
intension extension

Thus Lewis did not succeed in constructing a strictly intensional system. More comments on strictly intensional logic may be found in section 2.3.

[2] The following ways to relate non-declaratives to declaratives or propositions have achieved prominence in the field (illustrated here with schematic treatments of "questions"):

(a) $$\underbrace{\text{performative clause} + \text{“question”}}_{\text{declarative}}$$

(e.g. Ross (1970), Sadock (1971). Lewis (1972), Karttunen (1978), Groenendijk & Stokhof (1980))

(b) $$\underbrace{\text{mood operator} + \text{“propositional content”}}_{\text{question}}$$

(e.g. Ajdukiewicz (1929), Stenius (1967), Åqvist (1965), Hintikka (1976))

(c) $$\underbrace{\text{set of propositions}}_{\text{question}}$$

(e.g. Stahl (1969), Hamblin (1973), Karttunen (1978)).

The alternative analysis of non-declaratives incorporated in the present paper was developed in Hausser (1976c), Hausser (1978a), and Hausser & Zaefferer (1979). The goal of the present paper is essentially syntactic, whereas Hausser (1978a) is more literature oriented and directed towards motivating the distinction between moods and speech acts (here summarized in section 1.2) and the use of higher types as denotations of non-declaratives. The theory of the earlier papers is smoothly accommodated in our canonical analyses of non-declaratives. For reasons of economy and readability, a number of comparisons with other treatments of "questions", "answers", and related topics proposed in the literature have been removed from this version of manuscript. The criticism contained in these passages is analog to that of Hausser (1978a).

While our formal analysis of non-declaratives differs from all proposals indicated in (a), (b), and (c) above, it also shares some features with each of them. Our treatment is a denotational approach like (c). The combination of a mood-marker and an open sentence, furthermore, is similar to (b). The treatment of open sentential complements ("indirect questions") in section 5, finally, is similar in some respects to (a). Similarities may also be found with proposals by Katz & Postal (1964) and other transformational treatments. Thus the mood marker may be equated with the so-called Wh-form. For an overview of transformational analyses see Malone (1978).

[3] The notion of a responsive is analog to that of imperative and interrogative: interrogare → interrogative; respondere → responsive. I am grateful to Marleen Rozemond who argued convincingly for the term 'responsive' rather then 'respondative', as used in the 1980-version of Hausser (1978a), footnote 8.

[4] Searle (1965), "What is a speech act?"

[5] A notable exception is Davidson (1979). However, after describing the distinction between moods and speech acts, Davidson proposes to derive non-declaratives as well as declaratives from *two* underlying declaratives, e.g.:

"My next utterance is an imperative. You will put your that on." But such a treatment is clearly circular: the explanandum (i.e. the syntactic mood "imperative") reappears in the explanans (i.e. the first underlying declarative "What follows is an imperative"). Davidson (1979) as well as Hiż (1978) use the term "indicative" to refer to the declarative mood. This is an incorrect use of terminology, since "indicative" refers to verbal mood, while the syntactic mood in question is called " declarative" (see for example Webster's New Collegiate Dictionary).

[6] There is a particular spot in the paradigm (28), i.e. (27.1) which is especially suited to be *used* in the speech act of questioning. This specific *use potential* is a direct consequence of the syntactico-semantic properties of this particular expression, namely the tempus (present tense), the subject (first person pronoun), the direct object (second person pronoun), and the use of the verb *ask*. Thus (27.1) is an example of a *declarative* often or primarily used for making a question. (27.2), on the other hand, is an *interrogative* usually used to make a question. (27.1) and (27.2) are two sentences of different mood which may be used for the same speech act.

[7] This formula is developed in Hausser (1979b, c, 1980a).

[8] Presuming certain well-motivated changes such as strict intensionality (formally treated in Hausser 1978b, 1979c) and the use of context-variables introduced in Hausser (1979a, b).

[9] These phenomena are discussed in Hausser (1976b), (1978b), and (1974a). (1976b) and (1974a) are in need of revisions regarding the syntactic presentation, which is not up to the standard of a canonical analysis.

[10] The systematic category-type-correspondence was pioneered by Montague in PTQ; the present system differs only in that we assume a strictly intensional logic. Cf. Hausser 1979c, "A constructive approach to intensional contexts" for explicit definitions.

[11] Explicit formulations of lexical derivation rules may be found in Hausser (1981a, 1981b, 1982a).

[12] The surface compositionality constraint (SCC) is motivated and formally defined in Hausser (1978b).

[13] The formal system of this new type of syntax, called orthogonal syntax or ORTAX, was developed in Hausser (1980c) and is summarized in Hausser (1982b). The tree structures of this system where first presented in an informal talk at the Linguistics Department of Stanford University in November 1979. I adopted the name 'orthogonal tree' from a remark made by Ron Kaplan in a discussion after the talk.

[14] For discussion of this solution see Hausser 1982b, p. 3.39—3.47.
[15] Hausser (1978a), Hausser & Zaefferer (1979), Hausser (1976c). Belnap (1980) holds that "there is *no* requirement that the type (in the sense of type theory) of the translation have any intutive significance." For Belnap "the chief problem ... is the embedding problem ... and whatever has to be invoked to solve that problem can be treated like the postulated features or kinds of physical science (spin, charm)", p. 2, 3. In light of the formal solution to the embedding problem in section 5, our attempt to use intuitively plausible types of possible denotations for different moods may be seen as a bonus (certainly not as an objectionable feature of our analysis).
[16] The treatment of context-dependency presumed here is developed in Hausser (1979a, b). For our formal notion of context see also section 6.
[17] Cf. Hausser (1979a, b).
[18] It would be perfectly possible to treat these structures by means of continuous categories only, but for intuitive reasons the discontinuous connection between the interrogative moodmarker and the fronted wh-element has a certain plausibility.
[19] This was brought to my attention by Theo Vennemann.
[20] In Hausser (1978b) und (1980c) it is shown that a categorial grammar obeying the SCC is decidable.
[21] Hintikka (1976) uses the distinction between existential and universal quantification of the Wh-variable in his analysis of 'direct questions' or interrogatives, which according to our analysis are not ambiguous, however.

The idea that wh-variables arising in sentential complements should be quantified is central also to the treatments by Belnap (1980), Bennett (1979), and Karttunen (1978). Our solution likewise provides for quantification of the Wh-variables in open complements, but this treatment of "indirect question" is not assumed to carry over to "direct questions" (pace Belnap, Bennett, Karttunen and others), where we use lambdas instead of quantifiers to bind the Wh-variables. For this reason no ambiguity between universal and existential quantification arises in interrogatives.
[22] For an analysis of scope restrictions of English quantifiers see Hausser (1976b).
[23] Cf. Hausser (1979a, b). It seems that our assumption that (i) anaphoric pronouns are assimilated to a general treatment of context-dependency, and (ii) the compositional treatment of wide scope quantification in (66.3), jointly meets the challenge of v. Stechow (1980), who says on p. 24: "No syntactic rule involving variable binding has a compositional semantics".
[24] Leaving context-variables aside for the moment.
[25] Donñellan (1966), Kripke (1972, 1977).
[26] Hausser (1979a, c, 1980a, 1982).
[27] For a more detailed discussion see Hausser (1980a, 1982). Cf. also G. Lippit (1973) for an overview of various psychological theories concerning the interaction of a speaker with his context.
[28] Frege (1918) likens the semantic notion of truth to notion like weight or temperature in physics.
[29] For motivations from an ontological point of view see Hausser (1979c). A more extensive representation of the SID-approach to model-theory may be found in Hausser (1981).

References

Ajdukiewicz, K. (1929) ''Logiczne Podstawy Naucania'' (The Foundations of Teaching), 1928. Quoted here after Hiż (1978).

Ajdukiewicz, K. (1935) ''Syntactic Connexion'', in **Polish Logic**, 1920-1939, Storrs McCall (ed.), Oxford, Clarendon (1967), p.207-231.

Apostel, L. (1971) ''Further Remarks on the Pragmatics of Natural Language'', in Y.Bar-Hillel (ed.) **Pragmatics of Natural Language**, Reidel, Synthese Language Library, Vol. 41.

Åqvist, L. (1965), **A new Approach to the Logical Theory of Interrogatives**, Filosofiska Föreningen, Uppsala 1965. New edition 1975, TBL Verlag Gunter Narr, Tübingen.

Aristotle (1949), **Aristotles Metaphysics**, a revised text with introduction and commentary by W.D. Ross, Oxford.

Ballmer (1975), **Sprachrekonstruktionssysteme**, Skripten Linguistik und Kommunikationswissenschaften 15, Scriptor Verlag Kronberg.

Ballmer (1978), **Logical Grammar**, North Holland Linguistic Series 39, Amsterdam, New York, Oxford.

Bar-Hillel, J.A. (1953), ''A Quasi-Arithmtical Notation for Syntactic Description'', in Bar-Hillel (ed.), **Language & Information**, Reading, Mass.

Bartsch, R. and T. Vennemann (1972), Semantic Structures, Athenäum Verlag.

Belnap, N.D.jr. (1979, ''Questions and Answers in Montague Grammar'', mimeograph.

Belnap, N.D.jr. and Steel, T.B.jr. (1976), **The Logic of Questions and Answers**. Yale University Presse, New Haven and London.

Bell, J. and M. Machover (1977), **A Course in Mathematical Logic**, NorthHolland, Amsterdam.

Bennett, M. (1979), **Questions in Montague Grammar**, Bloomington (Indiana Linguistics Club).

Bressan, A. (1972), **A General Interpreted Modal Calculus**, Yale University

Cooper, R. (1975), **Montague' Semantic Theory and Transformational Syntax**. unpublished Ph.D. dissertation, University of Massachussetts at Amherst.

Davidson, D. (1967) ''Truth and Meaning'', **Synthese**, XVII, No.3. p.304-323. Reprinted in Rosenbaum and Travis (eds.) **Readings in the Philosophy of Language**, Englewood Cliffs, N.J.

Davidson, D. (1979) ''Moods and Performances'', in A. Margalit (ed.) **Meaning and Use**, Reidel, Synthese Language Library, Dordrecht.

Donnellan, K. (1966), ''Reference and Definite Descriptions'', **The Philosophical Review**, LXXV, No.3. Reprinted in Rosenberg, J.F. and C.Travis (eds), **Readings in the Philosophy of Language**, Prentice Hall, Inc., Englewood Cliffs, New Jersey (1971).

Dowty, D.R. (1979), **Word Meaning and Montague Grammar**, Reidel, Synthese Language Library, Vol.7, Dordrecht.

Frege, G. (1892), ''Über Sinn und Bedeutung'', Zeitschrift für Philosophie und philosophische Kritik, 100, p.25-50.

Frege, G. (1918), ''Der Gedanke. Eine logische Untersuchung'', in **Beitraege zur Philosophie des deutschen Idealismus**, Band I. 1918, p.58-77.

Geach, P.T. (1972), ''A Program for Syntax'', in Davidson D. and G. Harman (eds.) **Semantics of Natural Language**, p.483-497, Reidel, Synthese Language Library, Dordrecht.

Grice, P. (1957), ''Meaning'', in Steinberg, D. and L.S. Jacobovits (eds.) **Semantics**, Cambridge University Press.
Gruenendijk, J. and M. Stokhof (1980), ''On the Semantics of Wh-Complements'', in Gruenendijk and Stokhof (eds.) **Papers in Formal Philosophy**, Vol.III, University of Amsterdam.
Hamblin, C.L. (1973), ''Questions in Montague English'', **Foundations of Langauge** 10, 1973, pp.41-54.
Hausser, R.R. (1973), ''Presuppositions and Quantifiers'', in **CLS 9**, proceedings of the Ninth Meeting of the Chicago Linguistics Society, Chicago.
Hausser, R.R. (1974a), ''Syntax and Semantics of plural'', in **CLS 10**, proceedings of the Tenth Meeting of the Chicago Linguistic Society, Chicago.
Hausser,R.R. (1974b) Quantification in an Extended Montague Grammar, Ph.D. dissertation, University of Texas at Austin. Available over University Microfilms, Ann Arbor, Michigan.
Hausser, R.R. (1976a) ''Presuppositions in Montague Grammar'', in **Theoretical Linguistics**, Vol.3.3.
Hausser, R.R. (1976b), ''Scope Ambiguity and Scope Restriction'', in Bartsch, Gruenendijk, and Stokhof (eds.) **Papers in Formal Philosophy**, Vol.I, University of Amsterdam.
Hausser, R.R. (1976c), ''The logic of questions and answers'', unpublished manuscript.
Hausser, R.R. (1978a), ''Surface Compositionality and the Semantics of Mood'', in Gruenendijk and Stokhof (eds.) **Papers in Formal Philosophy**, Vol.II, University of Amsterdam. Reprinted in Searle, Kiefer, Bierwisch (eds.) **Speech Act Theory and Pragmatics**, (1980), Reidel, Synthese Language Library, Dordrecht.
Hausser, R.R. (1978b), ''Surface Compositional Semantics, chapter I: Methodological Deliberations'', unpublished manuscript, revised Stanford, November (1979), Munich, June (1980).
Hausser, R.R. (1979a), ''How do Pronouns Denote?'', in Heny and Schnelle (eds.) **Syntax and Semantics**, Vol.10, Academic Press, New York.
Hausser,R.R. (1979b), ''A New Approach to Context in Model Theory'', appeared in **Sull' Anaphora,** atti del seminario Accedemia della Crusca, Firenze MCMLXXXI.
Hausser, R.R. (1979c), ''A Constructive Approach to Intensional Contexts'', to appear in **Language Research,** Vol. 18, No. 2, Seoul, Korea, (1982)..
Hausser, R.R. (1980a), ''The Place of Pragmatics in Model Theory'', in Gruenendijk et al. (eds.), **Formal Methods in the Study of Language**, Mathematical Center Tracts 135, The University of Amsterdam. (1980).
Hausser, R.R. (1980c), ''Chapter III: Categorial Surface Syntax'', München, unpublished manuscript, 68 pages.
Hausser, R.R. (1981), ''The Speaker Simulation Device and the Foundation of Semantics and Pragmatics'', appeared in **Language and Linguistics,** No.7, Journal of the Language Research Institute, Seoul National University, Korea.
Hausser, R.R. (1982a), ''A Surface Compositional Categorial Syntax'', to appear in the proceedings of the '82 Workshop on Formal Grammar, Seoul, Korea.
Hausser, R.R. (1982b), **Surface Compositional Grammar,** to appear.
Hausser, R.R. and D. Zeafferer (1979), ''Questions and Answers in a Context Dependent Montague Grammar'', Guenther and Schmidt (eds.) **Formal Semantics and Pragmatics for Natural Languages**, Reidel, Synthese Language Library, Dordrecht.
Hintikka, J. (1976), **The Semantics of Questions and the Questions of Semantics**, Acta Philosophica Fennica, Vol. 28, No.4. North Holland Publishing Company.

Hiż,H. (1978) ''Difficult Questions'', in H. Hiż (ed.) **Questions**, Reidel, Synthese Language Library, Dordrecht.

Karttunen, L. (1978), ''Syntax and Semantics of Questions'', in H. Hiż (ed.) **Questions**, Reidel, Synthese Language Library, Dordrecht.

Katz, J. and P. Postal (1964), **An Integrated Theory of Linguistic Description**, Cambridge, MIT-press.

Kreisel, G. and J.L. Krivine (1970), **Modelltheorie**, Springer-Verlag, Berlin, Heidelberg, New York.

Kripke, S. (1972), ''Naming and Necessity'', in Davidson and Harman (eds.), **Semantics of Natural Language**, p.169-218, Reidel, Synthese Library, Dordrecht.

Kripke,S. (1977), ''Speaker's Reference and Semantic Reference'', in P.S. French et al. (eds.), **Midwestern Studies in Philosophy**, Vol II: **Studies in the Philosophy of Language, the University of Minnesota, Morris, 1977, pp. 255-276.**

Lee, Kiyong (1982), "On Case Shifting", **Linguistic Journal of Korea** 7.2. pp. 497–517.

Lewis, D. (1972), ''General Semantics'', in Davidson and Harman (eds.), **Semantics of Natural Language**, p. 169-218, Reidel, Synthese Language Library, Dordrecht.

Lewis, D. (1974), ''Tensions'', in Munitz and Unger (eds.) **Semantics and Philosophy**, New York University Press, p.49-62.

Link, G. (1979), **Montague Grammatik**, Wilhelm Fink Verlag, München.

Lippitt, G.L. (1973), **Visualizing Change**, University Associates, Inc La Jolla, California.

Malone, J.L. (1978) ''Generative-Transformational Studies in English Interrogatives'', in H. Hiż (ed.) **Questions**, Reidel, Dordrecht, p.37-86.

Montague, R. (1974), **Formal Philosophy, The Papers of Richard Montague**, edited and with an introduction by Richmond Thomason, Yale University Press, Newhaven.

Partee, B. (1978), ''Semantics-Mathematics or Psychology'', paper read at the SFB-99 Conference **Semantics from different points of view.** Universität Konstanz, September 1978.

Quine, W.v.O. (1960), **Word and Object**, MIT Press, Cambridge, Mass.

Ross, J.R. (1970), ''On Declarative Sentences'', in Jacobs and Rosenbaum (eds.) **Readings in English Transformational Grammar**, Waltham, Blaisdell.

Sadock, J.M. (1971), ''Queclaratives'', in **CLS 7**, proceedings of the Seventh Meeting of the Chicago Linguistic Society, Chicago.

Searle, J.R. (1965), ''What is a speech act?'', in Max Black (ed.) **Philosopy in America**, Allen & Unwin, p.221-239.

v. Stechov, A. (1980), ''Modification of Noun Phrase, a Challenge for Compositional Semantics'', to appear in **Theoretica Linguistics.**

Stenius, E. (1967), ''Mood and Language Game'', Synthese 17, pp.254-274. Tarski, A. (1935), ''The Concept of Truth in the Formalized Languages'', in **Studia Philosophica**, Vol. I, pp. 261-405.

Tarski, A. (1944), ''The Semantic Conception of Truth'', in Philosophy and Phenomenological Research, 4.

Tichý, P. (1971), ''An Approach to Intensional Analysis'', Nous 5, pp.273-297.

Ziff, P. (1967), ''On Grice's Account of Meaning'', in **Analysis**, XXVIII, No.1.

Jaakko Hintikka

New foundations for a theory of questions and answers

1. Semantics for knowing that

Any satisfactory theory of questions and answers must be based on a good theory of knowledge and knowing. In my earlier work on questions and answers, I used the notation of customary epistemic logic but left its semantics unanalysed.[1] The reason for this relative neglect was that I took the semantics in question to be familiar enough to my readers. Meanwhile, however, I have come to realize that this assumption is not fully satisfied for two different reasons. First, far too many philosophers and linguists still think of the notation of epistemic logic (and of comparable frameworks of semantical representation) as regimented versions of natural languages which receive their meanings from back translations of their sentences into ordinary discourse. Nothing could be more wrong, it seems to me. The only real advantage of a logical notation is that its semantics can be explained without recourse to natural languages in a simple and perspicuous manner. (Logical notation, I have sometimes put this point, must be thought of as a semanticist's "first language".)

Hence an explanation of the semantical foundations of one version of epistemic logic is in order here. This version is particularly helpful in connection with the analysis of questions and answers. Accordingly, I will begin by sketching briefly a semantical foundation for my version of epistemic logic, together with an associated syntactical technique (model sets and model systems technique) which will enable us to carry out actual proofs. This semantics will lead to certain changes in the customary formulations of epistemic logic, which is my second reason for paying more attention to it than I have done in the past.

The semantics in question is based on two main ideas. The first of them is the cornerstone of all the usual possible-worlds treatments of knowledge and other epistemic concepts. It is in effect a conceptualization of knowledge as an objective informational notion. Basically, what it amounts to is to characterize someone's, say *a*'s, knowledge at a certain time *t* by means of the states of affairs or courses of events ("possible worlds") it admits of as distinguished from those it excludes.

Ferenc Kiefer (ed.), Questions and Answers, 159–190.

The motivation of this construal of knowledge is familiar from the writings of (among others) Wittgenstein, Popper, and Carnap, and more generally from the theory of semantical information. Formally, this idea can be captured by means of a two-place reflexive relation R (the alternativeness relation) associated with each pair $\langle a, t\rangle$ of knowers and times. This relation is defined on a given set W of models ("worlds"). This set W is called a *frame*. The worlds in W bearing the relation R to a world w_o are called the a-alternatives to w_o at t. Intuitively speaking, they are those worlds that are compatible with everything a knows in w_o at t. (In what follows, I shall normally omit the time parameter.) No further conditions (besides reflexivity) are at this time imposed on W or on R. It is assumed, though, that of each individual occurring in the domain of any world w_1 it is true or false that it exists in any other world w_2. Furthermore, it is assumed that, in each world, a truth-value is assigned to each atomic sentence even when some of its singular terms are empty.

Now *knowing that* sentences can be evaluated in each $w \in W$. The relevant truth clauses will be the following:

(T.K) $K_a p$ is true at w iff p is true in all a-alternatives to w.
(T.~K) $\sim K_a p$ is true at w iff $\sim p$ is true in at least one a-alternative to w.

Here K_a is designed to capture the force of "a knows that." The condition (T.~K) may lead to difficulties in that it apparently involves the assumption of "logical omniscience" or "logical incontinence": whoever knows that p will *ipso facto* know all the logical consequences of p. This dubious assumption can be avoided by taking the members of W to be urn models rather than classical (invariant) models.[2] Especially natural candidates for the role of membership in W are the "almost invariant" worlds at some fixed level of analysis d.[3] However, the distinction does not matter in most of the rest of this paper, and will hence be disregarded here.

2. Model set technique for knowing that

In the model set technique and model system, the force of (T.K)–(T.~K) is captured by the following conditions on a model system Ω:[4]

(C.K) If $K_aS \in \mu \in \Omega$, then $S \in \lambda$ for each alternative λ to μ in Ω.
(C.~K) If $\sim K_aS \in \mu \varepsilon \Omega$, then $\sim S \in \lambda$ for at least one alternative λ to μ in Ω.

The idea on which these conditions and the whole model systems technique is based is that a model set (a member of a model system) is a partial description of a world. Model systems are sets of model sets. Model systems are thus the syntactical counterparts to frames. The alternativeness relation between the members of a model system matches the equally named relation between worlds. (Hence it, too, is reflexive). In spite of their being only partial descriptions of worlds, model sets are large enough to guarantee that the world described is logically possible.

When considered alone, a model set μ is defined by the following conditions:

(C.v) If $(S_1 \vee S_2) \in \mu$, then $S_1 \in \mu$ or $S_2 \in \mu$ (or both).
(C.&) If $(S_1 \& S_2) \in \mu$, then $S_1 \in \mu$ and $S_2 \in \mu$.
(C.E) If $(\exists x)\, S(x) \in \mu$, then, for some "$z$", $S(z) \in \mu$ and (in case "x" occurs in $S(x)$ outside the scopes of all intensional operators) $(\exists y)\,(z=y) \in \mu$.
(C.U) If $(x)\, S(x) \in \mu$, then $S(y) \in \mu$ for each "y" occurring in any member of μ. If "x" occurs in $S(x)$ outside the scopes of all intensional operators, we must also have $(\exists z)\,(z=y) \in \mu$ or $(\exists z)\,(y=z) \in \mu$.
(C.~) If $A \in \mu$, then not $\sim A \in \mu$.
(C.=) If $(x=y) \in \mu$, (or $(y=x) \in \mu$) and $A(x) \in \mu$, then $A(y) \in \mu$. Also analogously for $(x=a)$, $(a=x)$, and $(a=b)$.
(C.self=) Not $\sim(x=x) \in \mu$. Also analogously for $\sim(a=a)$.

It is presupposed in these conditions that negation-signs are always pushed toward the inside of sentences automatically as far as they go (by means of DeMorgan's laws, the law of double negation, and the equivalences $\sim(\exists x)=(x)\sim$ and $\sim(x)=(\exists x)\sim$).

In (C.U), $S(y)$ is like $S(x)$ except that all free occurrences of "x" have been replaced by "y" (but not necessarily vice versa); and likewise for $S(z)$ in (C.E).

In (C.~), A is an arbitrary atomic formula (or identity). In (C.=), $A(x)$ is an arbitrary atomic formula (or identity) containing "x", and $A(y)$ is like $A(x)$ except that "x" and "y" have been interchanged in some of their occurrences.

It turns out that (as derived conditions) we can allow A in (C.~) and (C.=) to be any sentence without intensional operators.

The quantifier conditions (C.E) and (C.U) have to be understood against the background of the following notation: "a", "b", ... are arbitrary free singular terms. They may pick out different individuals in different worlds. Each of the letters "x", "y", ... picks out always the same individual in different worlds. They can occur either free or bound. In their former use, they are like Russell's "logically proper names" or Kripke's "rigid designators". In their latter use, they embody Quine's often-argued point that quantifiers must range over real (well-defined) individuals; which well-definedness I am interpreting here as implying that the proper names of such individuals always pick out the same individual. Later we shall meet a slightly different notion of well-definedness.

The conditions (C.E)–(C.U) have the intended effect that existential assumptions are carried only by existential quantifiers. The viewpoint I have adopted means requiring that quantified variables range over only existing individuals in so far as the actual world is concerned. (More generally, we can speak of the world at which a sentence is evaluated.) Now we are considering x as a citizen of the actual world in $S(x)$ if and only if x occurs in $S(x)$ outside the scopes of all intensional operators. (More on this later in section 6). Hence we must have the clauses in (C.E) and (C.U) that mention $(\exists y)\ (z=y)$ or $(\exists z)\ (z=y)$ (or $(\exists y)\ (y=z)$ or $(\exists z)\ (y=z)$), respectively. However, as far as other worlds are concerned, the use of bound variables presupposes well-definedness but not existence. (For the notion of well-definedness used here see the next section.) Hence, no further requirements are needed in the quantifier rules. From these defining conditions for model sets and model systems we can read off a technique for showing that a sentence S is satisfiable, viz. by showing that it can be imbedded in a model set μ which occurs as a member of some model system Ω, $\mu \in \Omega$. This is the technique I shall use in this paper. It can be shown that it is sound and complete with respect to the underlying semantics.

The model set and model system technique can be generalized so as to include also mirror-image conditions regulating non-membership in model sets (belonging to a model system).[5] They are as follows (in the same notation as before):

($\bar{C}$.∨) If $(S_1 \vee S_2) \notin \mu$, then $S_1 \notin \mu$ and $S_2 \notin \mu$.
($\bar{C}$.&) If $(S_1 \& S_2) \notin \mu$, then either $S_1 \notin \mu$ or $S_2 \notin \mu$ (or both).
($\bar{C}$.E) If $(\exists x)\ S(x) \notin \mu \in \Omega$, then $S(z) \notin \mu$ for each "z" occurring in the members of any $\lambda \in \Omega$ (unless "x" occurs in $S(x)$ outside the scopes of all intensional operators; then we may instead have $(\exists y)\ (y=x) \notin \mu$ or $(\exists y)\ (x=y) \notin \mu$).
($\bar{C}$.U) If $(x)\ S(x) \notin \mu \in \Omega$, then $S(y) \notin \mu$ for some "y". If "x" occurs in $S(x)$ outside the scopes of intensional operators; then we may have instead $(\exists z)\ (y=z) \notin \mu$ and $(\exists z)\ (z=y) \notin \mu$.
($\bar{C}$.=) If $(x=y) \in \mu$ (or $(y=x) \in \mu$), $A(x) \notin \mu$, then $A(y) \notin \mu$.
($\bar{C}$.K) If $K_a S \notin \mu \in \Omega$, there is an alternative $\lambda \in \Omega$ to μ such that $S \notin \lambda$.
($\bar{C}$.~K) If $\sim K_a S \notin \mu \in \Omega$ and if $\lambda \in \Omega$ is an alternative to μ, then $S \notin \lambda$.

It can be shown that this expansion preserves the completeness of the model system method. Now we can also characterize logical truth and logical implication in a new (and for our later purposes in this paper, a better) way:

(i) S is logically true iff $S \notin \mu \in \Omega$ is impossible.
(ii) S_2 is logically implied by S_1 if $S_1 \in \mu \in \Omega$, $S_2 \notin \mu$ is impossible.

This also gives rise to an actual technique of establishing logical truths and logical implications. It consists in assuming the contrary, e.g. assuming in the case of (i) that $S \notin \mu \in \Omega$, and then reducing this assumption *ad absurdum*.

3. Semantics for knowing + an indirect question

The second main idea of my semantics pertains to the treatment of constructions of the form *knowing + a wh-clause.* As a first approximation, these will be construed as having the form

(1) $(\exists x)\ K_a A(x)$

This (1) has roughly the force "a knows who (say x) is such that $A(x)$", if it is assumed that "x" ranges over persons. As a special case we obtain

(2) $(\exists x)\ K_a(b=x)$

for (roughly) "*a* knows who *b* is", assuming again that our universe of discourse consists of persons.

The intuitive appeal of (1)–(2) as formal renderings of "knows who" statements is obvious. What more can conceivably be required of knowing who *b* is than knowing of some particular individual *x* that *b* is that individual? Even though the intended answer to this question turns out to need amplifications, it is in my judgment basically correct.

It easily turns out that this "translation" does not work unless the underlying semantics is somehow changed. These difficulties are highlighted by the logical truth (in the semantics so far developed) of sentences like

(3) $K_a(\exists x)(b=x) \supset (\exists x)K_a(b=x)$

for any free singular term "*b*". What (3) says (roughly) is that the identity of the bearers of *all* singular terms is known to anyone as soon as he or she knows that the term is not empty.

The fundamental insight on which my theory is based is that we can capture (with qualifications soon to be explained) the right logical force of "knowing who" by means of (1) if we modify our semantics *by allowing an otherwise* bona fide *individual x to be ill-defined in some worlds.* In such worlds, it does not make any sense to ask if *x* exists or not. In other words, one can fail to be able to trace *x* from a world w_1 in which *x* exists to another, say w_2, for two different reasons:

(i) *x* does not exist in w_2;
(ii) *x* is not well defined in w_2.

It is in the second case only that we shall say that the world line of *x* cannot be continued to w_2. (A world line is a notional line connecting the roles or embodiments of the same individuals in different worlds.) I shall even assume that truth-values (*true* or *false*) are associated with each atomic sentence *A* at a world *w* in which the individual symbols of *A* are well-defined, even if they should be empty. Only when the world line of at least one of the individual symbols of *A* cannot be extended to w is A undetermined in w. (For the notion of undeterminacy, see the next section.)

How does this change enable us to do justice to the logic of *knowing + a wh-construction?* It helps us because now we can incorporate the following natural idea into our semantics: A person, e.g. *a,* knows *who* (say x) is such that $B(x)$, if and only if there is some one person x whom *a* could recognize in all circumstances compatible with what he or she knows and of whom *a* knows that $B(x)$. This idea of "being able to be recognized" is now captured by the possibility of extending the world line of x to all the "worlds" compatible with everything *a* knows. (Notice that this does not exclude the nonexistence of x in some of these worlds. But in such worlds *a* must be able to tell, in principle, that this particular individual does not exist there.)

Now we can see what was wrong with our earlier semantics. There it was assumed that all world lines are extendible *ad libitum.* Now we can see that this would mean that the identity of all individuals is known to everyone. Thus the feasibility of (1) as the rational reconstruction of "*a* knows who (say x) is such that $A(x)$" presupposes letting some world lines break down when we try to extend them to new worlds.

Now we can also see the import of our notation more clearly. Whether they are bound or not, the symbols "x", "y", ... range over world lines (genuine, at least partly cross-identified individuals), whereas "a", "b", ... may pick out different individuals in different possible worlds. It is therefore the (unbound) symbols "x", "y", ... that are the true *individual* symbols of our canonical notation.

Notice that this new semantics is language-independent. The given set W of worlds, together with the alternativeness relation *and* the warp of world lines spanning the members of W, determines uniquely *a*'s knowledge of the identity of different individuals and different kinds of individuals. It is nevertheless useful to resort to freshly introduced symbols in formulating the explicit truth-condition for *knowing+wh-construction:*

> (T.Kwh) $(\exists x)\ K_aB(x)$ is true at $w \varepsilon W$ if and only if there is a world line such that if "x" picks out all the nodes of this world line, $K_aB(x)$ is true in w.

What we have thus reached is essentially a semantics for *indirect questions.* Admittedly, in its present from it applies only to indirect questions governed by the verb *knows*. However, for other epistemic verbs, such as *remembers, perceives, sees,* etc., a parallel semantics can be formulated. For others, such as *believes, thinks, hopes,* etc. a slightly modified treatment is possible. Two differences can be pointed out between these verbs and the ones listed before them: (i) for them, the alternativeness relation cannot be assumed to be reflexive; (ii) they don't possess the wh-constructions in natural languages. An explanation for (ii) is given elsewhere,[6] and (i) is trivial. Hence a large class of subordinate questions can be automatically handled by my theory, and it seems possible to extend it to the other indirect questions as well. I shall not try to do so here, however.

Before extending my theory to direct questions, I shall first see what kind of model set and model system treatment captures the semantics we have just formulated.

4. Failures of determinacy and their consequences: extensional notions

At first sight, very little needs to be changed in my earlier treatment. A closer look nevertheless shows that a large number of details have to be reconsidered.

There are two main reasons for these changes. The second one will be dealt with later in section 6. The first one is the following: The fact that world lines can break down means that some sentences are neither true nor false at some worlds. In other words, we are dealing with a special kind of three-valued logic rather than with the classical two-valued logic. The third "truth-value" (besides *true* and *false*) is called *undetermined*. If a sentence is true *or* false, we shall say that it is *determined*.

This has the further consequence that several logical concepts split into several. For instance, one kind of negation of S is true if and only if S is false, undetermined if S is undetermined. This negation will be called $\neg S$. The other negation of S is true if and only if S is not true. It will be called $\sim S$. Thus $\sim S$. is never undetermined.

Likewise, one kind of knowledge-operator will now say, when applied to S, that S is determined and true in all the relevant alternatives. If S is not false in any alternative to μ but is undetermined in some, $K_a S$ is undetermined. Otherwise it is false. We shall call this sense of knowledge K.

Another sense will say that S is true *if* determined in each alternative, otherwise false. This sense of knowledge will be represented by $\bar{K}$. It is fairly clear that these two different senses of knowledge are not sharply distinguished from each other in ordinary discourse.

Thus we have the following truth-tables:

S	"false if determined" $\neg S$	"not true" $\sim S$	"not false" $\sim\neg S$	"definite and true" $\neg\sim S$
true	false	false	true	true
undet.	undet.	true	true	false
false	true	true	false	false

$\neg\neg S = S$	$\sim\sim S = \neg\sim S$	$\neg\sim\neg S$
true	true	false
undet.	false	false
false	false	true

By means of the new logical particles, we can establish a number of logical equivalences. In order to help the reader to appreciate them, I shall first present informal explanations of some of the key symbols and symbol combinations:

$\neg S$ = "S is false if determined"
$\sim S$ = "S is not true"
$K_a S$ = "a knows that S is determined and true"
$\bar{K}_a S$ = "a knows that S is true if determined"
$\neg\sim S$ = "S is definite and true"
$\sim\neg S$ = "S is not false"
$\neg\sim\neg S$ = "S is definite and false"

The natural three-valued truth-tables for conjunction and disjunction are the usual ones:

S_1	S_2	$S_1 \vee S_2$	$S_1 \& S_2$
T	T	T	T
T	U	T	U
T	F	T	F
U	T	T	U
U	U	U	U
U	F	U	F
F	T	T	F
F	U	U	F
F	F	F	F

Here are some of the relevant equivalences:

(4) (i) $\neg\neg S \equiv S$
(ii) $\neg{\sim}S \equiv {\sim}{\sim}S$
(iii) ${\sim}{\sim}S \equiv \neg{\sim}S$
(iv) $\neg{\sim}\neg S \equiv {\sim}{\sim}\neg S$
(v) ${\sim}{\sim}\neg S \equiv \neg{\sim}\neg S$
(vi) ${\sim}\neg{\sim}S \equiv {\sim}S$
(vii) $\neg{\sim}{\sim}S \equiv {\sim}S$
(viii) ${\sim}{\sim}{\sim}S \equiv {\sim}S$

(5) (i) $\neg(S_1 \& S_2) \equiv (\neg S_1 \vee \neg S_2)$
(ii) $\neg(S_1 \vee S_2) \equiv (\neg S_1 \& \neg S_2)$
(iii) ${\sim}(S_1 \& S_2) \equiv ({\sim}S_1 \vee {\sim}S_2)$
(iv) ${\sim}(S_1 \vee S_2) \equiv ({\sim}S_1 \& {\sim}S_2)$

(6) (i) $\neg(x)\, S(x) \equiv (\exists x) \neg S(x)$
(ii) $\neg(\exists x)\, S(x) \equiv (x) \neg S(x)$
(iii) ${\sim}(x)\, S(x) \equiv (\exists x){\sim}S(x)$
(iv) ${\sim}(\exists x)\, S(x) \equiv (x){\sim}S(x)$

(7) $\bar{K}_a S \equiv K_a{\sim}\neg S$

(8) (i) ${\sim}\neg K_a S \equiv K_a{\sim}\neg S$
(ii) $\neg{\sim}K_a S \equiv K_a \neg{\sim}S$

Here (7) enables us to eliminate $\bar{K}_a$. Moreover, (4)–(6) and (8) make it possible for us to drive negation-signs deeper into our sentences in many cases. The following will be the irreducible occurrences of negation-signs:

(9) (i) $\neg A$
(ii) $\sim A$
(iii) $\sim \neg A$
(iv) $\neg \sim A$ (or $\sim\sim A$)
(v) $\neg \sim \neg A$ (or $\sim\sim \neg A$)

(10) (i) $\neg K_a S$
(ii) $\sim K_a S$
(iii) $\sim\sim K_a S$ (or $\neg \sim K_a S$)

5. Model sets and model systems modified

Before formulating the new conditions on model sets and model systems, a couple of explanations are in order.

With the possibility of undeterminacy, the import of the notions of model set and model system also changes somewhat. Before the change, a model set was (intuitively speaking) a partial description of a "possible world" (possible state of affairs or course of events, depending on the time element). The cash value of this idea is that it is possible to give an interpretation (assignment of truth-values) of all the sentences in a model set μ such that (i) all the atomic sentences and their negations in μ are true and (ii) all the other sentences of μ are likewise true.

After the introduction of possible undeterminacy, a model set μ is characterized by the following properties:

(i) It is possible to give a consistent assignment of truth-values (i.e., a valuation in a suitable model) to all the atomic sentences (including identities) and their negations such that they are all true.
(ii) If so, all the sentences of μ are true.
(iii) If μ is characterized by requiring that no member of a set λ of sentences belongs to μ, then here is a soluation which makes all members of μ true but no member of λ true.

The extension of this idea to model systems is obvious. We can then define a set of sentences ν to be satisfiable iff it can be imbedded in a member μ ($\nu \subseteq \mu$) of a model system Ω, $\mu \in \Omega$.

With these explanations in mind, it is easily seen that the following new conditions on model sets μ and model systems Ω are the correct ones:

(C.K) If $K_a S \in \mu \in \Omega$ and if $\lambda \in \Omega$ is an epistemic *a*-alternative to μ, then $S \in \lambda$.

(C.$\sim\sim$K) If $\sim\sim K_a S \in \mu \in \Omega$ and if $\lambda \in \Omega$ is an epistemic *a*-alternative to μ, then $\sim\sim S \in \lambda$.

(C.$\sim$K) If $\sim K_a S \in \mu \in \Omega$, then there is an epistemic *a*-alternative $\lambda \in \Omega$ to μ such that $\sim S \in \lambda$.

(C.$\neg$K) If $\neg K_a S \in \mu \in \Omega$, then there is an epistemic *a*-alternative $\lambda \in \Omega$ to μ such that $\neg S \in \lambda$.

(C.neg) If $S \in \mu$ or $\neg\sim S \in \mu$ or $\sim\neg S \in \mu$, then neither $\neg S \in \mu$ nor $\sim S \in \mu$ nor $\neg\sim\neg S \in \mu$.

The other defining conditions of model sets and model systems remain intact, except for the quantifier conditions. They will be discussed next.

The $\bar{\text{C}}$-conditions (conditions on non-membership) corresponding to (C.K)–(C.$\neg$K) are obvious.

6. Quantifiers and determinacy

The possibility of undeterminacy also affects the logical behavior of quantifiers. The reason is obvious. As has been emphasized particularly strongly by Quine, quantified (bound) variables range over well-defined individuals only. Hence an individual symbol, say "*y*", can be substituted for a bound variable, say "*x*", only if *y* is well-defined for all the worlds as a member of which we are considering *x*.

Now what are these worlds? Here we come to another leading idea of my approach to epistemic logic. In spite of the naturalness of the idea, it is not without subtleties, and it has frequently been misunderstood. (I have myself missed one of its subtleties in my earlier work.)

The idea is this: The worlds as a memberof which we are considering

x in $S(x)$ are shown by the sequences of nested intensional operators (operators whose scopes are within the scopes of earlier operators in the sequence) within the scopes of which x occurs in $S(x)$. If "x" occurs in $S(x)$ outside the scopes of all intensional operators, we are considering x as a member of the actual world w_0. (More generally, w_0 is the world at which we are evaluating $S(x)$). If "x" occurs in $S(x)$ within the scope of "K_a" (but not within the scope of any negation-sign), we are considering x as a member of all the epistemic a-alternatives to w_0.[7] If "x" occurs likewise within the scope of the nested operator "K_b" (in this order), we are considering x as a denizen of (epistemic) b-alternatives to (epistemic) a-alternatives; and so on.

Likewise, the worlds at which a free individual symbol "y" is assumed to be well-defined in a sentence is shown in the same way by the sequences of intensional operators within the scope of which "y" occurs in the sentence.

If we are considering occurrences of "y" in the sentences of different members of a model system Ω (when we are evaluating a sentence at $w_0 \in \Omega$), then its occurrences in the members of the b-alternatives to w_0 are naturally to be considered in the same way as its occurrences within the scope of "K_b", and likewise for other alternatives, alternatives to alternatives, and so on.

Hence the taks of formulating the quantifier conditions seems very easy. The condition (C.E) does not need any changes, and (C.U) can be formulated as follows:

(C.U) If (i) $(x)\, S(x) \in \mu \in \Omega$, (ii) "$y$" occurs freely in μ (or in the other members of Ω) within the scopes of all the same sequences of intensional operators as "x" occurs in $S(x)$, and (iii) in case "x" occurs in $S(x)$ freely outside the scopes of all intensional operators we have $(\exists z)\,(y=z) \in \mu$ or $(\exists z)\,(z=y) \in \mu$, then $S(y) \in \mu$.

Here $S(y)$ is like $S(x)$ except that all free occurrences of "x" have been replaced by free occurrences of "y".

However, this will not quite do without further explanations. First, because of the reflexivity of the alternativeness relation, we may be tacitly considering y in a sentence as a member of the world w_0 in which it is being evaluated by letting "y" occur within the scope of, say, "K_a". Hence we have to modify the condition (C.U) by replacing the phrase "all the same sequences of epistemic operators" by "all the same *or stronger* sequences of intensional operators". A sequence σ_1 of operators is said to be stronger than another one, say σ_2, iff σ_2 can be obtained from σ_1 by omitting some operators.

However, even this change is not radical enough. Indeed, here we come to the main improvement over my earlier work. Consider, for instance, a sentence of the form:

$$(11)\ (z)\ (A(z) \supset (\exists x)\ (x=z \,\&\, \neg\ K_b A(x)))$$

Here (11) apparently says of each actually existing individual which is A that it could be a not-A, as far as b knows. Each x mentioned in (11) is being considered as a member of *at least one* suitably selected epistemic a-alternative to the actual world (over and above the actual world itself). Since we are dealing with a bound variable, x must be well-defined at that world. However, in the treatment so far, something much stronger is being required. It is required that each x is well-defined in *all* epistemic a-alternatives. This makes quite a difference, and even distorts the intuitive meaning of (11). Hence we have to change our treatment of well-definedness requirements and quantifier conditions.

We need no verbal changes in (C.U), however. It suffices to redefine the notions of "the same" and "stronger than" when applied to sequences of intensional operators. The following changes are in order:

(i) We distinguish from each other *positive* occurrences of an intensional operator, i.e., occurrences within the scope of an *even* number of negation-signs, from *negative* occurrences, i.e., occurrences within an *odd* number of negation-signs. In the definition of sameness for sequences of intensional operators, positive and negative occurrences are treated as if they were different operators.

(ii) In judging whether two occurrences of certain symbols are within the scope of the same sequences of intensional operators, negative operators are considered the same if and only if they are *numerically* identical, that is, the very same occurrence of an operator and not just two occurrences of similar-looking operators (both negative). In contrast, the criterion of the identity of positive operators is simply their formal identity (same letter with the same subscript).

The intuitive import of this change is obvious. A negative operator says that *some* (at least one) alternative is of a certain kind. It does not say which one. Hence we cannot capture the same alternative world with another occurrence of a similar negative operator; we can reach it for sure only via numerically the same operator.

This intuitive idea can be given an explicit form by means of a game-theoretical treatment of epistemic logic. I shall not do so in this paper, however.

(iii) A sequence of operators σ_1 is said to be stronger than another one, say σ_2, iff σ_2 can be obtained from a sequence identical with σ_1 in the sense explained in (ii) by (a) omitting positive operators and/or (b) replacing positive operators by corresponding negative ones.

With these re-definitions, the earlier (modified) form of (C.U) is still applicable. The negative conditions corresponding to our reformulated (C.E) and (C.U) can be formulated as follows:

($\bar{\text{C}}$.E) If (i) $(\exists x)S(x) \notin \mu \in \Omega$ (ii) "y" occurs in μ (or in the other members of Ω) within the scope of the same sequences of operators as "x" occurs in $S(x)$, and (iii) in case "x" occurs in $\bar{S}(x)$ outside the scopes of all intensional operators, we have $(\exists z)(z = y) \in \mu$, or $(\exists z)(y = z) \in \mu$, then $S(y) \notin \mu$.

($\bar{\text{C}}$.U) If $(x)\ S(x) \notin \mu \in \Omega$, then for at least one "y" we have $S(y) \notin \mu$.

In view of the importance—and novelty—of the last few changes, it is perhaps in order to consider one more example.

One of the simplest examples is the following:

(12) I know who stole (could have stolen) the blueprints, for all that John knows.

The logical form of (12) in my epistemic logic notation is clearly

(13) $(\exists x)\ K_{\text{I}}{\sim}K_{\text{John}}{\sim}(x$ stole the blueprints)

If the person in question is Dr. Strangelove, then before the change it was required, not only that I know who Dr. Strangelove is, but that John knows who Dr. Strangelove is, in order for (13) to be true. Yet clearly (12) could be taken to be true if there is someone who is not known by John to have committed the crime, even if John does not know his identity.

This is relfected by the fact that before the changes (13) was implied by

(14) $K_{\text{I}}{\sim}K_{\text{John}}$ (s stole the blueprints)

only in conjunction with some extra premise like

(15) $(\exists x)\ K_{I}\ K_{John}\ (s=x)$,

whereas after the change (13) is logically implied by

(16) $K_{I}{\sim}K_{John}$ (y stole the blueprints)

even without any extra premises.

This concludes my reformulation of epistemic logic.

7. Direct questions

The basic ideas of my analysis of questions can be explained by means of an example of a simple wh-question which does not involve any intensional notions.

(17) Who killed Julius Caesar?

I propose to interpret such direct questions as requests for information (knowledge). This means analyzing a question like (17) into a request part (an *optative* or *imperative operator*) and a description of the epistemic state of affaris the questioner wants the addressee of the question to bring about. The latter is called the *desideratum* of the question. We shall usually formulate it in first-person terms.

This analysis of (17) yields a paraphrase somewhat like the following:

(18) Bring it about that [I know who killed Julius Caesar].

This illustrates the general fact that the desideratum of a direct question has the form of the corresponding indirect question governed by "I know". Hence the treatment developed in the first six sections of this paper is automatically applicable here, and indeed becomes an integral part of a theory of direct questions. This part is, furthermore, the central one. For one thing, the imperative operator is the same in all (direct) questions, whereas the desideratum varies from question to question. Hence it is the desideratum that determines all the distinguishing properties of different kinds of questions.

Here we shall concentrate on the desideratum. However, a few observations concerning the imperative operator are in order here.

(i) The force of the operator is relative to the presupposition of the question. (The notion of presupposition will be defined later in this section.) Its force is roughly this: "Assuming that the presupposition of the question is satisfied, bring it about that".

(ii) In obeying an order, the answerer is supposed to do something. This action is normally of a very special kind. It is supposed to change the epistemic (informational) state of the questioner, but not the part of the world the question pertains to.

(iii) The imperative operator is subject to sundry conversational pressures (expectations, implicatures). Different derived types of questions, for instance examination-questions, rhetorical questions, etc. can be distinguished from each other by means of the special force they impose on the imperative operator. This force can also be changed by explicit indications as to what the governing operator is. (For instance, "Who's kissing her now, I wonder.") Such indications can even turn a direct question into an indirect one.

The desideratum can be expressed in the notation of epistemic logic. This translation will contain the epistemic operator K_I. It contains other intensional operators iff the original direct question contained them. In our example (17) there are no such operators.

The desideratum of (17) is

(19) I know who killed Julius Caesar.

According to what has been said so far, the logical form of (19) is

(20) $(\exists x)\ K_I\ (x \text{ killed Julius Caesar})$

where the bound variable is ranging over persons.

Desideratum minus the epistemic operator "K_I" (more generally, desideratum minus the outmost layer of such operators) is called the *presupposition* of the question. The presupposition of (17) is (*vide* (20))

(21) $(\exists x)\ (x \text{ killed Julius Caesar})$

that is,

Someone killed Julius Caesar

which indeed is in a very clear sense a presupposition of (40), even though it does not agree with some linguists' recent use of "presupposition" as a technical term.

Presupposition minus the initial quantifier is called the *matrix* of the question. In our example it is

(22) (x killed Julius Caesar).

Unlike the desideratum and the presupposition, the matrix of a question is not closed; it contains a variable.

Different questions are distinguished from each other by the logical form of the desideratum. Here is a list of some of the most important kinds of questions:

Kind of question	*Form of the desideratum*
(i) Yes-or-no question	$K_I S \vee K_I \neg S$
(ii) Propositional question ("whether" question)	$K_I S_1 \vee K_I S_2 \vee \ldots \vee K_I S_i$
(iii) Simple wh-question	$(\exists x)\, K_I S(x)$
(iv) Question of identity	$(\exists x)\, K_I(d=x)$
(v) Multiple wh-question	$(\exists x_1)\,(\exists x_2) \ldots (\exists x_i)\, K_I\, S(x_1, x_2, \ldots, x_i)$
(vi) Nested wh-question	$(\exists x_1)\, K_I\, S_1(x_1)$ where $S_1(x_1)$ contains a propositional component of the form $(\exists x_2)\, K_I\, S_2(x_1, x_2)$, etc.
(vii) Free-variable wh-questions	$(y_1)\,(y_2) \ldots (y_k)\,(\exists x)\,(\exists u_i)\,(\exists u_2) \ldots (\exists u_k)\,((y_1=u_1)\,\&\,(y_2=u_2)\,\&\ldots\&\,(y_k=u_k)\,\&\,K_I\, S(x, u_1, u_2, \ldots, u_k))$

Presupposition	*Example(s)*
(i) $S \vee - S$	Is Mary home?
(ii) $S_1 \vee S_2 \vee \ldots \vee S_i$	Does Stig live in Sweden, Norway or Denmark?
(iii) $(\exists x)\, S(x)$	Who killed Julius Caesar?
(iv) $(\exists x)\, (b=x)$	Who is Cassius Clay?

Presupposition	*Example(s)*
(v) $(\exists x_1)\ (\exists x_2)\ \ldots\ (\exists x_i)$ $S(x_1, x_2, \ldots, x_i)$	For whom did Mary buy what?
(vi) $(\exists x_1)\ S_1(x_1)$	Who remembers what Bill saw?
(vii) $(y_1)\ (y_2)\ \ldots\ (y_k)\ (\exists x)$ $S(x, y_1, y_2, \ldots, y_k)$	Who is the best advisor to an aspiring politician? Which woman does every true Englishman honor above all others?

Comment: strictly speaking, the examples (vii) have a slightly different kind of a desideratum, viz. one in which the outside quantifiers have been restricted to a given class of entities (politicians or Englishmen, respectively). A more explicit representation of the forms of their desiderata is the following (with $k=1$)

(23) $(y)\ (P(y) \supset (\exists x)\ (\exists u)\ (y=u\ \ \&\ \ K_I S(x, u)))$

The corresponding presupposition is

(24) $(y)\ (P(y) \supset (\exists x)\ (\exists u)\ (y=u)\ \ \&\ \ S(x, u)))$

This list is not intended to be exhaustive. Furthermore, the categories listed are not all mutually exclusive. For instance, one and the same question can be multiple, nested, and a free-variable one, or any two of these. Notice that a question can be a nested one only if its explicit natural-language formulation contains intensional notions.

From what has been said it is clear how the notions of desideratum and presupposition are defined for all questions.

Likewise, it can be seen that the specific features of the concept of knowledge do not play an appreciable role in my theory so far. From the semantics developed in the early sections of this paper, it is seen that the theory is neutral with respect to virtually all intensional notions which have a "success grammar" (i.e. for which the alternativeness relation is reflexive), e.g. true belief, knowledge (in some stronger sense), etc.

8. The double-barrelled character of natural-language questions

An important insight is still missing from the formulation I have so far presented of my theory of questions. What is missing is the fact that (20) is not the only possible logical form of (19) (not the only possible rendering of the desideratum of (17)–(18)). The ordinary-language sentence (19) is intrinsically ambivalent between (20), which can be written equivalently as

(25) $(\exists x)$ $(x$ killed J. C. & $(\exists z)(z=x$ & $K_{\mathrm{I}}(z$ killed J. C.))),

and

(26) (x) $(x$ killed J. C. $\supset$ $(\exists z)(z=x \& K_{\mathrm{I}}(z$ killed J. C.))).

This observation can be generalized. In general, each wh-word is an ambidextrous (AC/DC, as my Californian friends put it) quantifier, which can be taken either existentially or universally.

It is not hard to find arguments for the presence of both ways of taking a wh-question, direct or indirect. Above, I have given some reasons for assuming the existential reading. In certain other theories, for instance in Karttunen's, only the universal reading is countenanced. On balance, the evidence thus clearly supports the two-barrelled interpretation.

Contextual (e.g. conversational) factors can filter out one of the two readings. In principle, however, both are always potentially present. Conversational expectations also generally favor the universal reading because it is stronger. It is easy to produce examples, however, where the existential force is being favored. Here is one:

(27) Janet knows how one can get from Heathrow to Oxford.

For the truth of (27) it is clearly not necessary that Janet should know all the reasonable ways of making the journey in question.

The reason why (26) is formulated in the way it is should be obvious from the earlier discussion. If we had written, instead of (26), the tempting sentence

(28) (x) $(x$ killed J. C. $\supset$ $K_{\mathrm{I}}(x$ killed J. C.))

we would be speaking only of such individuals as are well-defined for all the I-alternatives. (Since "x" occurs in (28) both inside the scope of a positive occurrence of "K_I" and outside it, any substitution-value of "x" must be well defined in these worlds.) This is not what we want to say. We want to say that each individual which in fact killed Julius Caesar is known by the questioner to have done so. Indeed, (24) does this, for in it "x" occurs only outside the scopes of intensional operators and thus ranges over actually existing individuals.

The double-barrelled character of wh-words does not affect the definitions above of the presupposition and matrix. However, what was listed above as the desideratum is now only the existential (or disjunctive) half of the desideratum. The other half is listed in the following table for different kinds of questions. Please note that the existential and universal readings of wh-questions are matched for propositional questions by analogous *disjunctive* and *conjunctive* readings.

Kind of question	*Universal (conjunctive) desideratum*
(ii) Propositional question	$(S_1 \supset K_I S_1) \& (S_2 \supset K_I S_2) \& \ldots \& (S_i \supset K_I S_i)$
(iii) Simple wh-question	$(x)(S(x) \supset (\exists z)(x = z \& K_I S(z)))$
(v) Multiple wh-question (vi) Nested wh-question	Different possible forms depending on the interpretation of the wh-word and the order of quantifiers and epistemic operators
(vii) Free-variable wh-questions	$(y_1)(y_2) \ldots (y_k)(x)(S(x, y_1, y_2, \ldots, y_k) \supset \supset (\exists u_1)(\exists u_2) \ldots (\exists u_k)(\exists z)((y_1 = u_1) \& (y_2 = u_2) \& \ldots \& (y_k = u_k) \& (x = z) \& K_I S(z, u_1, u_2, \ldots, u_k)))$

Different desiderata of multiple and nested questions are studied at length in my monograph, *The Semantics of Questions and the Questions of Semantics,* especially chapters 6, 8—9. (See note 1 above.)

9. Answers to simple questions

What are the uses of the theory I have so far outlined? Later, I will list some of the applications and actual or promising further developments of the theory. (See section 10 below.) Many of them are connected with the central question which is left unanswered by virtually all the other theories of questions, viz. the question: What counts as an answer to a given question? It is useful to distinguish from each other two kinds of answers, or rather two kinds of things a constructive response (we shall call such responses *replies*) can accomplish:

(i) It may satisfy the epistemic request of the questioner completely. Such replies will be called *conclusive* or *full* answers.

(ii) It may fail to do so but yet contribute some information toward satisfying the request. Replies of this latter kind will be called *partial answers*.

One possible linguistic indication of the partiality of an answer (reply) is that it can be paraphrased so that it is prefaced by: "I don't know, but ...". For instance, suppose a police lieutenant asks a sergeant: "Who robbed the bank last night?" and prompts the reply: "The same burglar who robbed the supermarket last week." This may be a conclusive answer, viz. in case the lieutenant knows who committed last week's crime. (Cf. below, this section.) However, it may also be a merely partial answer. Then it might have been equally appropriate for the sergeant to say, "I don't know, Sir, but it was ...".

When is a response, say, "Cassius", to a simple wh-question, say (17), a conclusive answer? The basis for an answer is implicit in what has been said. This reply is a conclusive answer if and only if it brings about the truth of the desideratum. (The desideratum is a description of precisely the state of affairs the questioner wants to be brought about.) But what is it that this response does bring about? Giving a singular term, say "Cassius", as a reply to a wh-question, is tantamount to responding to it by giving as a putative answer to it the substitution-instance of the matrix with respect to this term. In our example this substitution-instance is

(29) Cassius killed Julius Caesar.

Given the expected conditions (the answerer is honest and well-informed), this response brings about a situation in which the questioner can truly say

(30) K_I (Cassius killed Julius Caesar).

But this is not yet the desideratum of (17) (on the existential reading). This desideratum is

(20) $(\exists x)$ K_I(x killed Julius Caesar),

which is different from (30). Hence the question becomes: When does (20) entail (30)? On what further conditions does the truth of (20) guarentee that of (30)? This is a special case of the problem of the conditions on which existential generalization is valid in epistemic logic. As was pointed out above, this is the most important problem in the foundations of epistemic logic, a problem which is essentially tantamount to the problem of formulating the truth-conditions on quantified sentences (more accurately, sentences involving "quantifying in"). It is the main problem discussed in the early sections of this paper. (See especially sections 3–6 above.) From that earlier discussion we can read off directly an answer to our question concerning (30)–(20). The fact is that (30) logically implies (20) only in conjunction with an extra premise whose force is that of

(31) $(\exists x)$ K_I(Cassius$=x$)

and which is a rough translation of the ordinary-language sentence

(32) I know who Cassius is.

This is obviously the right condition. If the questioner does not know who Cassius is, the reply "Cassius" will not satisfy him; it will not enable him to know *who* it was that killed Caesar. (This point is even clearer if the reply had been, not a proper name, but e.g. a descriptive phrase like "Public Enemy Number One".)

This solution to a special case of the problem of answerhood can immediately be generalized to all simple questions (without intensional operators). If the desideratum of such a question is

(33) $(\exists x)$ $K_I S(x)$,

then "b" is a conclusive answer to the question if and only if

(34) $(\exists x)\ K_{\mathrm{I}}(b=x)$.

The following simple argument shows the sufficiency of the extra condition:

(35) $K_{\mathrm{I}}S(b) \in \mu \in \Omega$

Here the truth of $K_{\mathrm{I}}S(b)$ is what the response "b" brings about (put into the mouth of the questioner).

(36) $(\exists x)\ K_{\mathrm{I}}(b=x) \in \mu$

This is the conclusiveness condition.

(37) $(\exists x)\ K_{\mathrm{I}}S(x) \notin \mu$

This is the counter-assumption. From (36) we have by (C.E)

(38) $K_{\mathrm{I}}(b=x) \in \mu$

From (37) we have by ($\bar{\mathrm{C}}$.E) (because of the way "x" occurs in the members of μ, as shown by (38))

(39) $K_{\mathrm{I}}\ S(x) \notin \mu$

From (39) we have by ($\bar{\mathrm{C}}$.K)

(40) $S(x) \notin \lambda$ ($\lambda \in \Omega$ is an alt. to μ)

From (35) we now have

(41) $S(b) \in \lambda$

and from (38)

(42) $(b=x) \in \lambda$

By the extension of (C.=) mentioned in section 2 above, we obtain from (41)–(42)

(43) $S(x) \in \lambda$

This contradicts (38), however, proving that (34) and

(44) $K_I\, S(b)$

logically imply (33).

Moreover, it is seen from the argument that without an extra premise having the strength of our conclusiveness condition the implication in question is not forthcoming.

10. Answers to other questions

An important part of the systematic theory of questions is to find defining conditions for conclusive answers to different kinds of questions. Here I can only indicate, without argument, what these conditions are for a few selected types of questions.

In the case of propositional questions (including yes-or-no questions), we shall assume that N is the response in the case of the disjunctive reading. In the case of conjunctive reading, we shall assume that the response is "N_1, N_2, ..., and N_j". Otherwise we shall follow the same conventions as in the earlier lists.

(i) Yes-or-no question.
(45) $K_I(N \supset S) \vee K_I(N \supset \neg S)$
(ii) Propositional question,
(a) Disjunctive reading.
(46) $K_I(N \supset S_1) \vee K_I(N \supset S_2) \vee \ldots \vee K_I(N \supset S_i)$
(b) Conjunctive reading.
(47) $\bigwedge_{k=1}^{k=j} [\bigvee_{l=1}^{l=i} K_I(N_k \supset S_l)]$
(iii)–(iv) Simple wh-questions (which include questions of identity).
(a) Existential reading.
(b) Universal reading.

Two different kinds of responses can be considered:

(I) a list of singular terms, say "b_1, b_2, ..., and b_j"; or
(II) a response involving a general term, say "the B's".

(I) The conclusiveness condition is in this case
(48) $\bigwedge_{i=1}^{i=j} (\exists x)\ K_{\mathrm{I}}(b_i = x)$
(II) In this case, the conclusiveness condition is
(49) $(x)\ (B(x) \supset (\exists z)\ (z = x \,\&\, K_{\mathrm{I}} B(z)))$

This can be split into two components

(50) $(x)\ (B(x) \supset (\exists z)\ (z = x \,\&\, K_{\mathrm{I}}(z = z)))$
(51) $(x)\ (B(x) \supset K_{\mathrm{I}} B(x))$
(v) Multiple wh-questions.

The conclusiveness condition depends on the reading in question. Their theory has not yet been developed.

(vi) Free-variable wh-questions.

Let's assume that there is only one outside quantifier in the picture, i.e., that $k=1$.

Then the precise force of the conclusiveness condition depends on two things: First, whether the question is given an existential or a universal reading, and, second, whether the response is a list of pairs of singular terms or a general term (a function in the existential case, a two-place predicate in the universal one).

(a) Existential reading; response a list of ordered pairs of singular terms, e.g., $\langle a_1, b_1 \rangle$, $\langle a_2, b_2 \rangle$, ..., $\langle a_m, b_m, \rangle$ where each a_i occurs only once.

If the question in point is

(52) Whose advice has each British Prime Minister trusted?

a more colloquial form of the response might be

(53) Margaret Thatcher has trusted the advice of Mr. Thatcher; James Callaghan that of Denis Healey; Harold Wilson that of Marcia Williams; ...

Let's assume that the desideratum is of the form

$$(54)\quad (y)\ (P(y) \supset (\exists x)\ (\exists u)\ (y=u \,\&\, K_{\mathrm{I}}\ S(x,\ u)))$$

Then it can be shown that the conclusiveness condition is the conjunction of the following:

$$(55)\quad (y)\ (P(y) \supset ((y=a_1) \vee (y=a_2) \vee \ldots \vee (y=a_m))$$
$$(56)\quad \bigwedge_{i=1}^{i=m}\ (\exists x)\ K_{\mathrm{I}}(a_i=x)$$
$$(57)\quad \bigwedge_{i=1}^{i=m}\ (\exists x)\ K_{\mathrm{I}}(b_i=x)$$

(b) Let us assume that we are dealing with a question with the same desideratum but with a response of the form of a function, say $f(x)$. In our example, the answer might perhaps be "his principal private secretary".

Then the conclusiveness conditions might be

$$(58)\quad (y)\ (P(y) \supset (\exists x)\ K_{\mathrm{I}}(x=f(y)))$$
$$(59)\quad (y)\ (P(y) \supset (\exists z)\ (y=z \,\&\, K_{\mathrm{I}}(z=z)))$$
$$(60)\quad (y)\ (P(y) \supset (\exists z)\ ((z=f(y)) \,\&\, K_{\mathrm{I}}(z=z)))$$

(c) The universal-quantifier reading of the same qh-question is

$$(61)\quad (y)\ (P(y) \,\&\, (x)\ (\exists u)\ (\exists z)\ (S(x,\ y) \supset (y=u \,\&\, x=z \,\&\, K_{\mathrm{I}}S(z,\ u))))$$

If a reply has the form of a list of ordered pairs of singular terms (where a first member of a pair can occur more than once), say $\langle a_1, b_1\rangle$, $\langle a_2, b_2\rangle$, ..., $\langle a_m, b_m\rangle$, the conclusiveness conditions are (55)–(57) plus

$$(62)\quad \bigwedge_{i=1}^{i=m}\ (x)\ (S(x,\ a_i) \supset \bigvee_{j=1}^{j=n}\ (x=b_{ij}))$$

where b_{ij} ($j=1, 2, \ldots, n$) are all the b's such that $\langle a_i, b_{ij}\rangle$ is in the list that *is* the purported answer.

(d) The same with a two-place predicate, say $M(y, x)$, as the reply. The conclusiveness conditions can then be formulated as follows:

$$(63)\quad (y)\ (P(y) \supset (x)(M(x,\ y) \supset (\exists u)(\exists z)(y=u \,\&\, K_{\mathrm{I}}\ M(z,\ u)))$$
$$(64)\quad =(59)$$
$$(65)\quad (y)\ (P(y) \supset (x)(M(x,\ y) \supset (\exists z)(z=x \,\&\, K_{\mathrm{I}}(z=z))))$$

This concludes our quick survey of the conclusiveness conditions of some selected types of questions.

11. Prospects for the theory

The insights we have reached, especially the insights concerning the question-answer relation, open an immense wealth of further applications and developments. Collectively, they constitute the best cumulative evidence for my theory. Here I can only scratch the surface of this lode of further applications, by mentioning selected examples. Some of these applications have been carried out elsewhere, some have been mentioned before, and some others remain to be worked out.

(i) Once we have found the right conditions for conclusive answers, it is not very hard to develop a theory for partial answers, especially for their closeness to being conclusive.

For the basic ideas of such a theory, see chapter 3 of *The Semantics of Questions and the Questions of Semantics,* which overlaps with my paper, "Answers to Questions", in Henry Hiż, editor, *Questions,* D. Reidel, Dordrecht, 1979.[8] Further work nevertheless reamins to be done.

(ii) The basic part of my theory sketched above in this paper can be extended to which-questions, how- and why-questions. This extension, which largely remains to be carried out, promises interesting applications to the theory of explanation in science and in ordinary discourse. (For a preview of some results, see my paper, "Toward an Interrogative Model of Scientific Inquiry" in W. Callebaut *et. al.,* editors, *Theory of Knowledge and Science Policy,* Communication & Cognition, Ghent, 1979, pp. 208—20.

(iii) The conclusiveness condition is not a *presupposition* of a full answer; it does not have to be true *before* the reply is made. It need only be true *after* the adressee of the question has responded to it. Making it true is part of the function of the response.

Thus we obtain an important insight into the semantics and pragmatics of questions and answers. The function of a satisfactory response to question is (at least) twofold. It is not always (nor typically) sufficient that the addressee of (say) a wh-question offers a true substitution-instance as a reply to the question; the addressee must also see to it that the conclusiveness condition is or becomes satisfied. Thus an intended response to a wh-question has two functions:

(a) It must present to the questioner a true substitution-instance of the matrix.
(b) It must make the conclusiveness condition true with respect to the substitution-value in question.

Because of (b), no "tell me truly" analysis of questions can be satisfactory. (For a suggestion for such an analysis, see David and Stephanie Lewis reviewing Olson & Paul, *Contemporary Philosophy in Scandinavia, Theoria* vol. 41 (1975), pp. 39–60.) Notice also that it is the recognition of the second function of answers that opens the door to a theory of partial answers. True is true is true but conclusiveness can be a matter of degree.

In several other respects, our insight into the duality of the functions of replies helps us to understand the semantics and pragmatics of questions.

(iv) In general, being able to analyze the question-answer relation means that we can develop a theory of question-answer sequences and question-answer dialogues. These promise in turn extremely interesting applications to information-seeking through questioning, text semantics, etc. Some such applications already exist; see especially Jaakko Hintikka, "Information-Seeking Dialogues: A Model: in W. Becker and W. Essler, editors, *Konzepte der Dialektik,* Vittorio Klostermann, Frankfurt, 1980; Jaakko Hintikka and Merrill B. Hintikka, "Sherlock Holmes Confronts Modern Logic" in E. Barth, editor, *Theory of Argumentation,* Benjamins, Amsterdam; and Lauri Carlson, "Focus and Dialogue Games" in Lucia Vaina and Jaakko Hintikka, editors, *Cognitive Constraints and Communication,* D. Reidel, Dordrecht, 1981.

I consider the development of a genuine semantics for question-answer dialogues a major breakthrough in text semantics.

(v) As has already been indicated, the theory of multiple and nested questions is not only highly interesting subject in its own right, but yields also important suggestions concerning the foundations of semantics in general. These matters are discussed at length in my monograph, *The Semantics of Questions and the Questions of Semantics* (Acta Philosophica Fennica, vol. 28, no. 4), North-Holland, Amsterdam, 1976.

(vi) From the semantics outlined above in sections 1 and 3 for *knowing that* and *knowing + an indirect question,* respectively, it is seen that the two are relatively independent. Truth-conditions for knowing that tell which possible worlds are compatible with someone's knowledge, whereas truth-conditions for sentences of the form knowing + indirect question deal with the world lines that connect the members of the different worlds. It follows from this that the truth and falsity of sentences of the form $(\exists x)\ K_a(b=x)$ are partly independent of the truth-values of atomic sentences and identities. It also follows that the two kinds of truth-conditions can be varied relatively independently from each other. This makes it possible to study various semantical and pragmatic problems. This possibility is briefly discussed in my paper "Quine on Who's Who" forthcoming in the Library of Living Philosophers volume on W. V. Quine.

(vii) In general, the theory of questions and answers I have sketched above takes the basic semantics (alternative worlds and world lines connecting them) as given and develops the rest of the concepts and results relative to it. As a consequence, it applies automatically to every nonstandard use of questions in which only the basic semantics is different from the usual one. Since world lines define the values of quantified variables, this implies that my theory applies *mutatis mutandis* to wh-questions in which unusual entities constitute the ranges of the quantifiers that wh-words are. Examples are offered e.g. by wh-questions involving quantification over offices instead of officeholders. For instance: "Who appoints Supreme Court Justices?" when the intended answer is "The President" rather than "Jimmy Carter" (or whichever person happens to be the President).

More importantly, ostensive questions, that is, questions whose intended answers consist in pointing to a person or an object and saying e.g. "That one!" can be treated in the same way. It turns out that they merely presuppose that world lines presupposed by the wh-words in question are drawn by acquaintance, a possibility I have argued on independent grounds we must countenance. (Among other things, other kinds of world lines are needed to account for the semantics of direct-object constructions with such verbs as "knows", "remembers", "sees", etc.) As I have pointed out, my theory yields in this way even the right conclusiveness conditions for replies to ostensive questions.

Cf. here my *The Semantics of Questions*, note 1 above, chapter 3, section 6.

The contrast between normal (descriptive) questions and answers and ostensive ones can be illustrated by the following two question-answer pairs. The two questions can be thought of as being uttered by different persons on closely similar circumstances.

(66) Question (pointing): "Which building is that one?"
Answer: "That one is *The Bodleian*."

(67) Question: "Which building here is the Bodleian?"
Answer (pointing): "*That* one is Bodleian."

The former is a normal pair, the latter an ostensive one. The conclusiveness condition for the latter will be

(68) $(\exists x)\ K_{\mathrm{I}}(\text{that building}=x)$

where the quantified variable "x" ranges over the questioner's acquaintance-objects, usually visual objects. In other words, the ostensive reply in (67) is normally a conclusive one if and orly if the questioner sees what is being pointed to. Obviously, this is the condition for the satisfactoriness of ostensive answers.

(viii) More has to be said of the domains over which the different quantifiers range that are expressed in English by the different wh-words. This leads to highly interesting theoretical problems which among other things yield a partial rational reconstruction of Aristotle's doctrine of categories as well as insights into the reasons for its inadequacy. Some of these developments are sketched in my forthcoming paper, "Semantical Games, the Alleged Ambiguity of 'Is', and Aristotelian Categories", Synthese (1983).

(ix) On the basis of the double-barrelled character of the wh-quantifiers, a large number of features of the behavior of direct and indirect questions in English can be explained. For some such explanations, see my *The Semantics of Questions* ..., chapters 4–5.

This list is not by any means exhaustive. What is especially impressive about it in my judgment is not any single application as much as the naturalness with which all the different applications flow from the basic ideas of the theory.

Florida State University
Department of Philosophy

Notes

[1] See *The Semantics of Questions and the Questions of Semantics* (Acta Philosophica Fennica, vol. 28, no. 4), North-Holland, Amsterdam, 1976; "Questions about Questions" in M. Munitz and P. Ungar, editors, *Semantics and Philosophy,* NYU Press, New York, 1974, pp. 103—58; "Answers to Questions" in H. Hiż, editor, *Questions,* D. Reidel, Dordrecht, 1978 pp. 279—300.
[2] See Veikko Rantala, "Urn Models", *Journal of Philosophical Logic,* vol. 4 (1975), pp. 455—74; reprinted in Esa Saarinen, editor, *Game-Theoretical Semantics,* D. Reidel, Dordrecht, 1979, pp. 347—66.
[3] See Jaakko Hintikka, "Impossible Possible Worlds Vindicated", *Journal of Philosophical Logic,* vol. 4 (1975), pp. 475—84; reprinted (with additions) in Saarinen (note 2 above), pp. 367—79.
[4] For earlier expositions of the model set and model system technique, see my *Models for Modalities,* D. Reidel, Dordrecht, 1969; *Knowledge and Belief,* Cornell U. P., Ithaca, NY, 1962.
[5] This extension technique allows for the following alternative to (C.~K):
If $\sim K_aS \in \mu \in \Omega$, then $S \notin \lambda$ for at least one alternative λ to μ in Ω.
[6] See *The Semantics of Questions* (note 1 above), chapter 4, sections 4—6.
[7] Thus the value of an individual symbol "y" is determined in all of a's epistemic alternatives as soon as it occurs within the scope of "K_a". As a consequence, we can express the fact that a knows who b is by letting such a symbol pick out b in the actual world and to occur within the scope of "K_a" in some trivial way. I have used for the purpose the trivial identity "$y=y$", whence the statement in question assumes the form

(*) $(\exists y)\ (y=b \,\&\, K_a(y=y))$

This has unfortunately mislead some philosophers who don't understand the model-theoretical situation into barking up the wrong tree and wondering what is so holy about self-identity. (Cf. R. M. Chisholm, *Person and Object,* George Allen & Unwin, London, 1976, p. 223.) Of course nothing hangs on self-identity here. Instead of (*), I can equally well write e.g.

(**) $(\exists y)\ (y=b \,\&\, K_a(A(y) \vee \sim A(y)))$

where the expression within the scope of "K_a" is understood in the perfectly normal (*de dicto*) way.
[8] See note 1 above.

J. Hoepelman

On Questions*

I. Introduction

Since M. and A. Prior's paper on "Erotetic Logic" (1955), the logico-linguistic literature on questions has proliferated so enormously, that one feels slightly embarrassed to add yet another proposal to the existing ones. Nevertheless it seems to me, that there are certain phenomena which a theory of questions should be able to handle, but which are not dealt with jointly by the existing theories. These phenomena can be summed up under the following headings:

(1) Questions and argumentation.
(2) The role of negative questions.
(3) The function of the particles "yes" and "no" and their counterparts in other languages (and in older stages of English).
(4) The scope of questions.
(5) The relation between interrogative pronouns and relative pronouns.
(6) The problem of asking equivalent questions.
(7) Questions, tautologies and contradictions.

Let us briefly consider each of these points.

II.

Ad. 1. Questions can play a role in argumentation, just like imperatives can. (Rescher, 1966, p. 5). There are logical relationships between questions. To cite Åqvist (1965): "Some questions seem to be logical consequences of others, two questions may be logically equivalent, a set of questions may be consistent, or inconsistent, and so on" (p. 3).

* This paper was written under DFG-project Ro 245/10 led by Prof. C. Rohrer, University of Stuttgart. An abbreviated version has appeared in J.A.G. Groenendijk (et al.) "Formel Methods in the Study of Language" Amsterdam, 1981.

Ferenc Kiefer (ed.), Questions and Answers, 191–227.

Connections like these also seem to hold between questions and assertions.

Moreover expressions which one can reasonably assume to be of sentence type can be built up of "assertive" parts and of "question" parts. To give a few examples: From the two questions

(1) Have you seen a picture of Picasso?
and
(2) Have you seen a picture of Dali?

the following seems to be a consequence (still in an intuitive sense of course):

(3) Have you seen a picture of Picasso and a picture of Dali?

But also the following seems to be a consequence:

(4) Have you seen a picture of Picasso or a picture of Dali?

The following assertion and question seem to be incompatible (when asserted and asked by the same person of course):

(5) No one has ever seen the abominable snowman.
(6) Has John seen the abominable snowman?

We must be a little bit on guard in this case. One can very well imagine a fragment like the following, spoken at a meeting of the Royal Geographic Society:

(8) No one has ever seen the abominable snowman!
Has Sir Edmund Hillary seen him? Has his sherpa seen him?
Has Reinhold Messner seen him? No! No one has seen—etc.

In this case the questions are used rhetorically or, as Åqvist would say, in a secondary way, and one would suppose that it is *because of* this incompatibility that they cannot be accepted as real questions. The speaker could as well have said:

(9) — No one has seen the abominable snowman!
Sir Edmund Hillary hasn't seen him! His sherpa hasn't seen him!
Reinhold Messner hasn't seen him!—etc.

To give a few examples of combined assertion-question sentences:

(10) Hübner is a great chess-player all right, but can he stand the stress of the tournament?
(11) If John has an alibi for Saturday night, then who has killed Mr. Jones?
(12) So you have written papers on tense and on quantification, and on negation too?
(13) This pie doesn't taste good, you have forgotten the spinach or the tomatoes, or have you forgotten the garlic?
(14) You have spoken with the chairman, or was it his assistent?
(15) Is the red button turned on? Then push the green button and run away fast!
(16) Did they pay him? He went right to the tavern and spent his wages down to the last dime. (Bolinger, 1978, p. 101).

Ad. 2. Negative questions are an interesting and quite confusing phenomenon, that seems to have received too little attention in the literature. Compare the following questions and their answers:

(17) — Is two an even number?
— Yes./— Yes, two is an even number.
— No./— No, two is not an even number.
(18) — Isn't two an even number?
— Yes./— Yes, two is an even number.
— No./— No, two is not an even number.

Notice that one can give the same answers to the negative and to the positive question, and that these answers have the same force! One couldn't answer "Isn't two an even number?" in the following ways:

(19) *Yes, two is not an even number.
(20) *— No, two is an even number.

Nevertheless one cannot say that (17′)

(17′) Is two an even number?
and (18′)
(18′) Isn't two an even number?

are the same question. A moment's reflection on the situations in which you would ask (17′) or (18′) makes this clear. You are likely to ask (17′) when you hear somebody talk about the difference between even and odd numbers, a difference you have never heard of before. You didn't know that two is an even number. On the other hand, you will ask (18′) in a situation like this: You have always thought that two is an even number. Now you hear a talk of a famous mathematician on the properties of numbers and something in what he says make you think that two might not be an even number after all. So you ask: "Isn't two an even number?"

If you do not think that two is an even number, then it is inappropriate for you to task "Isn't two an even number", because it would make other people think that you hold "Two is an even number" to be true. And if you think that two is an even number, then asking "Is two an even number" is inappropriate, because it would make people think that that it is not the case that you hold "Two is an even number" to be true.

Ad. 3. The observations made above mean that we cannot consider "yes" and "no" as abbreviations for the assertion or the negation of the questioned sentence. We will see that some of the theories to be discussed lead to precisely the wrong results in this respect. Modern English has only "yes" and "no", but in French one has "oui", "si" and "non", in German "ja", "doch" and "nein", in Dutch "ja", "toch wel" and "nee". In sixteenth century English we have "yes", "no", "yea" and "nay". (comp. Bäuerle, 1979). The use of these particles is explained in the following scheme:

(22)

question	answer				
	modern English	old English	French	German	Dutch
Is two an even number?	yes/no	yea/nay	oui/non	ja/nein	ja/nee
Isn't two an even number?	yes/no	yes/no	si/non	doch/nein	{ja / toch wel} /nee

A theory of questions should explain the use of these particles.

Ad. 4. Mostly by means of stress one can indicate which element of the sentence it is that is actually questioned. E.g. (19) and (20) are two different questions:

(22) Did John meet Mary in the párk?
(23) Did John meet Máry in the park?

One can extend this set of examples simply by shifting the stress. A sentence like (22) can be paraphrased like

(22′) (I know that) John met Mary somewhere, but did he meet her in the park?

whereas (23) would give

(23′) (I know that) John met someone in the park, but was it Mary whom he met?

Putting stress on the auxiliary "did" does not seem to have this semantical effect; (24) seems not to be different from (25) apart from having more emphasis:

(24) Díd John meet Mary in the park?
(25) Did John meet Mary in the park?

A theory of questions should be able to deal with this phenomenon.

Ad. 5. In most of the languages I know, (some) relative pronouns and (some) interrogative pronouns have the same form. We may suppose that this is no coincidence. It may not be our first concern, and a theory of questions may be a very good one without explaining this sameness of form, but of two equally good theories I would prefer the one which, as an additional feature, does explain it.

Ad. 6.

(26) two plus two equals four
and
(27) three plus one equals four

are two logically equivalent sentences. Nevertheless, asking whether two plus two equals four is not asking whether three plus equals four, i.e. (28) and (29) are not equivalent questions:

(28) Does two plus two equal four?
(29) Does three plus one equal four?

Any theory which treats them as being equivalent is in need of revision and/or amendment, I think.

Ad. 7. It makes no sense to ask a contradiction or a tautology. A question like

(30) *Does John work and not work?

is anomalous, and so is a question like

(31) *Does John work if he works?

A theory of questions should be able to sort out such deviant ones as (30) and (31). Of course (32) is perfectly o.k. as a question:

(32) Does John work or not?

This only means that (32) should not be analyzed as an inquiry after the truth of the tautology "John works or John doesn't work". On the other hand, one *can* ask a logical truth (which is not a tautology) or falsehood, as is witnessed by (28) and (33):

(33) Is two plus two five?

But again a question like (34)

(34) Is two plus two four or not?

should not be construed as an inquiry after the truth of the tautology "two plus two is four or two plus two is not four".

III.

We will now discuss some representatives of the main tendencies in question theories, and see whether they can deal with the points made above. Our division of theories on questions is taken from Bäuerle (1979). As is well known, questions can be divided in three main categories, so called *wh-questions:*

(35) Who is the prime minister of the Netherlands?

yes—no questions:

(36) Is Amsterdam the capital of the Netherlands?

and *alternative questions:*

(37) Is Amsterdam or the Hague the capital of the Netherlands?

It is of course attractive to try to reduce these categories and there exist several proposals to do so, depending on the (formalized) conceptions of questions. (I closely follow Bäuerle hereafter).

III.1

The *propositional approach* is represented by such authors who claim that any question is to be identified with a list of sentences, possible answers, which are offered as choices, loosely speaking. E.g. Hamblin (1973) takes a question to denote an at least two membered set of poropositions. Statements on the other hand denote one membered sets of propositions. A wh-question like

(38) Who walks?

represents the set containing the propositions denoted by "Mary walks", "John walks", . . . (a possibly infinite list).

A yes—no question like

(39) Does Peter walk?

represents the set containing of the pair of propositions denoted by "Peter walks" and its negation.

Hamblin doesn't pay attention to alternative questions, but we may, with Bäuerle, assume that an alternative question can be thought to represent a set containing the propositions which correspond to the alternatives. Karttunen (1978) slightly modifies this approach in that he assumes a question to represent a set containing only the true answers to it. Karttunen's analysis is carried out within the framework of Montague grammar. We will take his paper as a representative of the propositional approach, and see how it copes with our problems. Karttunen doesn't treat direct questions, because he assumes that direct questions can be reduced to indirect ones by means of paraphrases like

(40) I ask you (to tell me) whether it is raining.

for

(40′) Is it raining?

and
(41) I ask you (to tell me) which book Mary read.
for
(41′) Which book did Mary read? (p. 165)

Therefore Karttunen concentrates on the semantics of indirect questions. It is perhaps not fair to make critical remarks in connection with these examples already, because they are not pursued in the paper and beause one can safely assume that Karttunen would have noticed these problems if he had worked them out. Let us say, then, that the following remarks are preventive criticism. If "Is it raining?" is analyzed as "I ask you (to tell me) whether it is raining", then presumably

(42) Isn't it raining?

will be analyzed as:

(42′) I ask you (to tell me) whether it is not raining.

One can satisfy this request in the case of (40) (I ask you (to tell me) whether it is raining) by the statement

(43) It is raining

and in the case of (42′) by the statement

(44) It is not raining.

You couldn't answer (42′) by the statement

(45) Yes, it is raining.

But the question-answer pair

(46) — (42) Isn't it raining?
— (45) Yes, it is raining

is perfectly normal.

Another problem, it seems to me, resides in the use of the phrase "I ask you . . ." It is to be expected that the semantics of the verb "ask" will be connected intimately with the semantics of direct questions, so analyzing direct questions as being built up from indirect questions plus "I ask you . . ." takes for granted that which is to be explained. It will perhaps be better to drop the "I ask you . . ." part and to take the imperative of "tell" instead:

(47) Tell me! whether it is raining.

We will return to the imperative later on.

The core of Karttunen's proposal is his *Proto-Question Rule* (p. 174)

(48) PQ: If $\phi \in P_t$, then $\ulcorner ?\phi \urcorner \in P_Q$
If ϕ translates to ϕ', then $\ulcorner ?\phi \urcorner$ translates to
$\hat{p}[{}^{\vee}p \;\&\; p = {}^{\wedge}\phi']$

Here Q is the category of indirect questions, defined as t//t. The proto-question "?Mary cooks" is translated to $\hat{p}[{}^{\vee}p \;\&\; p = {}^{\wedge}cook'_{*}(m)]$. This expression denotes a function from propositions to truth values, i.e. a set of propositions. If Mary cooks, then "?Mary cooks" denotes a set whose only member is the proposition that Mary cooks; if Mary doesn't cook, the empty set is denoted. Protoquestions are the building blocks out of which expressions of English are constructed, like "whether Mary cooks or John eats out", "whether Mary cooks or not" and "which girl cooks" by means of rules, of which we will cite the YES/NO QUESTION RULE as an example:

(49) YNQ: If $\ulcorner ?\phi \urcorner \in P_Q$ then $\ulcorner$whether or not $\phi\urcorner$ and $\ulcorner$whether ϕ or not$\urcorner \in P_Q$.
If $\ulcorner ?\phi \urcorner$ translates to ψ', then $\ulcorner$whether $\phi\urcorner$, $\ulcorner$whether or not $\phi\urcorner$ and $\ulcorner$whether ϕ or not$\urcorner$ translate to
$\hat{p}[\psi'(p) \vee (\neg \exists q \psi'(q)\ \&\ p = {}^\wedge \neg \exists q \psi'(q))]$

"Whether Mary cooks", "whether or not Mary cooks" and "Whether Mary cooks or not" are all translated to a formula that turns out to be equivalent to

(50) $\hat{p}[{}^\vee p\ \&\ [p = {}^\wedge \text{cook}'_*(m) \vee p = \neg {}^\wedge \text{cook}'_*(m)]]$

These fragments suffice to bring forward my main criticisms against Karttunen's proposal. In the first place, there is nothing which prevents a tautology or a contradiction to be asked in a yes/no question. Secondly, (this has also been pointed out by Higginbotham and May (1978 p. 21)), if the sentence ϕ occurs in the scope of "?" in a protoquestion, then the set denoted by the protoquestion will contain all propositions which are logically equivalent to ϕ. In the case of a question like (28) (Does two plus two equal four?) this would lead to the undesirable result that one could answer with "Yes. Five plus five equals ten". Thirdly, and we mentioned this point before, negative questions do not come out right. It is easily seen (by substituting a negated sentence for ϕ in the yes/no question rule) that negative sentences will be treated in exactly the same way as positive ones, so that we will be lead to an analysis of (42) (Isn't it raining) as (42′) (I ask you to tell me whether it is not raining), which, as I hope to have made plausible, is wrong.

In the fourth place—but this is an objection that can also be directed against other theories which try to explain direct questions via indirect ones—in certain cases sentences which combine an assertive and a question part lead to ugly results if one replaces the question by its proposed paraphrase. E.g. 1) (Hübner is a great chess-player all-right, but can he stand the stress of the tournament?) will lead to

(51) Hübner is a great chess-player all right, but I ask you to tell me whether he can stand the stress of the tournament

and it is easy to imagine a situation in which you utter (10) without it being the case that you require someone to tell you such a thing. Whether Hübner can stand the stress of the tournament is something "the future will learn" and it may very well be the case that you utter (10) knowing that there is no one around to whom you could sensibly direct a request like the one contained in (51). The point is even stronger in the case of (13) (This pie doesn't taste good, you have forgotten the spinach or the tomatoes, or have you forgotten the garlic?) which would lead to

(52) This pie doesn't taste good, you have forgotten the spinach or the tomatoes, or I ask you to tell me whether you have forgotten the garlic.

In all likeness the addressee will not be able to tell you what he or she has forgotten.

The points (3) (the function of "yes" and "no") and (4) (the scope of questions) are not dealt with by Karttunen—but in the case of (3) we fear that an eventual theory might lead to problems because of the difficulties with negative questions mentioned above. The scope of questions is quite another problem. It is not dealt with in any of the theories I have seen. We shall try to sketch a solution for it at end of this paper.

III.2

The *categorial approach* supposes that questions are to be considered as functions from categorial answers to propositions. Representatives of this line of thought are e.g. Cohen (1929) and Egli (1976). A question like

(53) Who comes?

can be analysed as

(54) $\lambda x_{NP}(x_{NP}\text{comes})$

and a question like

(55) When does he come?

as

(56) $\lambda x_{ADV_t}(x_{ADV_t}(\text{he comes}))$

(Bäuerle, op.c. p. 64)

Notice that in this approach it will be difficult to account for sentences which are built up from an assertive and a question part, like (11). Egli (1976) proposes the following reduction of yes—no question to categorial questions: Any assertion is assumed to consist of two parts, *modus* and *dictum*. The *modi* are "yes" and "no", and the structure of

(57) Will he come?

is supposed to be

(58) $\lambda x_M(x_M(\text{he will come}))$

(Bäuerle, op.c. p. 65)

Thus yes—no questions are reduced to categorial ones. Again, there seems to be nothing which prevents asking tautologies or contradictions in this approach (or at least to mark these questions in some way). And again, negative questions are not treated in the right way. If, as Bäuerle says, Egli considers "no" to be equivalent to "it is not the case that", then answering the negative question

(59) Isn't John ill?

with "no" will amount to the assertion that John is ill. But, as we have pointed out before, a dialogue like

(60) — Isn't John ill?
No, John is ill.

is deviant.

The same objection can be directed against Hausser's (1977) analysis of yes—no questions (as rendered by Bäuerle, op.c., p. 65). Hausser's analysis of the question

(61) Did John leave?

is carried out in Montague grammar and has the following form

(62) $^\wedge\lambda y_n(y_n(^\wedge leave'(^\wedge j)) \,\&\, ((y_n = \hat{p}(^\vee p)) \vee (y_n = \hat{p}(^\vee \neg p)))$

where y_n represents the modus variable "it is the case that" or "it is not the case that". Taking the negative

(63) Didn't John leave?

instead of (61), then substituing "yes" or "no" for y_n, one easily sees that according to this theory the answers to (63) will be

(64) Yes, John didn't leave
and
(65) No, John left

which is wrong.

III.3

As a third approach I would like to mention the epistemic-imperative theory of Åqvist (1968) and Hintikka (1974).

In Åqvist's theory a question like

(66) Is Linguistic Philosophy still alive?

is analysed as

(67) Bring it about that either I know that Linguistic Philosophy is still alive or I know that Linguistic Philosophy is not alive any longer.

and

(68) Which is the smallest prime greater than 500?

is analysed as

(69) Bring it about that there is an object of which I know that it is the smallest prime greater than 500.

(Åqvist, op.c. p. 4)

We will not go into the semantics for the imperative and for "know" presented by Åqvist, but just give a few of his formulae which are easily understood intuitively. This will be enough for our purposes. Let

(70) Brutus killed Caesar.

be represented by p, and

(71) Cassius killed Caesar.

by q.
Then the question

(72) Did Brutus kill Caesar or did Cassius?

will be analysed as

(73) $!(Kp \vee Kq)$

i.e. "Bring it about that I know that p or that I know that q". This leads to the definition of an operator $?_2(p, q)$ as follows:

(74) $?_2(p, q) =_d !(Kp \vee Kq)$

and in general

(75) $?_n(p_1, p_2, \ldots, p_n) =_d !(Kp_1 \vee Kp_2 \vee \ldots \vee Kp_n)$

for any number n. Single yes—no questions are made by means of $?_1$:

(77) $?_1 p = ?_2(p, - p)$

But now we see immediately that in Åqvist's theory too negative questions will be treated in the wrong way—no difference can be made between (70) and (78)

(78) Didn't Brutus kill Caesar?

And a question like

(79) Doesn't two plus two equal four?

certainly doesn't mean

(80) Bring it about that I know that two plus two is not four.

As may be seen in (75), Åqvist introduces a multiplicity of question operators already when dealing with questions on the propositional level. This trait is reinforced when question operators are combined with predicate logic (containing imperative and epistemic operators). Here an enormous proliferation of quantifiers is needed to deal with possible readings of interrogatives (see e.g. the tableau in Åqvist, op.c. p. 128). I think that Åqvist is right in the way he distinguishes these readings. But if a theory can be found which deals with them in a formally less complicated way, it is to be favoured.

There are other problems connected with the epistemic-imperative theory of questions. In Hintikka (1974) we find the following example (p. 4):

(81) Who will kill Cock Robin?

Hintikka observes that it is not correct to analyse (81) as

(82) Bring it about that I know who will kill Cock Robin.

According to Hintikka it is reasonable to assume that the state of affairs which the questioner wants to be brought about:

(83) I know who will kill Cock Robin

implies

(84) Someone will kill Cock Robin

So (82) could be interpreted as a wish to have Cock Robin killed. Therefore Hintikka proposes the paraphrase

(85) Assuming that Cock Robin will be killed, bring it about that I know who will kill Cock Robin.

I think that this paraphrase will not do either, especially not if we take yes—no questions into consideration. A sentence like

(86) Will you kill Cock Robin?

will amount to

(87) Assuming that you will kill Cock Robin, bring it about that I know whether you will kill Cock Robin

Hintikka interprets "I know whether p" as "I know that p or I know that not P" (p. 7); this leads to

(88) Assuming that you will kill Cock Robin, bring it about that I know that you will kill Cock Robin, or that I know that you will not kill Cock Robin.

Then, arguing on Hintikka's lines it will follow that

(89) Assuming that you will kill Cock Robin, I wish you to kill Cock Robin, or I wish you not to kill Cock Robin.

Of course you may entertain none of these desires.

Arguing on a more general level, one may ask whether it is not desirable to try to find a logic of questions which doesn't consist in a reduction to imperative and epistemic notions. There surely are connections between imperatives and questions. E.g. a request can be formulated as an order or as a question:

(90) Get me a glass of water!
(91) Will you get me a glass of water?
(92) Get me a glass of water, please. (Question?, Order?)
(93) Will you get me a glass of water, please?

With some effort one could try to reduce imperatives to questions as well as the other way around—although I doubt whether a complete reduction will be possible. So one could analyse (90) as

(94) You know what is going to happen to you if you don't get me a glass of water, don't you? It won't happen if you get me a glass of water.

Perhaps a better understanding of the connection between imperatives and questions can be achieved if we first try to develop a logic of imperatives and a logic of questions independently from one another. I will sketch a proposal for the latter in the next paragraphs.

IV.

As may already be guessed from the foregoing I favour a treatment of all questions as expressions of sentence type. With Åqvist I think that it may be profitable to assign truth values to questions, which would e.g. simplify the treatment of consequences of questions and the valuation of combined assertive-question sentences. Under certain circumstances a question can be considered to be a "true question", in others as "false"—or, if you don't like these expressions, as "correct" and "incorrect" (Åqvist op.c. p. 26). This can be the case (for a certain individual) without there being anyone around to whom the order "relieve me from my ignorance concerning ϕ" can be directed. Sticking to the level of propositional logic, I want to give a logic for the propositional operator "?" which can be read as "It is the question whether" (German: "Es ist die Frage ob", Dutch: "Het is de vraag of"). For a sentence p, when is it the question whether p? Certainly not when p is true or false. One would rather say that it is the question whether p, when the truth value of p itself is undetermined. Thus we might be led to an interpretation of "?" in Łukasiewicz' three valued logic, in which, apart from the values 1 (true) and 0 (false) one has the value 1/2 (undetermined) (Łukasiewicz, 1920). In this logic we have the following truth tables:

(95)

p	$\neg p$		$p \,\&\, q$			$p \vee q$			$p \rightarrow q$			$p \leftrightarrow q$		
		p \ q	1	1/2	0	1	1/2	0	1	1/2	0	1	1/2	0
1	0	1	1	1/2	0	1	1	1	1	1/2	0	1	1/2	0
1/2	1/2	1/2	1/2	1/2	0	1	1/2	1/2	1	1	1/2	1/2	1	1/2
0	1	0	0	0	0	1	1/2	0	1	1	1	0	1/2	1

For "?" one could propose the following table:

(96)

p	?p
1	0
1/2	1
0	0

The three valued system of Łukasiewicz can be extended to an n-valued logic (for any natural number n) and to an infinitely valued logic. An n-valued logic is obtained by taking the values

$$(97)\quad 1=\frac{n-1}{n-1}, \frac{n-2}{n-1}, \ldots, \frac{1}{n-1}, \frac{0}{n-0}=0$$

and the following rules for evaluating complex formulae, where /p/ denotes the value of p and min (a, b), max (a, b) the minimum and maximum of a and b, respectively.

$$(98)\quad \begin{aligned} /-p/ &= 1-/p/ \\ /p\&q/ &= \min(/p/, /q/) \\ /p \vee q/ &= \max(/p/, /q/) \\ /p \rightarrow q/ &= \begin{Bmatrix} 1 \\ 1-/p/+/q/ \end{Bmatrix} \text{ according as } /p/ \text{ is } \begin{Bmatrix} \leqslant /q/ \\ > /q/ \end{Bmatrix} \end{aligned}$$

For the infinitely valued logic one takes 0 and 1 and all the rational fractions in between them and in addition the rules (98). It is not difficult to see that this three valued logic doesn't give us an intuitively satisfying account of "it is the question whether". In the first place, both the formula "p∨ ¬ p" and the formula "p& ¬ p" can get the truth value 1/2 (if the value of p is 1/2), in which case the value of "?p∨ ¬ p" and "?(p& ¬ p)" would be 1. The case of "?(p& ¬ p)" seems most clear: One doesn't ask a question like "Does John walk and not walk?". The case of "?(p∨ ¬ p)" having truth value 1 does not seem unplausible at first sight. After all, one might argue, it is because the value of p is undetermined that one can ask "Does John walk?", "Doesn't John walk? and "Does John walk or not?". But this would mean giving up the possibility of explaining the difference between positive and negative questions which was pointed out above. In the three valued system the following are equivalent:

?p, ? ¬ p, ?(p∨ ¬ p), ?(p& ¬ p)

This, I think, is highly unintuitive.

There are other three valued systems of propositional logic (I take all this from Rescher (1969)), such as Bochvar's, Kleene's and Heyting's. I will not explain these systems here, but they lead to unintuitive results if we try to interpret "it is the question whether" in terms of them. E.g. in Heyting's system "$\urcorner ? \urcorner p$" would be valid (where $\urcorner$ is negation as defined in this system) and in Bochvar's system

"?(p&q)" "?(p∨q)", "?(p → q)" and "?(p ↔ q)"
are all equivalent.

At this point, let us think about negative questions once more. It is true that you are uncertain about "John is ill" if you ask either

(99) Is John ill?
or
(100) Isn't John ill?

But I don't think that if you ask (100) you desire an answer in the negative more than if you ask (99). On the contrary, my intuition is that if one asks (100) one expects a positive answer. We might say that there are two kinds of uncertainty here, which are "directed" differently. Therefore, we can try to give a semantics for "?" not in Łukasiewicz three-valued system, but in its four valued extension, in which there are two undetermined values. Let us call this system $Ł_4$. The tables for p and $\neg$ p will, and the table for ?p might look like the following in $Ł_4$:

(101)

p	$\neg$ p	?p
1	0	0
2/3	1/3	1
1/3	2/3	0
0	1	0

We have to give ?p the value 1 in case p has the value 2/3, for if we would assign 1 to ?p in case /p/=1/3, it would be possible for ?(p& $\neg$ p) to take the value 1 (as one can easily verify).

Now ?p, ? $\neg$ p and ?(p∨ $\neg$ p) are no longer equivalent. The system has a few other pleasant properties. E.g. neither (102), nor (103) are valid:

(102) $?p \rightarrow ?\neg p$
(103) $?\neg p \rightarrow ?p$

I like this, because, as we pointed out above, if it is appropriate to ask "Is John ill" it is not appropriate to ask "Isn't John ill" and conversely. A few formulae which *are* valid are

(104) $?\neg p \rightarrow \neg ?p$
(105) $?p \& ?q \rightarrow ?(p \& q)$
(106) $?(p \& q) \rightarrow ?p \vee ?q$
(107) $?(p \vee q) \rightarrow ?p \vee ?q$

All of these are intuitive, I think (remember the examples given at the beginning of the paper). Still, I am not entirely happy with this system. It is still possible to assign the value 1 to a formula of the form

(108) $?(p \vee \neg p)$

(in case $/p/=2/3$ or $1/3$), but I think that we cannot construe

(109) Is John ill or not?

as an inquiry after the truth of the sentence

(110) John is ill or John is not ill

If it were, what would be more natural than to answer this question with "yes"?

In fact, anyone with a knowledge of the state of John's health would *have* to answer the question with "yes". But in fact one can very well answer (109) with "no", and anyone who gets this answer will know that John is not ill. So we turn to another system of four valued logic, and will see if it presents us with more satisfactory results.

V.

If we have two many-valued logics, C_n and C_m respectively, the *product system* $C_n \times C_m$ can be given in the following way (I follow Rescher op.c. p. 97 on these pages):

(111) a) The truth values of system $C_n \times C_m$ are to be ordered pairs (v_1, v_2) of truth values, the first of which, v_1, is a truth value of C_n and the second of which, v_2, is one of C_m.

b) The truth value of a proposition is to be (v_1, v_2) in $C_n \times C_m$ iff it truth value is v_1 in C_n and v_2 in C_m.

c) Correspondingly, negation ("$\neg$") and arbitrary binary logical connectives ("$\emptyset$") are to be so specified for $C_n \times C_m$ that their truth tables are governed by the rules:

$\neg (v_1, v_2) = (\neg v_1, \neg v_2)$ and
$(v_1, v_2) \emptyset (v_3, v_4) = (v_1 \emptyset v_3, v_2 \emptyset v_4)$

We will now turn our attention to the particular four valued product system $C_2 \times C_2$, which is the product of the classical two valued propositional calculus with itself. Rescher tells us that later in life Łukasiewicz had great partiality for this system which he considered to be of principal importance from a philosophical point of view (which is not the reason why we chose it). The tables for the connectives in $C_2 \times C_2$ are as follows:

(112)

p	$\neg$p	q \ p	p&q	p∨q	p → q	p ↔ q
			11 10 01 00	11 10 01 00	11 10 01 00	11 10 01 00
11	00	11	11 10 01 00	11 11 11 11	11 10 01 00	11 10 01 00
10	01	10	10 10 00 00	11 10 11 10	11 11 01 01	10 11 00 01
01	10	01	01 00 01 00	11 11 01 01	11 10 11 10	01 00 11 10
00	11	00	00 00 00 00	11 10 01 00	11 11 11 11	00 01 10 11

To this we add the following table for "?" (the intuitive reason for doing it this way will become apparent later)

(113)

p	?p	(and so: $? \neg p$
11	00	00
10	00	10
01	10	00
00	00	00)

We will now give a few examples of interesting valid and non-valid formulae containing "?" in this system. Valid are e.g.:

(114)
$\neg ?(p \vee \neg p)$
$\neg ?(p \& \neg p)$
$\neg ??p$
$\neg ? \ldots ?p$ (for any number of ?'s)
$? \neg p \rightarrow \neg ?p$
$?p \rightarrow ? \neg ? p$
$?p \rightarrow ? \neg ? \neg \ldots \neg ?p$ (any number of $? \neg ?$'s)
$?(p \rightarrow q) \rightarrow (?p \rightarrow ?q)$
$?(p \rightarrow ?q) \rightarrow (?p \rightarrow ?q)$
$?(?p \rightarrow q) \rightarrow (p \rightarrow ?q)$
$?(p \vee q) \rightarrow (?p \vee ?q)$
$(?p \& ?q) \rightarrow ?(p \& q)$
$?(p \& q) \rightarrow ?p \vee ?q$
$?p \& ?q \rightarrow ?(p \vee q)$
$?p \rightarrow (p \rightarrow q)$
$(?(p \rightarrow q) \& p) \rightarrow ?q$

The reader can easily verify this for himself (a tedious job). A few interesting non-valid formulae are:

(115)
$?p \rightarrow ? \neg p$
$? \neg p \rightarrow ?p$
$(p \leftrightarrow q) \rightarrow (?p \leftrightarrow ?q)$
$? \neg p \rightarrow (p \rightarrow q)$

That $p \leftrightarrow q$ doesn't imply that $?p \leftrightarrow ?q$ is of course particularly satisfying in the light of our discussion of equivalent questions. We see that the interpretation of "?" in $C_2 \times C_2$ retains the desirable properties we already found in $Ł_4$, and has a few more. It is e.g. valid that $p \vee \neg p$ is not asked and likewise for $p \& \neg p$. Moreover $?(p \rightarrow q) \rightarrow (?p \rightarrow ?q)$ is valid in $C_2 \times C_2$ (but not in $Ł_4$) and so is $(?(p \rightarrow q) \& p) \rightarrow ?q$, a formula which we will need when discussing the scope of questions. We will now say that a positive yes—no question, like (99) (Is John ill?) is of the form ?p, a negative yes—no question like (100) (Isn't John ill?) is of the form $? \neg p$ and a yes—no question like (109) (Is John ill or not?) is of the form $?p \vee ? \neg p$. In this last case we should be careful. It has been maintained e.g. by Bäuerle (op.c. p. 62) that alternative questions like

(116) Did you meet my brother or my sister?

cannot be answered by "yes" or "no". A fortiori a sentence like (109), if considered as an alternative question with two mutually exclusive alternants, cannot be answered by "yes" or "no". I think that this claim is only partially right. A sentence like

(117) Have you ever seen a film by Keaton or Chaplin?

can perfectly well be answered by "yes" or "no".

Also the following dialogues seem to be acceptable

(118) — Here is John. Look at the red spots on his face! Is he ill or not?
— Yes. He probably got the measles./ — No. That's marmelade.

Not in all cases answering questions like (116) with a "yes" or a "no" is acceptable. There seems to be an ambiguity here. If you ask (116), may be all you want to know is whether the addressee saw either one of your brother or sister (for then it might e.g. be the case that you know that your father is safe). Here a single "yes" is justified as an answer. Another possibility, however, is that you want to know which one of your brother and sister was seen by the addressee. Now a "yes" alone will not do. We may explain this ambiguity by assuming that (116) can formally be expressed in two ways:

(119) ?(you saw my brother-or-sister)
(120) ?(you saw my brother) or ?(you saw my sister)

The case of sentences like "Is John ill or not" is a little bit different. Although, as we have seen, a "yes" can be acceptable as an answer to a question of the form "ϕ or not", most likely, a father who asks his son

(121) — Have you passed this exam or not?

will not be content with a "yes" alone. This, I feel, is even more the case when instead of (121) the following had been asked:

(121^1) — Have you passed the exam or haven't you?

At the end of this paper a solution for this problem will be suggested which will depend on the respective scopes of "not" and "?".

We are now in a position to say more on the function of the expressions "yes" and "no".

VI.

We have seen that we cannot consider "yes" and "no" as abbreviations for "it is the case that—" and "it is not the case that—" followed by the sentence that has been asked. I agree with Bäuerle (op.c., p. 68—69) that "yes" and "no" are not to be taken as answers, but as "discourse elements that relate the answer to the question in some way or other". Let us see how we can make this more precise in the theory of questions proposed above.

If the question

(122) Is four an even number?

is addressed to someone, then, assuming that the person who asks it is honest, the addressee will know that the truth value of

(123) Four is an even number

for the person who asks (122) is 01. Let us say that the person who asks (122) suffers from an *uncertainty of the second kind.* The addressee can try to remedy this uncertainty by answering

(124) Yes./Yes, four is an even number.

or

(125) No./No, four is not an even number.

By (124) he indicates that the person who asks, should entertain a *certainty of the first kind* about "Four is an even number", i.e. that he can hold its truth value to be 11. By (125) the addressee indicates that the person who asked (122) should entertain a *certainty of the second kind* about "Four is an even number", i.e. that he should hold its truth value to be 00. To put it briefly, "yes" indicates the following change: 01 ⇒ 11, and "no": 01 ⇒ 00. Now consider negative questions.

(126) Isn't four an even number?

can be answered by

(127) Yes./Yes, four is an even number.

(128) No./No, four is not an even number.

Hearing (126) the addressee knows that the person who asks suffers from an *uncertainty of the first kind,* i.e. that for him the truth value of "Four isn't an even number" is 01, and therefore the truth value of "Four is an even number" 10. The addressee's answers "yes" and "no" are the same and indicate the same as in the case of the positive question: They try to change the uncertainty of the first kind into a certainty of the first kind (truth value 11) or a certainty of the second kind (truth value 00). Briefly: "yes" 10 ⇒ 11 and "no" 10 ⇒ 00. Thus we see that "yes" and "no" in modern English are ambiguous in a way. Sixteenth century English, having "yes", "no", "yea" and "nay" would give the following picture:

(129) "yea" 01 ⇒ 11
"nay" 01 ⇒ 00
"yes" 10 ⇒ 11
"no" 10 ⇒ 00

	English (mod.)				(16th. c.)				French				German				Dutch			
	yes	no	yes	no	yea	nay	yes	no	oui	non	si	non	ja	nein	doch	nein	ja	nee	ja toch	nee
01	11	00			11	00			11	00			11	00		well	11	00	wel	
10			11	00			11	00			11	00			11	00			11	00

Now we can also explain why the following answers to (122) and (126) respectively:

(130) *Yes, four is not an even number.
(131) *No, four is an even number

are incorrect:
"Yes" would indicate that the truth value to be entertained by the person who asks either (122) or (126) is to be 11, whereas asserting "four is not an even number" indicates that it has to be 00. Conversely "no" indicates that the truth value of the questioned sentences should be 00, whereas asserting "four is an even number" indicates the truth value 11.

VII.

There is another way to look at the product logic $C_2 \times C_2$ (again I follow Rescher (op.c. p. 113)). Let w_1 and w_2 be two alternatives (possible worlds). To any proposition we will assign the truth value 1, 2, 3, 4 according as it is

(132) a) true in w_1 and in w_2
b) true in w_1 but not in w_2
c) false in w_1 but true in w_2
d) false in both w_1 and w_2

For negation and conjunction we will get the following truth tables:

(133)

p	¬p	p & q: p \ q	1	2	3	4
1	4	1	1	2	3	4
2	3	2	2	2	4	4
3	2	3	3	4	3	4
4	1	4	4	4	4	4

If you compare these tables with those given for $C_2 \times C_2$, replacing 11 by 1, 10 by 2, 01 by 3 and 00 by 4, you will find out that they are exactly the same, and this holds for the other connectives as well.

We may now intuitively reinterpret our calculus of questions, by saying that a person's certainty rests on the comparison of two alternatives or worlds, of which the second has greater "authority" (in an epistemological sense) than the first. The first world may be thought of as the world as it might be for all the questioner knows, the second one as the world of the authority he is addressing himself to (a person, perhaps "Nature", God, or what have you) *as the questioner conceives of it.* This is one of the reasons why I have assigned 10 to "?p" in case 01 is assigned to "p". If a proposition p might not be true in "your" world, but seems to you to be true in the world of your "epistemological authority" then *for you* it is appropriate to ask "?p", but you will not think that for your "epistemological authority" it is the question whether p. The other reason for saying that /?p'=10 if /p/=01 is that in this way I want to render the intuition that questions cannot be true. We now can say that they have a value, but cannot be a certainty of the first kind.

VIII.

Armed with our new machinery, let us now turn to wh-questions and see what we can do with it. It is clear that in addition we will need the language of predicate logic. Let us assume that putting "?" in front of any expression of sentence type, results in a new expression of sentence type. Let us also assume that we have two models M_1 and M_2,

(134) $M_1=(D_1, F_1)$
$M_2=(D_2, F_2)$

where D_1 and D_2 are domains of individuals, $D_1 \subseteq D_2$, and F_1, F_2 are assignments to the constants, $F_1 \subseteq F_2$. In M_1 values are assigned to the individual variables by the functions $g_1, g_1', \ldots$, in M_2 by the functions $g_2, g_2', \ldots$.

We make the product system $PC_2 \times PC_2$ according to the following rules:

(135) a) The truth values of $PC_2 \times PC_2$ are to be ordered pairs of truth values (v_1, v_2), the first of which, v_1, is a truth value of PC_2 in M_1 according to the assignment g_1, the second of which, v_2, is a truth value of PC_2 in M_2 according to the assignment g_2.

b) The truth value of an expression of sentence type ϕ under the assignment $g_{1,2}$ is to be (v_1, v_2) in $PC_2 \times PC_2$ if its truth value in M_1 is v_1 under g_1 and v_2 in M_2 under g_2.

c) For expressions of sentence type the connectives are specified according to the following rules:

$$\neg (\phi_{M_1, g_1}, \phi_{M_2, g_2}) = (\neg \phi_{M_1, g_1}, \neg \phi_{M_2, g_2})$$

$$(\phi_{M_1, g_1}, \phi_{M_2, g_2}) \text{ ø } (\ddot{U}_{M_1, g_1} \text{ ø } \ddot{U}_{M_2, g_2}) =$$

$$= ((\phi_{M_1, g_1} \text{ ø } \ddot{U}_{M_1, g_1}), (\phi_{M_2, g_2} \text{ ø } \ddot{U}_{M_2, g_2}))$$

c) where ϕ_{M_1, g_1} is the value assigned to ϕ in M_1 under g_1.

For "?" we have the following rule:

d) i. Let ϕ be a closed formula without individual constants. Then

$?\phi_{g_{1,2}} = 10$ iff $\phi_{g_{1,2}} = 01$. Otherwise $?\phi_{g_{1,2}} = 00$.

ii. Let $\phi(x_1, \ldots, x_n)\ (a_1, \ldots, a_m)$ be a formula containing the n free variables $x_1, \ldots, x_n$ and the m individual constants $a_1, \ldots, a_m$ and no others (m or n may equal 0). Then

$?\phi(x_1, \ldots, x_n)\ (a_1, \ldots, a_m)_{g_{1,2}} = 10$ if
$\phi(x_1, \ldots\ x_n)\ (a_1, \ldots\ a_m)_{g_{1,2}} =$
$= 01$ *and* $g_2(x_1), \ldots, g_2(x_n), F_2(a_1), \ldots, F_2(a_1), \ldots,$
$F_2(a_m)\ \varepsilon D_1$

Otherwise $?\phi(x_1, \ldots, x_n)\ (a_1, \ldots, a_m)_{g_{1,2}} = 00$.

We order the truth values as follows: $00 < 01 < 10 < 11$, and define (Ax) and (Ex):

e) $(Ax)\phi_{g_{1,2}} = \min\ g'_{1,2}(\phi_{g'_{1,2}})$, $(Ex)\phi_{g_{1,2}} = \max\ g'_{1,2}(\phi_{g'_{1,2}})$, where $\min\ g'_{1,2}(\phi g'_{1,2})$ is the minimum truth value of ϕ for all $g'_{1,2}$ which are like $g'_{1,2}$ apart possibly from the assignment to x, and likewise for $\max\ g'_{1,2}(\phi_{g'_{1,2}})$.

If we now assume that $D_1 = D_2$, then formulae of the following form will be valid:

(136) $(Ax)?\phi \rightarrow ?(Ax)\phi$
$(Ax)?\phi \rightarrow ?(Ex)\phi$
$?(Ex)\phi \rightarrow (Ex)?\phi$

The last of these formulae isn't very intuitive, but it doesn't hold when we assume that $D_1 \subset D_2$. The converse formulae of the above do not hold if $D_1 = D_2$, nor if $D_1 \subset D_2$.

If we add "=" to our set of predicate constants then (among others) the following will hold:

(137) $(Ax)\ (Ay)\ (Az)\ (x=y\ \&\ ?(y=z) \rightarrow ?(x=z))$

which is an instance of

(138) $(Ax)\ (Ay)\ (x=y\ \&\ ?P(y) \rightarrow ?P(x))$

The following do *not* hold (which is as it intuitively should be)

(139) $(Ax)\ (Ay)\ (?(x=y)\ \&\ P(x) \rightarrow ?P(y))$
(140) $(Ax)\ (Ay)\ (?(x=y)\ \&\ ?P(x) \rightarrow ?P(y))$

IX.

Now I propose to give a wh-question like

(141) Which men work?

the following intuitive reading:

(142) For every man x, is x a man which works?

In Montague grammar we could achieve a formal rendering of (142) in the following way:
First we form *man which works,* which is translated to $\hat{x}(\text{man}_*'(\check{\ }x)\ \&\ \text{work}_*'(\check{\ }x))$, then we form *is he*$_n$ *a man which works?,* which is translated

to ?(Ey) $(\text{man}_*{}'(\check{}y)\&\text{work}_*{}'(\check{}y)\&\check{}y=\check{}x_n)$ then, from the expressions *every man* and *is he*$_n$ *a man which works?* we form, by a rule of quantification, the expression *Which men work?,* which is translated to

(143) $(Ax)\ (\text{man}_*{}'(\check{}x) \rightarrow ?(Ey)\ (\text{man}_*{}'(\check{}y)\&\text{work}_*{}'(\check{}y)\&\check{}y=\check{}x))$

Likewise.

(144) Which man works?

will be read as

(145) There is a man x: is x a man which works?

And by the same steps as those sketched above, we would arrive at the translation

(146) $(Ex)\ (\text{man}_*{}'(\check{}x)\&?(Ey)\ (\text{man}_*{}'(\check{}y)\&\text{work}_*{}'(\check{}y)\&\check{}y=\check{}x))$.

(147) Who works?

seems to be ambiguous, and can be treated as

(147′) Which persons work?
and
(147″) Which person works?

respectively, leading to the translations

(148) $(Ax)\ (\text{person}_*{}'(\check{}x) \rightarrow ?(Ey)\ (\text{person}_*{}'(\check{}y)\&$ $\text{work}_*{}'(\check{}y)\&\check{}y=\check{}x))$
and
(149) $(Ex)\ (\text{person}_*{}'(\check{}x)\&?(Ey)\ (\text{person}_*{}'(\check{}y)\&$ $\text{work}_*{}'(\check{}y)\&\check{}y=\check{}x))$

We see that a question of the form

(150) Where ϕ?

could also be rendered in two ways:

(151) $(Ax)\ (place_*'(\check{}x) \rightarrow ?(Ey)\ (place_*'(\check{}y) \& f\ y) \& \check{}y = \check{}x))$
and
(152) $(Ex)\ (place_*'(\check{}x) \& ?(Ey)\ (place_*'(\check{}y) \& \emptyset(\check{}y) \& \check{}y = \check{}x))$

I think that this corresponds to a real ambiguity, the difference between what Åqvist calls "monadic complete list what-questions" and "monadic at-least-what questions" (Åqvist, op.c. pp. 85—91).

Multiple questions seem to pose no particular problems in this framework. (See e.g. Karttunen/Peters, 1979.)

(153) Which student does each professor recommend? (Karttunen/Peters 1979, p. 1)

can be arrived at in the following way:

First we form *he*$_1$ *recommends he*$_2$.
Then we form *student which he*$_1$ *recommends,*
then *a student which he*$_1$ *recommends,* followed by
is he$_3$ *a student which he*$_1$ *recommends?,* the translation of which will be

(154) $?(Ey)\ (student_*'(\check{}y) \& recommend_*'(\check{}x_1, \check{}y) \& \check{}y = \check{}x_3)$

Out of (154) and *a student* we then make *which student does he*$_1$ *recommend?* by a rule of quantification, and translate it to

(155) $(Ex)\ (student_*'(\check{}x) \& ?(Ey)\ (student_*'(\check{}y) \& recommend_*'(\check{}x_1, \check{}y) \& (\check{}y = \check{}x))$

Finally, again by a rule of quantification, from *each professor* and *which student does he*$_1$ *recommend?* we form

(156) Which student does each professor recommend?

which has the following translation:

(157) $(Az)\ (professor_*'(\check{}z) \rightarrow ((Ex)\ (student_*'(\check{}x) \& ?(Ey)\ (student_*'(\check{}y) \& recommend_*'(\check{}z, \check{}y) \& \check{}y = \check{}x)))))$

It is easy to see how one can arrive at the other possible reading of (153), namely by first pushing *each professor* into *student which* he_1 *recommends.* As a last example we directly give the translation of

(158) Which professor recommends which student for the job?

(159) $(Ez)\ (\text{professor}_*{}'({}^{\vee}z)\&?(Ev)\ (\text{professor}_*{}'({}^{\vee}v)\&$
$(Ex)\ (\text{student}_*{}'({}^{\vee}x)\&?(Ey)\ (\text{student}_*{}'({}^{\vee}y)\&$
$\text{recommend}_*{}'({}^{\vee}v,\ {}^{\vee}y)\&{}^{\vee}y={}^{\vee}x))\&{}^{\vee}z={}^{\vee}v))))$

I will conclude this chapter by putting forward a few suggestions on the structure of sentences containing "know wh-". In the first place we notice that the English verb "know" can be used in (at least) two different ways, as examplified in

(160) John knows Peter

and

(161) John knows that Peter comes.

Dutch and German have two different verbs for these uses, namely "kennen" and "weten (D.)/wissen (G.)". I think that

(162) John knows who comes

in which *know* is used in the first sense, can be read as:

(163) There is someone who comes and John knows him.

It is easy to see how (162) could be dealt with in Montague grammar: We form *a person who comes* and *John knows* him_n and by a rule of quantification we get *John knows who comes* which is translated to

(164) $(Ex)\ (\text{person}_*{}'({}^{\vee}x)\&\text{come}_*{}'({}^{\vee}x)\&\text{know}_*{}'(j,\ x))$

(162) (John knows who comes) in its plural reading will be formed analoguously and translated to

(165) $(Ax)\ (\text{person}_*{}'({}^{\vee}x)\&\text{come}_*{}'({}^{\vee}x) \rightarrow \text{know}_*{}'(j,\ x))$

If *know* is used in the second sense, then I think that (162) has several readings. (162) may be read as

(166) There is a person who comes and John knows that he comes or as

(167) For a person x, John knows whether x comes or not

Again it is easy to see how we can form (166) in Montague grammar: We make *a person who comes* and *John knows that he*$_n$ *comes* and by a rule of quantification we get *John knows who comes,* translated to

$$(168)\quad (Ex)\ (\text{person}_*'(\check{}x) \& \text{come}_*'(\check{}x) \& \text{know}_*'(j,\ \hat{}\text{come}_*'(\check{}x))$$

and analoguously for the plural reading.

I suppose that (167) can be dealt with along the following lines: From *John knows that he*$_n$ *comes* and *John knows that he*$_n$ *doesn't come* we form *John knows whether he*$_n$ *comes or not.* From this and *a person* we form *John knows who comes,* which is translated to

$$(169)\quad (Ex)\ (\text{person}_*'(\check{}x) \& \text{know}_*'(j,\ \hat{}\text{come}_*'(\check{}x)) \vee \vee \text{know}_*'(j,\ \hat{}\neg\ \text{come}_*'(\check{}x))$$

Finally I would like to point out that there might still be another reading for (162) namely

(170) For a certain person of whom it is the question whether he comes, John knows whether he comes or not.

It is clear how we could deal with the part of this sentence following the comma. The part preceding it can be handled in the following way: we make *he*$_m$ *comes?* and out of this and *person* we make *person who comes?* Then we make *a person who comes?* and out of this and *John knows whether he*$_n$ *comes or not* we make *John knows who comes* which is translated as

$$(171)\quad (Ex)\ (\text{person}_*'(\check{}x) \& ?(\text{come}_*'(\check{}x)) \& \text{know}_*'(j,\ \hat{}\text{come}'(\check{}x)) \vee \vee \text{know}_*'(j,\ \hat{}\neg\ \text{come}'(\check{}x)))$$

The plural readings for (162) are treated accordingly.

X.

Finally I will make a few remarks on the scope of questions. We have seen that questions like

(172) Does Jóhn kiss Mary in the park?
and
(173) Does John kíss Mary in the park?

are two different questions. Intuitively it is clear what this difference consists in: in (172) the speaker is uncertain about the person who kisses Mary, in (173) the speaker is uncertain about what John does to Mary in the park.

In an earlier paper I have proposed a treatment for denial in Montague grammar (Hoepelman, 1979), which I will extend to questions. Compare the following sentences:

(174) Jóhn doesn't kiss Mary in the park.
(175) John doesn't kíss Mary in the park.

Here, too, the difference is intuitively clear. In (174) the speaker accepts that someone kisses Mary, but he denies that it was John who does the kissing. In (175) the speaker accepts that John does something to Mary in the park, but he denies that it is kissing. In (Hoepelman, 1979) I introduce a dummy element for each basic category of the Montague Grammar, which in the case of terms could be read as "something" (or "someone" if terms are split up in *human* and *non-human*). Let us denote the dummy of category a by O_a. Then (174) is analysed as

$$(176)\ \neg (Ex)(Ay)(park_*'(\check{}y) \rightarrow \check{}x = \check{}y \& in'(\check{}x)\, \hat{z}(kiss_*'(\check{}z, m))(\hat{}j)) \& (O'_T)(in'(\hat{P}(Ex)(Ay)(kiss_*'(\check{}y) \rightarrow \check{}x = \check{}y \& P\{x\}))\, \hat{z}(kiss_*'(\check{}z, m))$$

where O'_T is the translation of the dummy of category T.

Generally speaking, if $\phi(O'_a, d_a)'$ is obtained from ϕ' by replacing the element d_a of type a by the translation O'_a of a dummy element with the same type, then the proposed translation for a sentence ϕ in which d is the denied element will be

(177) $(\phi(O_a, d_a))' \& \neg (\phi')$.

As this translation gives certain undesirable results when we try to handle the scopes of adverbs like "necessarily" (in e.g. "necessarily Jóhn kisses Mary in the park"), Gabbay (personal communication) proposed to replace (176) by (177):

(178) $(\phi(O_a, d_a))' \& \S((\phi(O_a, d_a))' \rightarrow \phi')$

where § is the adverb in question. It is easily seen that (179) is equivalent with (176) in case $\S = \neg$.

If we now apply the same technique to question sentences, then (172) can be given the form:

(180) $(\phi(O_T, \text{john}))' \& ?((\phi(O_T, \text{john}))' \rightarrow \phi')$

which, by the formula $p \& ?(p \rightarrow q) \rightarrow ?q$ is seen to imply

(181) $(\phi(O_T, \text{john}))' \& ?\phi$

Let us now return to "-or not?" questions, as announced at the end of chapter five. Suppose that you want to prove to someone that four is an even number. After long and complicated calculations you look him in the face triumphantly and ask

(182) Is four an even number or not?

"Yes", he has to admit. But if you had asked

(183) Is four an even or an odd number?

the answer could have been neither "yes" nor "no". As we have seen, an "-or not?" question sometimes (perhaps most of the time) behaves like (183) in this respect. My hypothesis is,that in such cases the *not* is the denial of a specific element of the sentence. To take a simple example, I suppose that in such cases

(184) Is John ill or not?

has the following form:

(185) $?(\mathrm{Ill}(\mathrm{John})) \vee ?((\phi(O_{adj}, \mathrm{ill})) \& \neg (\mathrm{Ill}(\mathrm{John})))$

which clearly is not of the form $?p \vee ? \neg p$.

Universität Stuttgart
Institut für Lingvistik

Bibliography

Åqvist, L., 1965. ''A New Approach to the Logical Theory of Interrogatives. Analysis & Formalization.'', University of Uppsala.
Bäuerle, R., 1979. ''Questions and Answers'', in: R. Bäuerle, U. Egli, A. v. Stechow (Eds.) **Semantics from Different Poins of View.** Springer Verlag, Berlin.
Bolinger, D., 1978. ''Yes-No Questions are not Alternative Questions'' in: H. Hiž (Ed.), **Questions**., D. Reidel Publishing Company, Dordrecht/ Boston.
Cohen, R., 1929. ''What is a Question?'' **The Monist**, 39, p.350-364.
Egli, U., 1976. ''Zur Semantik des Dialogs''. Papiere des SFB 99, Konstanz.
Hamblin, C.L., 1976. ''Questons in Montague English'', in: B. H. Partee (Ed.) **Montague Grammar**, Academic Press, New York.
Hausser, R., 1977. ''The Logic of Questions and Answers''. Photocopied. (Reference taken from Bäuerle, 1979)
Higgingbotham, J.
May, R., 1978. ''Questions, Quantifiers and Crossing''. Photocopied. (Columbia University/Rockefeller University).
Hintikka, J., 1974. ''Questions about Questions''. in: M.K. Munitz, P.K. Unger (Eds.) **Semantics and Philosophy**, N.Y.U. Press, New York.
Hoepelman, J., 1980. ''Negation and Denial in Montague Grammar''. **Theoretical Linguistic 7.**
Karttunen, L., 1978. ''Syntax and Semantics of Questions'', in: H. Hiž (Ed.) **Question,** D. Reidel Publishing Company, Dordrecht/Boston.
Karttunen, L., Peters, S., 1979. ''Interrogative Quantifiers''. in: C. Rohrer (Ed.), **Time, Tense and Quantifiers, Niemeyer, Tübingen.**
Łukasiewicz, J., 1920. ''O logice trojwartosciowej'' (On three valued logic) (as mentioned in Rescher: Many valued Logic).
Prior, A.,
Prior, M., 1955. ''Erotetic Logic''. **Philosophical Review**, vol 64, pp. 43-59.
Rescher, N., 1966. ''The Logic of Commands''. Routledge & Keegan Paul, London.
Rescher, N., 1969. ''Many Valued Logic''. McGraw-Hill, New York.

Aravind K. Joshi

Varieties of Cooperative Responses in question-answer systems[1]

1. Introduction

1.1 In this paper, we will briefly review the types of cooperative responses desirable in question-answer (Q-A) systems. The overall scope of this paper will be limited in the following ways:
1. We will not be concerned with the details of how the specific responses are to be generated. Rather we will only briefly describe several types of cooperative responses and discuss some related issues.
2. Although a variety of cooperative behaviors can be expected from a helpful system in a Q-A environment (as discussed later), we will limit ourselves to only certain types of cooperative responses (to be specified later).
3. This is not a survey paper. **The material discussed here is based on the work carried out by a group of investigators[2] at the University of Pennsylvania over the past four years and some work that is in progress at present.**

1.2 We will be primarily concerned with Q-A systems which are designed for interacting with data bases. A data base (DB) for our present purpose can be regarded as a body of knowledge about a certain domain, consisting of a set of entities, their attributes, and relations among them, organized in some specific maner. For example, a university student data base might consist of entities such as

students, faculty, courses, grades,etc.

Students may have attributes such as

name, social security number, age, graduate or undergraduate,etc.

Some relations might be (students) **take** (a course), (faculty) **advise** (a student), (students) **enroll** (in a course), etc.
It is useful to make the distinction between the structure and content of

Ferenc Kiefer (ed.), Questions and Answers, 229–240.

the DB. The structure of the DB would be characterized by statements such as

students are either graduates or undergraduates.
students take courses.
faculty teach courses.
graduates teach courses
faculty advise students.

etc.

Content of the DB would be characterized by statements such as

John Smith is a graduate student.
John Smith teaches course CIS 500.
John Hamilton is a professor.
John Smith's age is 26.
etc.

The content of the DB can change from time to time (e.g. students leaving or entering, assignments of instructors to courses changing from year to year, etc.) The structure of the DB remains constant or if it does change, it changes much more slowly, i.e. over a much longer period of time as compared to the content.

1.3. The early work in natural language (NL) Q-A systems consisted of providing a very limited use of natural language. The NL interface was essentially a substitute for some formal query language. Two interesting developments took place subsequently.
1. Even though the NL interface provided was limited, users of such systems (because the interaction was via NL) began to expect more and more the kind of interaction they might expect in normal situations where NL is used. One specific expectation is that the NL interface deal with the situation when the user's view of the DB as expressed in NL is different from the system's view.
2. The DB's themselves increased in complexity (with respect to size, structure, and dynamic aspects) and the users could not be expected to know about the structure or even about the entire contents of the DB (i.e., one could not always assume that the user's view of information in the DB and how it is organized is the same as the system's view).

Thus we have to deal with the situation where the user's view of the DB and the system's view of the DB are disparate. Most of the types of cooperative behaviors we will be concerned with are related to this issue. Other types deal with responses explaining the structure of the DB and implicit requests for monitoring states of dynamic data bases.

2. Certain Types of Cooperative Responses:

2.1. The disparity between the views of the user (U) and the system (S) can be with respect to the content of the DB. Such a failure can be called extensional.

Example:

U: How many students received the grade A in CIS 500 in Fall 1980?
One of U's presumptions here is that
CIS 500 was offered in Fall 1980.

Suppose this is false. In this case, a response **None** to U's query would be misleading, because it would implicitly confirm the false presumption. A helpful response here consists of correcting the false presumption.

S: CIS 500 was not offered in Fall 1980.

This type of response can be called a **corrective indirect response.** If one presumption, say, P1 'entails' another, say, P2, the failure of P1 would, of course, cause P2 to fail also. A good strategy here is to correct the least (respect to a partial ordering) failing presumption(s).

2.2 Often there may not be any inconsistency between the views of U and S, however, the direct reponse has to be accompanied by supportive information in order to meet U's expectations as discerned from U's view of the DB.

U: What are the phone numbers of all professors in Computer Science?

A response listing only the phone numbers, say, 4958, 7945, 7754, ...

is useless unless accompanied by the associated names of the professors. Hence, the appropriate response is

S: Smith, 4958, Jones, 7945, Hamilton, 7754, ...

Such a response can be called **a supportive indirect response.** Such responses are related to the so-called ''conclusive answers'' of Hintikka (this volume).

2.3 Sometimes additional information beyond the direct response can be provided. (This case should be distinguished from the one discussed in Section 2.2). The simplest situation when such a response is useful is when the direct response to a yes-no question is **No.**

U: Is John Smith a senior?

Assume that **John Smith** is not a senior. The direct response is then **No.** The system, S, can try to vary the 'focus' of the query.[3] In other words S tries to answer a different but related question. Assume that the system has determined **senior** as the focus. A helpful response here would be

S: No, he is a junior.

Such a response would be called a **suggestive indirect response.**

Responses described in (2.1), (2.2), and (2.3) above and other related reponses are provided in the CO-OP system developed by Kaplan (1979). Further details of design and implementation are given in Kaplan and Joshi (1978), Kaplan, Mays, and Joshi (1979), McKeown (1979), Kaplan (1981). Some theoretical issues are discussed in Kaplan (1979), Joshi (1979, 1981), and Kaplan (1981).

2.4 We now consider the case where the disparity between the views of U and S is not with respect to content but with respect to the structure of the DB. Such failures can be called intensional. Extensional failure is based on the current contents of the DB, while an intensional failure is based on the structure or organization. For example, (2a) presumes among others) (2b), (2c), and (2d).

(2a) U: Which faculty members teach the course CIS 500?
(2b) Faculty members teach courses.
(2c) Faculty members teach CIS 500.
(2d) CIS 500 is a course.
etc.

(2b) above is subject to intensional failure if the DB does not permit the relation **teach** between the entities **faculty** and **course.** An extensional failure of (2b) will occur if indeed the teach relation exists between faculty and **course** but there are no instances in the DB of a faculty member teaching any course. Note that (2b) is a precondition for the truth of (2c) which is an extensional presumption.

Although a presumption which fails intensionally will of necessity fail extensionally, it is important to differentiate between them since an intentional failure that occurs will occur consistently for a given DB structure, whereas extensional failure is a transitory function of the current content of the DB.[4]

Example:
U: How many undergraduates taught courses in Fall 1980?

Assume the DB structure permits the relation **teach** between **faculty** and **course**, as well as between **graduate students** and **course** (as graduate students are often conscripted to teach some introductory undergraduate courses in Computer Science!). Since the relation **teach** is not permitted between **undergraudate students** and **course**, the presumption in U's query that

Undergraudates teach courses

which is an intensional presumption, is false. Hence, at the least S must correct this false structural presumption. A response **None** would be misleading as in Section 2.1. However, S can be more helpful. While checking for the truth or falsity of the presumption

Undergraduates teach courses.

the system has come across some information which is likely to be useful to U. Of course, what this information is depends on how the information about the DB structure is organized and how it is searched by S. Let us assume that in our case S searches over the domain and range of the relation **teach** in the representation of the DB structure. Then a helpful response S could produce would be as follows.

S: Undergraduates do not teach courses **(corrective response)**
Faculty members teach courses.
Graduate students teach courses.

Cooperative responses for intensional failures of the type described above have been investigated by Mays (1980 a, b, c). The distinction between extensional and intensional failures is not always so sharp as discussed above. Some failures depend on the currency of data. For example, (see Mays 1980 b) in a naval DB the question **''What is the position of the Kitty Hawk?''**presumes that the current data about position is available. If the update takes place at the same time (or almost at the same time) as the physical event takes place then on some occasions the current data is available (i.e., when the time at which the question was asked, say t_q, coincides with the time when the update was received, say t_u). Now suppose that $t_q \neq t_u$, S could then respond as follows.

S: I don't know the current position but the position at the last update was X.

Note that in this case, U's presumption that the data about the position is current has failed extensionally. If however, the time lag between the processing of the update and time of actual occurrence of the event is always sufficiently long, then the same presumption (that the data about position is current) can be regarded as failing intensionally because **the data about position is never current.** Thus the helpful corrective response is to let the user know that the current data about position is never available (Mays 1980 b).

2.5 When S discerns that U has some misconceptions about the structure of the DB (as in Section 2.4 above) the corrective response may have to be more than a sentence i.e., it may have to be a text length response. (We already have a very simple instance of this in the Example in Section 2.4). A similar situation arises when U is interacting with the system not for the purpose of retrieveing some specific content but for acquainting himself/herself with the structure of the DB. U's query is then directly concerned with the structure of the DB. In such cases, it is not enough to present the information available in DB schemas. It is necessary to present structural differences between entities, or describe relationships that hold between entities. This type of response could be used not only for specific questions about the DB structure, but also as supportive explanations for yes-no questions or as explanations for structural presumption failures (Sections 2.2 and 2.4).

Since these responses can be several sentences, it is not sufficient to present the information as a succession of sentences; the set of sentences needs to be organized as a text, using certain organizational principles such as compare and contrast, top-down description, illustration by example, etc., as well as appropriate syntactic devices.

Example:

U: What is the difference between a part-time student and a full-time student?

A possible response is:

S: Both are graduate students, going for MS or PhD degrees. Full-time students, however, take 3 or 4 courses per semester, while part-time students take only 1 or 2, usually in addition to holding a full time job. Consequently, it takes a part-time student longer than a full-time student to finish the degree.

A yes-no question like:

U: Is John Smith taking 4 courses?
might be answered by
S: No John Smith is a part-time student and part-time students take only 1 or 2 courses per semester.

McKeown (1980 a, b) has investigated such responses and is currently designing a system in the context of a DB system.

2.6 So far we have been concerned with DB's where implicitly we have assumed that the DB is static. However, this is not always the case. DB content is updated from time to time. This environment of a dynamic DB requires that the system take initiative and provide additional information along some new dimensions going beyond those considered in Sections 2.2-2.5. We will not describe the full range of responses needed in this dynamic context. We will describe briefly one interesting situation, which we will call **implicit alerters.** In a dynamic DB the user will often request that the system monitor certain states (more precisely changes of states). For example, the user may request **"Let me know if John Smith's grade point average drops below 3.0."**This is a request for setting up an alerter (monitor). We will call such an alerter an explicit alerter as the user has explicitly requested the setting up of this monitor. However, sometimes the user's query, under certain circumstances, can be interpreted (in addition to being a query requesting some information) as an implied request for setting up a monitor.

Example:

A pre-registration period is a specific period in the semester preceding the semester for which the students are expected to register (e.g. a specific period in Spring 1981 for Fall 1981 registration).

Let us assume that we are in the pre-registration period, and U asks the question:

U: Has John Smith registered for CIS 500 yet?

If John Smith has indeed registered then the answer is **Yes.** If he has not then the answer is No; however, in this case, since the stated event could still take place, the system could interpret the question as an implied request for an alerter and respond as follows.

S: No, but I will let you know if he does.

The decision to set up an implicit alerter depends at least on the structure of the query, knowledge about the domain, and the discourse context. These issues about when implicit alerters should be set up, and equally importantly, when they should be turned off are being investigated in Mays (1980) and Mays et al. (1981).

3. A general formulation:

Most of the responses described in Section 2 are concerned with the situation when there is a disparity between the user's view of the structure and content of the DB and that of the system's. It is useful to try to place this work in a more general framework for handling misconceptions. This is clearly a very difficult problem as we are involved here with almost all the major problems in interactive discourse. However, we can limit ourselves deliberately to some very particular aspects of cooperation and try to construct a general framework for dealing with misconceptions. Such an attempt has been made by Joshi (1981) using the notion of mutual beliefs (MB). MB here refers to that part of shared beliefs of the system (S) and the user (U) that are discerned by S and U only as a result of the interaction, more precisely a certain segment of the interaction. MB is to be distinguished, for example, from other shared beliefs about general knowledge of the domain, which remains invariant from interaction to interaction. We can define cooperative behavior as both giving a truthful and informative response (i.e., for example, providing the requested information) and 'squaring away' the discrepancies in MB's discerned during the interaction. That is, (i) S truthfully and informatively answers U's question by providing the requested information, and (ii) at the end of the interaction (with respect to the given query), if S has discerned any misconceptions on behalf of U about the structure or content of the DB (again with respect to the given query) then S informs U about it and similarly U informs S.

This 'squaring away' response need not be completely symmetric. In fact, in man-machine interactions when the machine plays the role of a helpful agent, these asymmetries are likely to be accentuated (see Joshi (1981) for further details).

There are two important situations to consider here. (i) S discerns a misconception on the part of U and unless the resulting MB's are 'squared away' there is no way S can truthfully and informatively respond to U's query. Hence S must clarify the situation first and then respond to U's modified request. The responses in Section 2.1 and 2.4 are examples of this situation. (ii) Although S has discerned that there is some misconception on the part of U, it is possible for S, based on the information provided by U, to truthfully and informatively answer U's reqiest. At this point S has responded to U's request and the interaction could end. In fact, following certain conventions of cooperation, it would be quite appropriate for the interaction to end at this point. However, according to our definition of cooperativeness the relevant MB's have not been squared away. Hence, S and U must continue the interaction until the MB's are squared away.

Situations described in (ii) above arise, for example, when a part of the description of an entity is adequate to identify the referent and therefore answer the question. The remaining part of the description may or may not match because, for example, the system and the user may have different beliefs about it. In this case, the system, in addition to answering the question, must square away any disparities in the mutual beliefs. For example consider the follwing interaction:

U: Has the car Reg. No. 576 belonging to John Smith been found?

Assume that **Reg. No.**(registration number) is a unique identifier for cars in the DB. Also assume that U believes that the car belongs to John Smith; however the system (S) believes that it belongs to Harry Jones (because, for example, the ownership has changed recently and the DB has been updated). Note that S can respond to the question, although part of the description has not matched. Hence, S gives the direct response followed by a 'squaring away' response.

S: Yes. However, did you know that the car does not belong to John Smith? It now belongs to Harry Jones.

If the interaction is completely symmetric, U would respond by

U: I didn't know that.

The above example is a simple illustration of what we have in mind. Joshi (1981) as suggested a revision of Grice's maxim of quality to account systematically for the behavior described above. The modification is as follows. Under the revised maxim of quality, (i) S should not say anything which is false, (ii) further, based on S's assessment of MB's, it should not be possible for U, from what S has said, say Q, to infer something which S believes to be false. If there is such a possibility then after saying Q, S should provide further information to 'square away' the MB's. In other words, S should not say anything which may imply (for U) something which S believes to be false. (For further details and implications of this view, see Joshi (1981)).

4. Conclusion:

We have briefly reviewed certain types of cooperative responses in Q-A systems. In particular, we have considered the situation when the user's and the system's view of the structure and/or the content of the DB are disparate; and we have illustrated the different types of responses by means of examples. We have also considered responses which explain the struture of the DB and responses which are implicit alerters for monitoring stater of a data base that is being updated from time to time. We have also briefly described a general formulation of a specific type of cooperative behavior consisting of giving a truthful and informative response and 'squaring away' any discrepancies in the mutual beliefs discerned during the interaction.

The material discussed in this paper is based on the work carried out by a group of investigators at the University of Pennsylvania.

University of Pennsylvania
The Moore School of Electrical Engineering

Notes

[1] This work is partially supported by a grant from the National Science Foundation, MCS 79-08401. An earlier version of this paper was presented at the Conference on Questions and Answers, Visegrad, Hungary, May 1980.

[2] Kathy Filliben, Jerry Kaplan (now at the Stanford University), Sitaram Lanka, Eric Mays, Kathy McKeown, Tim Finin, Bonnie Webber, and the author. The work reported here is only a part of the overall activity in natural langage proccessing at the University of Pennsylvania.

[3] By 'focus' we mean the linguistic notion of focus and not the notion of 'local focus' used in some recent work in artificial intelligence, especially that of Candy Sidner.

[4] We do not imply that the DB structure is not subject to change. However, such a change usually implies a fundamental modification of the organization of the domain that is modelled by the DB.

References

We have listed here only those references which pertain to the cooperative responses described in this paper. This is not a bibliography for works on question-answer systems.

Joshi, A.K., ''Influence of the problem context'', **Parasession on Topics in Interactive Discourse, Proceedings of the 18th Annual Meeting of Association for Computational Linguistics, Philadelphia,**June 1979.

Joshi, A.K., ''Role of mutual beliefs in question-answer systems'', to appear in the **Proceedings of the Colloquium on Mutual Knowledge,**Social Science Research Council (SSRC) of Great Britain, held at Guildford, England, September 1980. (To appear as a book edited by N. Smith, published by the Academic Press, 1981).

Kaplan, S.J. and Joshi, A. K., ''Cooperative responses: An application of discourse inference to data base query systems, **Proceedings of the 2nd National Conference of Canadian Society for Computational Studies of Intelligence,**Toronto, Canada, July 1978.

Kaplan, S.J., ''Cooperative Responses from a Portable Natural Language Data Base Query System,'' **PhD dissertation, Department of Computer and Information Science, University of Pennsylvania, Philadelphia, PA, June 1979.**

Kaplan, S.J., "Loaded questions," **in Elements of Discours Understanding** (eds. A.K. Joshi, B.L. Webber, and I.A. Sag), Cambridge University Press, to appear in June 1981.

Mays, E., ''Correcting misconceptions about data base structure'', **Proceedings of the Conference of Canadian Society for Computational Studies of Intelligence,**Victoria, British Columbia, Canada, May 1980 (a).

Mays, E., ''A semantic data model for natural language interface: application of cooperative systems,'' **M.S. Thesis, Department of Computer and Information Science,** University of Pennsylvania, Philadelphia, PA 1980 (b).

Mays, E., ''Failures in natural language systems: application to data base query systems,'' **Proceedings of the first meeting of the American Association for Artificial Intelligence**(AAAI), Stanford , California, August 1980 (c).

Mays, E., Lanka, S., Joshi, A.K., and Webber, B.L., ''Natural language interaction with dynamic knowledge bases: monitoring behavior'', submitted to the **International Joint Conference on Artificial Intelligence (IJCAI),** 1981.

McKeown, K.R., ''Generating relevant explanations: natural language responses to questions about data base structure'', **Proceedings of the first meeting of the American Association for Artificial Intelligence (AAAI),**Stanford, California.

McKeown, K.R., ''Generating Descriptions and Explanations, ''Natural Language Response to Questions about Data Base Structure'', **Technical Report,** Department of Computer and Information Science, University of Pennsylvania, Philadelphia, March 1980 (b).

McKeown, K., "Generating natural language: Deciding what to say next," submitted to the **International Joint Conference on Artificial Intelligence,** 1981.

Manfred Pinkal

Questions of believing

1. Preliminary Remarks

Questions of believing are the topic of this paper, in a threefold sense: First, the paper is concerned with some questions of belief semantics. Second, and mainly, a specific aspect of the semantics of belief questions will be analyzed, of questions like (a), the propositional component of which is embedded in a construction with a verb expressing the attitude of belief.

(a) Do you believe that John loves Mary?

Third, the basis of my theoretical remarks are intuitions about readings and meaning of belief questions and of answers to such questions. Intuitions in this area are no strong intuitions, in general; particularly, the intuitions I start from are neither evident nor are they verified by empirical methods. Whether they are correct is, at least to some degree, rather a question of believing.

The starting point of my considerations has been a property of belief questions in German and French (and in several different languages), which is not very salient, at first sight. In German, three standard answers are provided for (b), the correlate of question (a), and there is a clear difference in content between all three of them:

(b) Glaubst du, dass Hans Maria liebt?
(c) Ja (, ich glaube es)
(d) (Ja,) Hans liebt Maria
(e) Ich glaube, ja

The same holds for French (cf. (b')—(e')), but not, e.g., for English.

(b') Crois-tu que Jean aime Marie?
(c') Oui, je le crois
(d') Oui, il l'aime
(e') Je crois que oui

Ferenc Kiefer (ed.), Questions and Answers, 241–256.

(c)/(c') and (d)/(d') may be translated to (c'') and (d''), resp.

(c'') Yes, I do
(d'') Yes, he does

However, it is difficult to find an English translation for (e)/(e′). These are definitely no plain surface inversions of a (c) answer. The belief construction in (e) does not merely echo the belief construction in question (b); it is rather an independent and semantically motivated modification of the affirmative answer[1]. Its communicative content is best reflected by (e''), but (e'') misses the point.

(e'') I think so

The embedded *ja/oui* cannot be interpreted in the sense of (c''), since under this reading (e) would turn out to be an implicite iterative belief construction, which is highly implausible in the context given. If, on the other hand, the *ja* of (e) is assigned a reading according to (d''), (e) coincides with (c). However, (c) and (e), as well as (c') and (e'), differ in content. In the following, I will, among other things, comment on the question how to obtain this difference, and my answer will have some implications for the semantics of belief questions and the semantics of belief.

Before starting, let me make three more short preliminary remarks. First, the sample sentences employed in this paper are mainly taken from German. The reason why no English evidence is referred to, is that the semantics of *believe* is more restricted that that of *glauben* and *croire* : certain phenomena, e.g., the one described above, which can be observed in German and French do not occur—or at least do not occur in such a clear mode—in English.

I mainly use *German* examples simply because German is the language I am best acquainted with. I will give interlinear versions and English paraphrases where this is necessary. It seems necessary, first of all, to indicate the content of the verb *glauben: glauben* is more ambivalent and flexible than its English counterpart, and it can be used to express a definitely weaker epistemic attitude than *believe;* consequently, in some contexts it is better translated by *think* or *suppose* (cf. (e'') above). This wide semantics is not ideosyncratic for German; it is shared, e.g., by French *croire*. Thus, it seems not to be a casual ambiguity, but a semantic phenomenon of greater distribution and greater significance.

Second, my comments on the semantics of belief questions will be completely informal—apart from some formulations in section 5. I could have given a formal account of belief semantics in terms of a well-established system of epistemic logic or logic of subjective probabilities, which would have been uncontroversial and unproblematic, as far as the topic of this paper is concerned[2], and the same could have been done for the semantics of questions. However, the arguments following are not dependent on particular semantic stipulations, and the interesting results are located in the borderline area between semantics and pragmatics for which a proper formalisation has yet to be developed, anyway.

The latter statement already anticipates my third remark: You should not expect important contributions to the traditional issues of question theory, or to the problems in the center of the contemporary discussions on propositional attitudes[3]. It is rather some borderline phenomena, one aspect of the interplay between semantic conventions and pragmatic principles, this paper primarily is about.

2. Assertory belief sentences

German *glauben* and French *croire* are ambivalent, more flexible than English *believe* . One may account for this fact by attaching two readings to each of these verbs, a ''strong'' and a ''weak'' one. The strong reading can be paraphrased by *take to be true* ; the weak one by *take to be probable at least to some specific degree* .[4]

This strong/weak reading distinction correlates with the difference between first person (singular present) use of *glauben* , and third person (to say it more general: 'normal') use. That first person use of *glauben* behaves irregular, in some sense, is a well-known and early recognized fact, the clearest evidence for which is provided by Moore's paradox of saying and disbelieving: (f) is a completely normal contingent sentence, whereas (g) is highly peculiar, if not contradictory.

(f) John loves Mary, but Bill doesn't believe it.
(g) John loves Mary, but I don't believe it.

Now, German *glauben* (as well as its counterparts in other languages with ''flexible belief'') in its first person use is additionally irregular in that it has to be assigned nearly always the weak reading (cf. (h)), whereas normal use (i) is ambivalent between strong and weak reading, but tends to assume the strong one.

(h) Ich glaube, dass Hans Maria liebt
(i) Bill glaubt, dass Hans Maria liebt.

As I think, Moore's paradox and this semantic asymmetry between first and third person reading are due to the same fundamental fact, i.e. the narrow connection between (strong) belief and assertion which has been discovered early, and has been stated by different philosophers in different ways.[5] I will give a short account of how this asymmetry might be explained, and will come back to the topic in section 5.

To assert a proposition Φ conversationally implies that one believes it —this is an immediate consequence of Grice's maxim of quality (cf. Grice (1975)). On the other hand, to believe a proposition Φ (in the strong sense) justifies the assertion of Φ.[6] The former statement refers to a very general pragmatic principle, whereas the latter concerns semantics, i.e. the semantics of (strong) belief. Both assumptions together amount to a conversational equivalence between plain assertion, like in (j), and assertion of strong belief, like in the supposed strong reading of (h).

(j) Hans liebt Maria.

Strong interpretation of (i) implies that the speaker feels sure about (j) to a degree which justifies assertion; and this again is exactly what plain assertion of Φ allows to conclude conversationally.

According to the manner maxim of Grice, the briefer and more perspicuous of two equally informative sentences has to be employed, provided no secondary (e.g. stylistic) purposes are pursued. Thus, since (h) is used very frequently instead of plain assertion, it cannot be used in the reading which is equivalent to plain assertion: it has to be exclusively used in its weak version, unless particular contextual circumstances prevail which, e.g., induce a contrastive interpretation.[7]

3. Belief Questions

To give an informal explication of the weak first person use, the verb *glauben* has been assigned two readings, in the preceding section.

Which of these readings is conversationally admitted in belief questions? This question can be precisified, for third person direct question as well as indirect belief question in general turn out to be completely regular counterparts of the normal assertory use:

(k) Glaubt Bill, dass Hans Maria liebt?
(k') Does Bill believe that John loves Mary?
(1) Es ist gleichgültig, ob du glaubst, dass Hans Maria liebt.
(l') It doesn't matter whether you believe that John loves Mary.

The interesting remaining case is the second person present direct question. How has (b) to be interpreted according to the rules of conversation?

(b) Glaubst du, dass Hans Maria liebt?

Strong reading, as it seems, can be excluded, with an argument directly corresponding to the argument for first person assertory use. The briefest, and most straightforward way to find out whether Bill (strongly) believes that John loves Mary is to ask him (m)/(m'):

(m) Liebt Hans Maria?
(m') Does John love Mary?

Belief question, in strong interpretation, and plain direct question, ask for the same information (provided the relation between strong belief and assertion stated in the preceding section actually holds); therefore, (b) —strong reading—is ruled out by the Gricean manner rules, as unnecessarily complicated.

Actually, certain differences in communicative function of (b) and (m) can be saved even in case *glauben* is restricted to strong interpretation. By the direct question, the addressee is requested to commit himself to the truth of either the fact that John loves Mary, or the fact that he doesn't. And this is slightly different from what is requested by a belief question, which might, under this aspect, be properly paraphrased by (n).

(n) Given the case, I would ask you now (m): are you disposed to commit you to the truth of the affirmative answer?

This difference has some concrete conversational consequences: (m) can be used as an order to find out whether John loves Mary, (b) cannot.

(b) as opposed to (m), on the other hand, can be used to ask a sincere information question although one feels already sure about the truth of (j), and expects the addressee to be disposed to give the wrong answer; direct question, in this case, is a request to undergo an untenable commitment. Thus, although the information yielded by direct answers to (m) and (b), would be more or less identical in the case of strong reading of *glauben,* the respective communicative 'side effects' differ.

However, in German (French, and other 'flexible belief' languages) it is not merely these side effects which make belief questions grammatical constructions in their own right. The communicative importance of belief constructions is e.g. clearly shown by the *wh*-belief questions in German. Since there is a constraint upon *wh*-movement in German which prevents movement from inside *dass*-complements, there is no conservative syntactic means to form the belief correlate to questions (o) and (p).[7a]

(o) Wer liebt Maria?
(p) Wer liebt Hans?
(o') Who loves Mary?
(p') Who does John love?

Nevertheless, *wh*-belief questions are often used in German, and they are built either by ignoring the constraint, at the cost of a quite low degree of acceptability ((q), (r)); or by employing an ideosyncratic semi-parenthetic construction which has as far as I can see no parallels in German and can hardly be categorized in conventional syntactic terms ((s), (t)).[8]

(q) Wer glaubt du, dass Maria liebt?
(r) Wen glaubst du, dass Hans liebt?
(s) Wer, glaubst du, liebt Maria?
(t) Wen, glaubst du, liebt Hans?

Besides this syntactic evidence, German native speakers' intuitions are definitive about a strong difference between plain question and belief question. Since strong reading does not establish a sufficient difference, belief questions will have to be restricted to the weak reading. As a consequence of this decision, (b) turns out to be an exact erothetic equivalent to the first person assertory use (h). This solution appeared to be most reasonable and obvious, from the beginning. But, how then to explain the difference between the three standard affirmative answers (c), (d) and (e), which has been stated in section 1?

4. Answers

Standard answers to belief questions in German (and French) are (c), (d) and (e). Strong interpretation of *glauben* renders (c) and (d) equivalent with respect to their informativeness. Weak interpretation of *glauben* leads to different interpretations for (c) and (d). (d) is an implicative answer: it entails the direct affirmative *ja* , which counts as a paraphrase of (h), under the weak reading. This, however, means that answers (c) and (e) coincide, which is in contradiction to intuitions and conversational principles.

The inadequacy can, however, be removed by looking once more at the pragmatics of belief questons. First person assertory belief sentence and second person belief question are similar in that restriction to strong belief renders an informational equivalence to direct assertion and question, resp., and therefore can be excluded. This accounts for the fact that second person belief questions lack the 'tendency to strong reading', which third person questions share with third person assertions. But apart from this minor agreement the conversational consequences are different: Implicatures of assertions cannot be directly transferred to the corresponding questions. To assert the unequivocal and less complicated sentence in case one is sure about the facts concerned is a strategy which will not go wrong, under normal conversational circumstances. To ask the more restrictive and less complicated question in case one wants to be made sure about a fact can carry certain drawbacks with it. The claim to a less informative answer than unrestricted affirmation or negation is, is given up in advance.[9] Thus, although a specification of (b) towards strong reading is blocked by rules of conversation, the strong reading alternative is not excluded, when (b) is uttered. A proper paraphrase of (b), the adequacy of the two-readings interpretation taken for granted, is

(u) Do you believe, at least in the weak sense, that John loves Mary?

Now, the direct answer turns out to be the most general one: it leaves open whether the truth of (h) is taken for granted or merely taken to be probable to some degree. Both (d) and (e) are more informative than (directly) requested: (d) asserts belief in the strong sense, (e) asserts unspecified belief, and implicates that it is not belief in the strong sense.

At first glance, it seems to contradict to this interpretation that (d) and (e) as indirect answers are the most usual ones, whereas (c) normally is felt to be somewhat unsatisfactory, at least in writing or in ''neutral'' pronounciation.[10] But this is a fairly general phenomenon which can be observed with questions having a highly general propositional component, containing, e.g., an existential quantification, or a disjunction. The answer *yes* for both (v) and (w) is not the answer the speaker usually wants to hear (whereas *no* is conversationally appropriate in either case).

(v) Did anybody of you take my car-keys away?
(w) Do you want coffee or tea?

(b), as well as (v) and (w), is usually intended to evoke an implicative answer, an answer which comments on the strength of certainty of the matter in question.

The comments I made on German belief questions are intended to hold for French and other languages with flexible belief, to, but not for English. I should say a word about English belief constructions, here. Uses of the verb *believe* cannot shift from strong to weak reading, since there is no distinct weak reading of *believe* (its place is occupied by *think*). Since for *believe* the same conversational effects hold, as for strong reading *glauben,* first person assertory sentence as well as second person question both deviate in their content from 'normal' use: first person present use has an emphatic or irrational component[11] ; belief questions are employed to obtain the communicative side effects mentioned at the end of section 3. Questions like (a) are, as far as I know, not unusual but of much lesser distribution, than *glauben*-sentences in German.

5 Semantic considerations

To explain the ambivalence and flexibility of *glauben/croire* in their different uses, two readings have been employed, which we introduced in section 2 by the informal paraphrases *to take to be true* and *to take to be probable at least to some specific degree.* Actually, I do not believe that there exist two readings, as far as the strong/weak belief distinction is concerned. To give the reasons for this opinion, I have to go a bit into the details of the semantics of attitude verbs which express beliefs.[12]

glauben indeed has at least three different readings, but on a completely different level than the one of strong/weak distinction. These readings are attached to different syntactic frames, which losely correspond to English constructions with the verb *believe*. One of them (*glauben/believe* + complement) has been exemplified and dicussed in this paper, so far. For the two other variants, verb + indirect object + complement and verb + *an/in*-PP or *daran, dass* -clause (the latter without direct counterpart in English), examples are given in (x) and (y).

(x) Bill glaubt Harry, dass Hans Maria liebt.
(x') Bill believes Harry that John loves Mary.
(y) Bill glaubt daran, dass Hans Maria liebt.
(y') Bill believes in John's loving Mary.

The common semantic basis of the three versions of *glauben/believe* sentences seems to be their bearings upon possible actions of the person(s) referred to by their subject. To believe that Φ, as well as to believe somebody that Φ or to believe in Φ is, roughly speaking, to take Φ for granted with respect to one's actions and decisions.[13] What is different between the three versions, are the sources of the certainty about Φ. Belief is—to put things again very sloppily —epistemically based in the complement case, based on a social, communicative act (Harry's assertion of (j)), in (x), and it is irrational, unconditional, 'doxastic' in a narrow sense, in case (y).

I finish this digression here, and restrict myself to the 'epistemic' version again. To state a belief of a person in terms of a simple complement construction involves a reference to the current epistemic state of this person, the portion of world knowledge available to him.[14] Now, the most straightforward way to relate a person's belief to his current epistemic state is to define *glauben/believe* in terms of subjective probabilities with respect to the epistemic state of that person. Strong and weak reading could then be represented by two alternative thresholds for likelihood, as is already suggested by their informal paraphrases. The following paraphrase of *A glaubt, dass* Φ is a first cautious step towards a precisification of the meaning of *glauben* .

(z) With respect to his actions/decisions, A takes Φ for granted because he ascribes to Φ a probability greater than p_1/p_2 on the basis of his current epistemic state.

A probabilistic precisification of the strong/weak belief distinction running roughly along these line has been proposed, e.g., by Kutschera in (1976). In this version, some shortcomings of the strong/weak distinction can be shown quite easily.

First, it is impossible to specify proper threshold values for strong as well as for weak belief. 1 (≙ absolute certainty) is obviously to restrictive for strong belief, 0,5 (≙ more likely than the negation) will usually be too weak for the weak version. Since there are no further prominent candidates, the respective thresholds have to be considered as vague.

Secondly, the required strength of belief corresponds to the importance of the actions/decisions under consideration: in this respect, to believe that you had three eggs for breakfast, is (gradually) different from believing that you have got enough money with you for having a breakfast, and this again differs, with respect to the strength of certainty required, from believing that you switched off the gas after frying the eggs (''normal'' circumstances provided). There should be said much more about the relationship between strength of certainty and (classes of) actions. However, I hope that the main point of the argument is clearly shown by the argument, though: probability thresholds for verbs of believing have to be defined as context-dependent, and they can assume definitely more than two possible values.

Thirdly, the strong/weak reading distinction cannot be properly accounted for as an ambiguity: In third person use *glauben* is normally employed without being desambiguated. With respect to the strong/weak distinction *glauben* rather behaves like the adjective *tall:* as *tall* tends to have quite precise standard readings (e.g. 'tall for a male adult middle-European'), it may be used in a less restrictive sense, and without being specified whether it is intended to have one or the other precise denotation, *glauben/croire* tends to adopt "the strong reading", but can also be used in a less precise way.[15]

To sum up, both supposed readings of *glauben* are vague, both are context-dependent, and they establish no ambiguity, but are rather related like different possible precisifications of a scalar adjective. After all, their semantic descriptions differ only in that they refer to different places on the same scale. Thus, it seems plausible to dispense with the two readings, and to treat *glauben* as a context-dependent scalar term. Formulation (z) then, would have to be replaced by (z'), where $\mathcal{A}_s$ is the class of actions/ decisions under consideration in the situation of utterance s, and $p_s \in [0.5,1]$ depends in its actual value on $\mathcal{A}_s$.

(z') With respect to $\mathcal{A}_s$, A takes Φ for granted because he ascribes to Φ a probability greater than p_s, on the basis of his current epistemic state.

This 'definition' of *glauben* has to be that complicated because it has to take into account at least the following essential semantic properties:

(i) the narrow relation to a—contextually variable—class of actions;
(ii) the narrow connection with the epistemic state of the speaker;
(iii) the fact that action level and epistemic level are set into relation by the notion of 'likelihood requiring to take a thing for granted'.

Of course, (z') is only intended to indicate one (although a relevant) dimension of the semantics of belief, and even with respect to that dimension it bears serious shortcomings. Two major ones are that, on one hand, (z') employs vague concepts which should be made more precise (e.g. the concept of action, the attitude of 'taking a thing for granted'), and, on the other hand, certain parts of (z') must be regarded as overspecifications: In normal situations of utterance, $\mathcal{A}_s$ is rarely completely precise, p is never, and $\mathcal{A}$ and p are related to one another only by means of a weak correlation, a kind of ''fuzzy mapping''.

Whereas the first shortcoming can only be remedied by giving the concepts in question a sound pragmatic foundation, the latter problem can be solved in a quite straightforward semantic way: (z') can be embedded (a formal semantic precisification of its terminology provided) in a system of supervaluation semantics, by reinterpreting the 'situation index' s as an index ranging over idealized complete precisifications, and reconstructing situations as sets of specifications. The immediate effect is a fuzzification of the situation parameters (of $\mathcal{A}$ and p, in the case of (z')); the interrelation between different parameters can be described probabilistically (cf. Fine (1975), Pinkal (1979)).

6. More answers

The semantic considerations of section 5 lead to reinterpretations of the semantic/pragmatic phenomena discussed before which seem to be more natural than the ones provided by the two-readings approach. The first thing to be explained in terms of the 'scalar analysis' of *glauben* is the intuitive plausibility of the strong/weak reading distinction itself. This distinction seems to be due to the special status assertions have, compared with different types of actions.

In some respects, assertion of Φ is a (generic) action which is a completely regular candidate for membership in the context-dependent class of relevant actions $\mathcal{A}$. In several different respects, assertion differs: Assertion is a distinct and very frequently used action type. It is hard to conceive of actions the consequences of which are more straightforwardly dependent on the truth of Φ in a systematic way, than it is the case with assertions of Φ. Finally, assertions of Φ are related to the question of Φ 's being true in a way which induces a relatively invariant and fairly high probability threshold for the context-dependent value assignment of *glauben* : In asserting Φ , the speaker commits himself to the truth of Φ not only on a more or less abstract intellectual level, but assumes—to some extent—the responsibility for negative consequences of actions the addressee could perform, relying on the truth of Φ. From these reasons, 'to take Φ for granted with respect to assertion of Φ' is a standard precisification of *glauben* , as well as 'tall for an adult' is a standard precisification for *tall* .[16] This standard precisification, which is completely due to pragmatic features of assertory actions, as compared with different $\mathcal{A}$-candidates, is what I called the strong reading of *glauben* . By contrast, all weaker precisifications are subsumed under the 'weak reading', but I suppose there does not exist one weak reading of *glauben* (maybe a maximally imprecise use).

Explanations of the first person irregularity and the tendency to strong reading in normal use follow directly form these considerations. The semantic assumption which has been introduced in section 2 for this purpose, turns out to be a trivial consequence of how strong belief is established, i.e. as standard precisification in terms of the generic act of asserting Φ. Normal third person use tends to strong reading since vague concepts tend to assume their standard precisification (provided there exists one). First person use allows all precisifications of $\mathcal{A}$, with the exception of those containing the assertion of the belief object—this would directly cause the conversational problems discussed in section 2.

In the case of second person belief questions, the restriction to the standard precisification is blocked. Uses of belief questions will therefore tend to be of relatively low precision. According to (z'), the belief question (al) can be reformulated as (bl):

(a1) Do you believe that Φ?
(b1) Is there any precisification s admitted by the situation of utterance such that you take Φ for granted with respect to $\mathcal{A}_s$ because you ascribe to Φ 's truth a probability greater than p_s?

The respective paraphrases of answers (c), (d) and (e) are:

(c1) Yes, there is.
(d1) Yes, there is such an s, and assertion of Φ is member of $\mathcal{A}_s$.
(e1) Yes, there is such an s, and assertion of Φ is not member of $\mathcal{A}_s$.

The fact that (d) and (e) are normally preferred to the direct answer (c) seems, in the scalar analysis, still more natural than in the two-reading approach. Belief questions contain a kind of existential quantification—as vague questions do in general—and therefore request an implicative answer. Cf. (f1), and the answers (g1) and (h1).

(f1) Is John rich?
(g1) He makes more than 100.000 dollars a year.
(h1) His daughter drives a Lamborghini.

Plain affirmation will be felt to be insufficient, in most cases. What is requested by the speaker of (f1), is a direct or indirect precisification of the predicate *rich* such that it holds true of John.

Example (f1) indicates a necessary correction of my analysis of belief questions.

There are not only two, but arbitrarily many ways to precisify the content of scalar adjectives. Likewise, there is not only the alternative (d1) vs. (e1) available to the addressee of (b) as possible implicative answers, but rather a wide variety of precisifying responses. Two ways of precisification are typical, in accordance with the informal analysis given in (z'): Precisifications of p, using an epistemic one-place sentence operator which indicates a degree of subjective certainty (*probably, certainly, it is most likely that*), and precisifications of $\mathcal{A}$, either specific ones, like (j1), as an answer to (i1), or general idiomatic ones, like (k1).

(i1) Glaubst du, dass ich rechtzeitig dort sein werde?
(i1') Do you think I'll be in time?
(j1) Du solltest lieber den Wagen nehmen.
(j2) You'd better take the car.
(k1) Darauf kannst du Gift nehmen.
(k2) You may gamble on it.

(d) and (e) are prominent candidates for answers to belief questions because they concern the standard precisification. However, there are more answers to belief questions. This is additional evidence in favor of the scalar analysis (z').

Belief questions (in German and French, at least) usually have vague denotations, and they request the addressee to properly precisify their denotation by uttering implicative answers. This is, in short, the result of this paper, as far as belief questions are concerned. Additionally, I hope to have illustrated one aspect of the semantics of verbs expressing beliefs, and, in doing so, given an example of the intensive interplay between semantics and pragmatics, in the field of propositional attitudes.

Notes

[1] Constructions of the kind exemplified by (e) are, at least in German, restricted to *glauben* and a couple of semantically narrowly related verbs (*denken* , *meinen*), but not acceptable, e.g., with *wissen* (= know).

[2] Cf. Hintikka (1962) for the first, and Lenzen (1980) for the second.

[3] Expecially, this paper does not contribute to the problems of contradictory belief and lacking intersubstitutability of cointensional expressions in belief contexts, in a direct way.

[4] Cf. Kutschera (1976), Lenzen (1980). I will come back to this suggestion later on.

[5] Cf. Carnap (1947) for the linguistically relevant aspect of the topic.

[6] As far as the current argument is concerned, I need not care about the fact that propositions are strictly speaking no god candidates for objects of assertion and belief, either.

[7] I should note that Gazdar's treatment of implicature in (1979) provides an elegant and very suggestive solution to the first person weak reading problem. He also refers to Grice, reinterpreting his quantity maxim in terms of two more or less precisely applicable rules which roughly have the following form: first, when a sentence A with a lexical item is uttered which can be located in a quantitative scale, sentences A' obtained by replacement of this item by different ones ranging higher in the scale (if there are any such items), are conversationally excluded by the former; second, when a sentence A occurs as a

constituent of another sentence B which does not entail it, ''speaker does not know whether A'' is a possible implicature of B. According to these rules, (h) implicates (h') and (h''):

(h') Speaker believes that he does not know that John loves Mary.

(h'') Speaker does not know whether John loves Mary.

(h') and (h'') both exclued the strong reading, in a way.—I chose a less elegant, but, as I hope, likewise satisfactory version to explain the first person weak reading.

[7a] Actually, things are more complicated than I put them here. There are various transitions between grammaticality and ungrammaticality caused by violation of movement restictions, dependent on the particular main verb and the moved constituent (cf. Kawashima (1979)). However, this does not affect the relevant argument that *wh*-belief questions actually used are felt to be of a dubious status of grammaticality.

[8] The *glaubst du* constituent is not parenthetic: its position behind the *wh*-NP is completely fixed; the phonetic realization is untypical for parentheses, without main accent, enclitic to the *wh*-phrase; in writing (s) and (t) one hesitates to place punctuation signs.

[9] Of course, the addressee may give a modified answer like (e) also if he was asked (m), and he will do so if he observes the principle of cooperativeness, but this is not directly claimed by the question.

[10] In normal discourse, at least two more *ja*-answers have to be distinguished, one with 'decisive', the other with 'deliberative' intonation.

[11] This seems to be similar to Japanese talking about one's own belief (*shinjiru*), which has an emphatic connotation, as opposed to talking about supposed beliefs of a third person (*shinjite iru* ; Japanese, like English, has two verbs (*shinjiru/omou*) for expressing the attitude of strong and weak belief, resp.

[12] It is only one aspect of the belief semantics I will comment on in the following, and what I am going to say is often simply stated rather than argued for. A more detailed account of the aspect of belief semantics under consideration is given in Pinkal (1981).

[13] There is a lot of natural language evidence for the narrow connection between belief semantics and the level of actions; see, for the latter, Pinkal (1981).—In the *believe in/glauben an* -version, only those cases are considered where the NP governed by the preposition can be interpreted as a nominalized clause.

[14] Things are actually more complicated, since the ''unmarked'' version may be used neutrally with respect to the basis of the belief, rather than epistemically.

[15]''Less precise'' must not be lumped together with ''more general'': the most general reading is the weakest one, but this is not what is meant here.

[16] It is important to realize that neither of the two precisifications need to result in a sharp denotation. Both expressions will regularly remain vague, and contextually variable to some extent. According to the last paragraph of the preceding section, a precisification has to be considered as a restriction to a subset of the set of possible complete specifications which may be, but usually is not, a one-membered set.

Universität Düsseldorf
Seminar für Allgemeine Sprachwissenschaft

References

Carnap, R. (1947): Meaning and Necessity, Chicago: Univ. of Chicago Press.

Fine, K. (1975): ''Vagueness, truth and logic''. Synthese 30, p. 265-300.

Gazdar, J. (1979): Pragmatics. Implicature, Presupposition, and Logical Form, New York: Academic Press.

Grice, H.P. (1975):''Logic and Conversation'', in Cole, P./Morgan, J. (eds.): Syntax and Semantics, Vol. 3: Speech Acts. New York: Academic Press

Hintikka, J. (1962): Knowledge and Belief, Ithaca: Cornell Univ. Press.

Kawashima, A. (1979): ''Zur Frageform des Glaubenssatzes: Wohin glauben Sie, dass er fährt?'', Artes Liberales 24, p.23-37.

Kutschera, F.v. (1976): Einführung in die intensionale Semantik. Berlin: de Gruyter.

Lenzen, W. (1980): Glauben, Wissen und Wahrscheinlichkeit, Wien: Springer (forthcoming)

Pinkal, M. (1979):'' How to refer with vague descriptions'', in Bäuerle, R. et al. (eds.): Semantics from different points of view, Berlin: Springer.

Pinkal, M. (1981): ''Some semantic and pragmatic properties of German *glauben* '', in: Rieser, H./Eikmeyer, H.J. (eds.): Words, Worlds and Contexts. New Approaches in Word Semantics, Berlin: de Gruyter.

Petr Sgall

Relevance of Topic and Focus for Automatic Question Answering

1. After a systematic empirical investigation of the questions of topic and focus (comment), or theme and rheme, our research team has come to certain conclusions (see Sgall, Hajičová and Benešová, 1973; Sgall and Hajičová, 1977), which include several rather strong hypotheses. Though, of course, they do not cover the whole domain of word order, intonation and their functions, they appear to present a useful basis for a detailed description of the main features of the domain (leaving aside, for the time being, such specific cases as some kinds of contrast, sentences with more than one intonation centre, some non-projective constructions, etc.).

It seems to be possible to describe the system of natural language—the relationship between underlying structures (tectogrammatical representations) and the phonetic shape of sentences—as a system standing close to context-free languages (Plátek and Sgall, 1978). The tectogrammatical representation of a sentence has the form of a dependency tree labelled by complex symbols, which are ordered with respect to their so-called communicative dynamism; every tectogrammatical representation contains at least one element belonging to its focus, and it may also contain one or more elements constituting its topic (in a more detailed description, see Hajičová and Sgall, 1980, we understand the notion of dynamism as derived from that of contextual boundness of the nodes).[1]

The main verb is always more dynamic that its contextually bound participants (dependent nodes) and less dynamic than the non-bound ones. The non-bound participants are ordered according to their types—e.g. in English inside the focus Actor/Bearer precedes (is less dynamic than) Addressee, which precedes Patient (Objective); Patient, in its turn, precedes Origin, Instrument, etc. This systemic ordering of the participants is determined by the grammar of the given language (more specifically, by the generative component of its description, which has been specified in the quoted paper as a pushdown grammar). On the other hand, with the participants included in the topic the ordering of dynamism is not always identical with the systemic ordering; the scale of dynamism of the elements included in the topic may have different shapes, and the speaker's choice depends here first of all on the patterning of the text.[2]

Ferenc Kiefer (ed.), Questions and Answers, 257–272.

The semantic relevance of topic, focus and dynamism can be characterized by the following three points: [3]

(i) The scopes of quantifiers are determined, to some extent, by the relative degrees of dynamism of noun phrases, cf. (1) to (3)—at least in their primary readings; the capitals denote here the bearer of the intonation centre.

(1) (a) Many men read few BOOKS.
(b) Few books are read by many MEN.
(2) (a) John talked to few girls about many PROBLEMS.
(b) John talked about many problems to few GIRLS.
(3) (a) Everyone in this room speaks two LANGUAGES.
(b) Two languages are spoken by everyone in this ROOM.

Even without overt quantification there is a similar distinction in the truth conditions of such sentences as (4) and (5).[4]

(4) (a) English is spoken in New ZEALAND.
(b) ENGLISH is spoken in New Zealand.
(5) (a) One smokes in the CORRIDOR.
(b) In the corridor one SMOKES.

(ii) If a sentence is negated, then in the primary case it is just its focus that is in the scope of negation; if the verb is contextually non-bound (and thus included in the focus), the event identified by the verb is negated, as in (6), or (7), while if it is contextually bound, (and thus included in the topic), it is not negated readings of (8).

(6) Our defeat was not caused by HARRY.
(7) Jim didn't come because of his wife's ILLNESS.
(8) Jim didn't come because of the topic of today's LECTURE.
(...He just came to meet MARY.)

The fact that the focus (or, more precisely, its relationship to the topic) is negated in a negative sentence is closely related to the underlying assumption that in the positive counterpart of the sentence the focus is asserted ''about the topic'', the topic being assumed as given, i.e. presupposed; these issues are dealt with in Hajičová (1973).

(iii) The phenomenon described by Kuno (1972) as exhaustive listing is connected with focus only, and, moreover, only with a specific kind of focus viz. the focus does not include the verb, or it includes only such a lexically void verb as the copula.[5]

While exhaustive listing seems to belong to the layer of Gricean conversational maxims, the points (i) and (ii) concern directly the truth conditions of the sentences. As has been pointed out by Sgall, Hajičová and Procházka (1977), the tectogrammatical representations of sentences may be characterized as a linguistic counterpart of Carnap's intensional structure or of Frege's sense. Two sentences differing in sense can correspond to a single proposition (can share their truth conditions, their intension), as is the case in (9) or in (10):

(9) (a) The number of tables in this room is equal to an even prime number.
(b) The number of tables in this room is equal to the square root of four.
(10) (a) Charles sold a car to Tom.
(b) Tom bought a car from Charles.

In many cases this identity of truth conditions, though not of sense, is connected with sentences differing just in their topic-focus articulation:

(11) (a) John talked to a girl about a PROBLEM.
(b) John talked about a problem to a GIRL.
(12) (a) The man reads the BOOK.
(b) The book is read by the MAN.

A procedure of translation between the tectogrammatical representations and appropriate representations of propositions is then needed. For the subclass of sentences the focus of which includes just a noun phrase Materna and Sgall (1980) attempt to characterize their counterparts in a language of intensional logic (based on the theory of types and on possible worlds semantics.) [7]

Our approach characterizes topic and focus in accordance with the presystematic view according to which it is the focus (comment) what is asserted about the topic, when a sentence is uttered. At the same time we characterize these notions by means of the operational tests using negation or question. It thus seems that these notions, which exhibit interesting properties of different kinds, may be useful also in the domain of automatic question answering. Similar notions have already been used to various purposes; thus, first of all, Aravind Joshi and Steve Kuhn (1979) use a similar dichotomy in a framework of natural language inferencing (however, in their understanding ''focus'' comes much closer to subject). In accounting for the structure of task oriented dialogues, Barbara Grosz (1977) analyzes focus switching at a time-point in the discourse, working with notions close to David Lewis' ''prominence'' or our ''activation'' (foregrounding) of the items in the stock of shared knowledge (and other attitudes) of the speaker and his audience: the objects mentioned in the focus of a sentence become salient, i.e. the speaker may assume that their counterparts in the memory of the hearer are foregrounded enough to be easily identified (which may concern also objects foregrounded by the given situation itself), and it is then probable that some of these objects will be mentioned in the topic of the next utterance (see Sgall, 1980).[8]

Before coming to our main point, concerning the relevance of topic and focus in questioon answering, we add a few remarks on the identification of topic and focus in the surface sentences (§ 2) and on the topic-focus articulation of interrogative sentences (§ 3).

2. It is not easy to identify the topic and focus of a printed sentence, especially in such a language as English, where the surface word order is grammatically bound to a great extent, so that in many cases the hierarchy of communicative dynamism is rendered by means of a marked position of the intonation centre in the spoken language, which has almost no counterpart in the written (printed) texts. Some hints may be found in Sgall and Hajičová (1977). As for technical texts, which are concerned in most question answering projects, it is possible to work with the following assumptions:

(i) The participants standing to the left of the verb may be understood as belonging to the topic (this concerns the subject as well as the adverbials; exceptions occur with a subject having the indefinite article, which in some cases is included in the focus).[9]

(ii) If there is only one participant standing to the right of the verb, then this participant belongs to the focus.

(iii) (a) If there are more than one participants to the right of the verb and the rightmost of them is a local or temporal adverbial, then it should be checked whether the lexical meaning of this adverbial is specific (its head being a proper name, a narrower term, or a term not belonging to the subject domain of the given text) or general (a pronoun, a broader term); in the former case it is probable that the adverbial belongs to the focus, as in (13) and (14), while in the latter case it rather belongs to the topic, as in (15) or (16).

(13) Several teams carried out experiments with this method during the last two years.
(14) Several teams carried out experiments with this method in Stanford and Princeton.
(15) Several teams ... during the last decades.
(16) Several teams ... in this country.

(iii) (b) If there are more than one participants to the right of the verb and the rightmost one is not a local or temporal adverbial, then this rightmost participant is the most dynamic element of the sentence, its focus proper:

(17) Several teams carried out experiments with this method to find out whether it is adequate.

(iv) Given an isolated written English sentence, there are no reliable criteria distinguishing whether its verb belongs to its topic or to its focus. In most cases it is possible to assume that the verb belongs to the focus if it is a lexically specific verb (with a rather narrow meaning); if the verb is general (**be**, **have**, **become**, **carry out** ,...), then it may be assumed that it belongs to the topic.

Points (i) to (iv) may be useful if only a single sentence can be examined. However, in many cases it is possible to take into account the preceding context. It is then advisable to register the activated (salient) items we mentioned at the end of § 1. This can be done by a method similar to that illustrated by Grosz (1977); however, a principle similar to that of a pushdown store should probably be used: the element that was mentioned as the focus proper of the last utterance is the most salient in the given time-point of the discourse, while the elements that were used in other positions of this utterance get a somewhat lower status in the activated part of the stock of shared knowledge, and those that have not been mentioned in one or several subsequent utterances may fade away (if they do not have a specific position of a ''hypertopic'', which may concern e.g. those mentioned in the title or heading). Such a register makes it possible to decide in the unclear cases (in the points (iii) (a) and (iv) above, or in what concerns the participants standing between the verb and its rightmost participant) whether a given participant belongs to the topic (which is the case when it is contained in the register), or to the focus. It should be noted that also this method has its limitations: on one side the set of activated items should include not only items mentioned in the text, but also their parts, counterparts and other items connected with them by associative relations; on the other side, if a specific kind of contrast is involved, it is possible that also an item included in this set is mentioned as a part of the focus of the next utterance, cf. (18) and the requirement of ''recoverability'' in Halliday (1967, p.204) or of ''identifiability'' in Chafe (1976).

(18) Among these three cases our remark concerns only the first TWO.

3. In interrogative sentences the topic-focus articulation is connected with several unclear questions which have been intensively dicussed in Czech linguistic writings (by Mathesius, Firbas, Daneš, Křižková-Běličová, Hajičová and others).[10] One of the main results of these discussions consists in the fact that the interrogative formative itself cannot be understood as the only possible part of the focus of these sentences. In **yes-no** questions the interrogative character (as well as the other attitudinal aspects, to the extent in which they are structured by the system of language) may be regarded at the tectogrammatical level as one of the parts of the complex label of the root of the tree (i.e. of the main verb). The topic-focus articulation of these sentences appears to be similar (and conveyed by similar means of expression) as that of declarative sentences.

As for **wh**-questions, in most cases the interrogative element as well as the last word they contain belong to the focus. However, it is not always clear which of them is the focus proper (the most dynamic part of the sentence), or whether also some other sentence part belongs to the focus. It seems (cf. Hajičová, 1976a;b) that the interrogative element is the only part of the focus in case it is the bearer of the intonation centre, as in (19) or (20):

(19) WHEN did he come?
(20) WHICH cigarettes do you like best?

Since we are interested here in the domain of question answering systems, we need not discuss the distinction between questions and other uses of interrogative sentences (cf. Hausser, this volume). It was just necessary to give a general outline of the topic-focus articulation of interrogative sentences, to be able in the sequel to discuss the relationships of the topic-focus articulation of a question and of an appropriate (direct or indirect) answer to it.

4. Issues concerning topic and focus have been studied for different purposes within the field of question answering. We cannot give here a survey of these purposes (one of which is that of paraphrasing the question, see McKeown, 1979). Our aim is to point out that for a declarative sentence **S** to be a direct answer to a given **wh**-question conveyed by an interrogative sentence **I** it is not enough that **S** shares the (underlying) structure of **I**, only the **wh**-element (with its head, in some cases being substituted by a specific lexical unit (possibly with some modifications, adjuncts, etc.); it is also necessary that the topic-focus articulation of **S** corresponds to that of **I** in a certain way, which has to be specified.

If we restrict our investigation to interrogative sentences having normal intonation, we may assume that **I** has a surface structure which can be characterized, with many simplifications, by (21):

(21) **wh** —(**do** Sb) Verb ($Compl_1$ ($Compl_2$ (...$Compl_n$)...))

where **wh**stands for the interrogative phrase (i.e. either for an interrogative NP such as **who**, or for a NP containing an embedded interrogative element, e.g. **which table**), the syntactic role of which is subject, object, or adverbial, the parentheses indicate optionality, and Compl $_i$ stands for subject (Sb), object or adverbial, which may have the form of a NP (under which also prepositional phrases are classed in our approach), of an embedded clause, or of an adverb.

It may be assumed that in a sentence of this shape $Compl_n$ is the focus proper, while **wh** — perhaps also every $Compl_j$ for a given $1 < \mathbf{k}$, $\mathbf{k} \leq$, $\mathbf{j} < \mathbf{n}$, and Verb belong to the focus, while Sb (with some possible exceptions, and probably also $Compl_i$ (or even the other Compl $_i$., with $1 < \mathbf{i} < \mathbf{k}$) belong to the topic of **I** (cf. Sect.2).

As for the answer **S** , we assume that:

(a) the item referred to by the focus proper of **I** , as the most salient (activated) element in the given time point of the discourse, is referred to by the topic proper of **S** ;

(b) the element of **S** corresponding to **wh** -, i.e. the element carrying new information in **S**, is the focus of **S** (the whole, not only the proper focus);

(c) the elements corresponding to other elements of **I** belong to the topic of **S** .

The validity of (a) to (c) can be checked by means of such examples as (22):

(22) (**I**) When did the chemical industry recently cause a tragedy? (**S**) A tragedy was recently caused by the chemical industry in October.

It may be assumed that in the preferred reading of (22) **(I) a tragedy** is its focus proper, while **when** and **cause** belong to the focus, too, and the subject constitutes the topic proper, **recently** (temporal setting) representing the more dynamic part of the topic. According to (a), then, **a tragedy** is the topic proper of **S** , which is in accordance with its leftmost position as the subject of (22) (**S**); according to (b), **in October** is the focus proper of **S**, which is rendered, in (22) (S), by this phrase having the rightmost position; according to (c) the remaining three elements belong to the topic of **S**, which actually is the case in the preferred reading of (22) (**S**).

It is known that the topic, or some parts of it, may be either deleted or substituted by pronominal elements, as in (23) to (26); however, it is an interesting question to examine how these possibilities are restricted, i.e. how the implausibility of (27) can be predicted, or how it can be explained that (28) does not—if I am not mistaken—contain a deleted Actor.

(23) (It was) in October.
(24) It caused one in October.
(25) It did in October.
(26) One was caused by chemical industry in October.
(27) It did it in October.
(28) A tragedy was caused in October.

According to the general assumptions of our approach, the degrees of salience (activation) of individual sentence parts change in that the more an element was dynamic in **I**, the more activated it is in the time point of **S** , and, if other factors influencing the scale of communicative dynamism do not intervene (see Note 2 above), a more activated item should be referred to by a less dynamic element of **S**. In English the subtle questions of the scale of communicative dynamism are by far not so transparent as in the languages with the so-called free word order (most Slavonic languages, Latin, partly also German), and a thorough investigation of the given questions is beyond the frame of the present paper. Let us only note that in case the interrogative sentence used as a question contains a series of quantifiers such as there are in (1) to (3), the change of activation we just spoke about causes that the meaning of **S** does not match completely that of the question, as the following example illustrates (with the German version serving to point out the scale of communicative dynamism of the answer):

(29) Since when does John talk to few girls about many problems?
(30) John talks about many problems to few girls since half a year.
(31) Über viele Probleme spricht John mit wenigen Mädchen seit einem halben Jahr.

It is (32) rather than (30), which may serve as an answer to (29), since the scale of dynamism determines the scope of quantifiers and is thus semantically relevant.

(32) John talks to few girls about many problems since half a year.

4.2 In the experiment with a question answering system (based on the method TIBAQ, see Sgall, in press; Hajičová and Sgall, in prep.; Jirkú, 1981) that is being prepared by the Prague group of mathematical linguistics, we use a simplified technique to cope with this problem: **wh**- is transferred to the end of **I** during the syntactico-semantic analysis, and then a sentence sharing the scale of dynamism with this counterpart of **I** is chosen as an answer, if it can be found. If no such direct answer is found, an indirect answer (containing the prefixed words "I (only) know that") is looked for. In this way the changes of the scopes of quantifiers are avoided, and also a rather acceptable handling of exhaustive listing is ensured.

Certainly, at first glance (34) looks quite innocently as an answer to (33):

(33) What operations can be carried out by means of the device X?
(34) Integration and derivation can be carried out by means of the device X.

However, it should be borne in mind that a sentence with normal intonation (and we have supposed only such sentences to appear in our discussion, or in the experiments we are discussing) has the intonation centre at its end. In such a case (34) certainly can be followed e.g. by ''Also multiplication and other arithmetical operations can'', which means that (34) is not an exhaustive answer to (33), though (33) really appears to require an exhaustive answer and (what is worse) (34) pretends to give one, since due to the fact that its verb is contextually bound it is a sentence with a focus of the exhaustive-listing type. Similarly the pair (35) does not contain an appropriate answer to the given question, since the author of the question would mistakenly believe that the new information given by the answer is exhaustive (down to a certain threshold, at least), which it evidently is not, in the ''real world''.

(35) What does Britain import from India?
—A large part of our tea is imported from India.

The proper answers to the two questions can be found in a given set of propositions only if such propositions are found there that correspond to such sentences as (36) and (37), where the word order (and the normal intonation) is semantically relevant.

(36) The device X carries out the operations of the types Y, Z.
(37) From India, Britain imports...[11]

4.3 There is yet another aspect of the relevance of topic and focus to automatic question answering: During the work on the TIBAQ first experiment we have found that the inference rules which should enrich the set of assertions found in a technical text (for the system to be able to answer also questions which cannot be directly answered by any sentence contained in the given text) may also delete some types of adjuncts. For instance, if the underlying text contains such a sentence as (38), then the system should be able to answer (39) and (40).

(38) The device X is used in systems like Z to carry out Y.
(39) For what purpose is the device X used?
(40) In what systems does one use the device X?

One possible way how to get answers to these questions is to formulate rules which will derive (41) and (42) from (38) (more precisely, we should speak here about the tectogrammatical representations of these sentences):

(41) The device X is used to carry out Y.
(42) The device X is used in systems like Z.

Similarly, (44) should be derived from (43):

(43) From Finland we import wooden furniture.
(44) From Finland we import furniture.

The rule may be formulated in such a way that it deletes individual parts of the focus of an assertion, under two conditions: (a) the whole focus cannot be deleted, and (b) if a nominal adjunct is deleted, the remaining part of the NP cannot be connected with the delimiting feature Definite (the former restriction is conditioned by the fact that any assertion has to contain a focus; the motivation of the other restriction can be illustrated if **the** (or **our**) **wooden furniture** is substituted for the Objective of (43)).

On the other hand, a part of the topic cannot be deleted by such a rule, since e.g. (46) certainly cannot be inferred from (45) (while (48) can be inferred from (47)):

(45) Mathematical operations of such types as multiplication or integration are carried out by operational amplifiers.
(46) Mathematical operations are carried out by operational amplifiers.
(47) Operational amplifiers carry out mathematical operations of such types as multiplication or integration.
(48) Operational amplifiers carry out mathematical operations.

5.1 Jane Robinson has reminded us very convincingly that in a coherent dialogue a question cannot be understood only in a literal way. In the domain of automatic question answering one of the main problems connected with this issue is the so-called stonewalling (see Kaplan and Joshi, mimeo). Let us add only one remark concerning this aspect of the cooperativeness of question answering systems:

One of the points in which the systems could be made more cooperative is that they should give at the output also such information that cannot be regarded as a direct answer to the given question, but can serve as probably useful for the user in case no direct answer has been found. Such indirect answers, which can be marked e.g. by such a prefix as ''I (only) know that...'', may be given if the system has found relevant information concerning e.g. only some of the hyponyms of a noun that is at stake, or also in case the topic-focus articulation of the answer is not in accordance with that of the question (cf. Section 4 above, where we have already mentioned such examples).[12]

5.2 Our last point concerns the relationship between the topic of a sentence and that of a text. It cannot be claimed that every text has a single topic, and even the authors who started with such an assumption have found that such a case is only a specific one. In the general case it is possible to speak only of parts of texts connected by the same topic.[13] The so-called thematic progressions (now see esp. Daneš, 1974; but also e.g. Yuganov, 1979, pointing out that in real texts these progressions often do not appear in a pure form) illustrate the elementary possibilities (the topic of the preceding utterance retained in the following one, or the focus of the preceding utterance serves here as the topic, etc.) A systematic elaboration of the hints given in Sgall (1980) as for the hierarchy of salience of the items within the stock of information shared by the speaker and the hearer might be useful for a characterization of the role of the topic-focus articulation of sentences in the structure of a text.

One of the main open questions in this domain is that of the distinction between a ''full'' and ''partially formulated'' question. If such a question as (49) is understood as full, then it can be directly answered only by a complete list of all the visitors of Prague at the given day.

(49) Who came to Prague yesterday?

The usual case in human dialogues is that such a question is connected with a non-formulated background restricting the universe of discourse in a certain way (according to the relationship between the speaker and the hearer and to other aspects of the given situation, (49) may be understood as meaning ''Who among our common friends...'', or "Who among the participants of the conference we organize...", etc). In question answering the simple case is just to assume that the user knows how the universe of discourse is restricted by the stock of data included in the system; in this case the system itself need not use any further restrictions. A more sophisticated system should be able to extract from the preceding context some information on restrictions of the given kind, similarly as on possible antecedents of anaphorical relations. Thus, if e.g. (49) was answered by a list, in (50) **who** should be understood as referring only to members included in this list, even if the anaphorical pronoun is not present, if the system is oriented towards the organization of a conference.

(50) Who went to the hotel first?

The use of the terms 'topic' and 'focus' or 'comment' in different approaches to artificial intelligence differs (as is the case in various linguistic schools). Some of these differences may be removed rather easily (e.g. the term 'focus', as used by Grosz, corresponds to 'the activated part of the stock of shared knowledge' in our terms), in other cases the "translation" is more difficult. The Polytext system, as described by Karlgren and Walker (present volume), works with a dichotomy of 'topic' and 'comment' that concerns single utterances as well as their sequences; a further elaboration of the dichotomy as used there might be usefully based on an approach connected with an explicit definition of the topic and the focus of a sentence. As we have seen, the patterning of a text is open to different possibilities in this respect, so that it is advisable to study one type of texts after another, to get results useful for the information system concerning the given domains.

Charles University
Institute of Numerical Mathematics

Notes

[1] The distinction between subject prominent and topic prominent languages (see Li and Thompson, 1976) may be of great usefulness for analytical studies, but does not appear to be really basic (see Sgall, 1977; now cf. also Noonan's, 1977, remarks concerning the rather unclear position of German in this dichotomy, esp. p.384, note 21).—More than one patterning has to be distinguished in the underlying structure of a sentence, so that e.g. Barri (1978) is not putting the right question: topic and focus have to be studied **besides** the immediate constituents (or dependency) structure rather than **instead of** it.

[2] Such issues are relevant here as (i) the distinction between the topic proper and a local or temporal setting, (ii) a contrastive topic, (iii) a difference between the surface position of

enclitical particles and their amount of communicative dynamism, (iv) the question whether in general the least dynamic element of the topic occupies the first or the second (or the rightmost?) position in the surface word order of the topic (see Rylova, 1980, where the second position is preferred).

[3] It seems that exactly the coincidence of these three aspects corroborates the view that a concept of focus specified on their basis may be useful for a linguistic description, since this concept corresponds to a phenomenon having its important place in the linguistic patterning of the domain of content. Purely syntactic definitions (such as that given by Kiss, 1980) have to be examined as for their semantic relevance (which certainly can differ from one language to another).

[4] Cf.also such pairs as ''This motion must be approved by the COMMITTEE'' vs. ''This motion must be APPROVED by the committee''; if I am not mistaken, the preferred reading of the former sentence does not imply whether it is probable that the motion will be approved, while with the latter sentence the probability of approval is involved.

[5] If focus is defined as a single participant of the verb, as is the case with Anna Szabolcsi (1980), then it should exhibit the property of exhaustive listing; but if Szabolcsi's example (14) can be continued not only by..., **but Eve**, but also by..., **but plays with this kids**, or even by..., **but the door banged**, then (14) probably is more exactly translated by English ''Peter does not beat Mary'', where the verb, and perhaps even the subject belongs to the focus, too. ''It is not MARY, whom Peter beats'' is appropriate only with the first continuation.

[6] Hintikka's (1975) epistemically possible worlds and constituents of depth **d** (i.e. complexes of experience one can have by observing at most **d** individuals together) may be used to define the concept of proposition in such a way that it can be understood as the sense of a sentence, and, moreover, his concept of depth gives the possibility to distinguish not only between linguistic meaning and cognitive content, but also between different layers of the latter, as far as the complexity of inference is concerned; in other words, the tripartition of linguistic competence (allowing for 'oculist' and 'eye-doctor' to be treated as synonyms), general human intellectual abilities (allowing to infer ''Jim bought a car from Tom'' from ''Tom sold a car to Jim'', and a higher intellectual capability (necessary e.g. to infer that 10^3 is smaller than 2^{10} can be described on this base.

[7] However, it is necessary to take more possible combinations of contextually bound and non-bound elements into account than was done in the quoted paper, or also in Hoepelman's contribution to the analysis of questions (in the present volume), which appears to surmount successfully many of the difficulties that often pass unnoticed; another attempt at an intensional treatment of topic and focus is given in Kosík and Sgall (in prep.).—All these approaches, based on Tarskian semantics, are undermined by the ''any-thesis'' (now see Hintikka, 1980), but Zuber's (1978) argument, according to which the semantics of **any** can be described by using the existential quantifier in some cases, should be reexamined.

[8] Cf. Hendrix (1979), where it is pointed out that an activated element activates also other elements (connected with it by association), and shown how this can be handled within the framework of partitioned networks.

[9]. Also in languages with ''free'' word order (e.g. in Russian) the leftmost NP may convey new (irrecoverable) information; on the other hand an indefinite (specific) NP may also bear known information, i.e. belong to the topic. These and similar possiblities are often neglected in the writings on topic and focus (partly also in Sandra A. Thompson, 1978).

[10] Now see esp. Hajičová (1976a;b) and the writings quoted there.

[11] We assume that the list constituting the focus of this answer contains several more important items than tea, i.e. whatever be the threshold of importance chosen, tea cannot be the single item included in an appropriate answer (we assume that the universe of discourse has not been restricted to a domain that would allow for such an answer to be appropriate).

[12] If this approach is broadened by further relaxing the conditions on an indirect answer, it is possible e.g. to answer Aravind Joshi's question ''Which programmers work on projects 6471?'' by ''I only know that X_1, X_2, ...X_n work on the project Y_1, Y_2, ...Y_n, respectively.''

[13] Cf. Marciszewski (1976); Bayer (1979); also Dijk (1977) prefers to speak about the ''topic of (a part of) a discourse'', or ''the topic for this passage'', etc. (esp. pp.132-142), rather than to maintain that the text as such (or every text) has its topic.

References

Barri N. (1978), Theme and Rheme as Immediate Constituents, Folia linguistica 12, 253-265.

Bayer J. (1979), Diskursthemen. Presented at the 14th Linguistic Colloquium, Bochum.

Chafe, W. (1976), Giveness, Contrastiveness, Definiteness, Subjects, Topics, and Point of View. In: Li (1976), 25-55.

Daneš F. (1974), ed., Papers on Functional Sentence Perspective, Prague.

Dijk, T. A. van (1977), Text and Context. Explorations in the Semantics and Pragmatics of Discourse, London—New York, Longman.

Grosz B. (1977), The Representation and Use of Focus in Dialogue Understanding. SRI Project 5844

Hajičová E. (1973), Negation and Topic vs. Focus. Philologica Pragensia 16, 81-93.

Hajičová E. (1976a), Question and Answer in Linguistics and in Man-Machine Communication. SMIL, Statistical Methods in Linguistics, No. 1, 36-46.

Hajičová E. (1976b), Struktura doplóvací otázky a odpovědi z hlediska aktuálního členění. Slovo a slovesnost 27, 300-307.

Hajičová E. and P. Sgall (in prep.), Toward Automatic Understanding of Technical Texts. Prepared for The Prague Bull. of Mathematical Linguistics 36.

Hajičová E. and P. Sgall (1980), A Dependency-Based Specification of Topic and Focus. SMIL, No. 1-2. 93-140

Halliday M. A. K. (1967), Notes on Transitivity and Theme in English. Journal of Linguistics 3, 37-81; 199-244; 4 (1968), 179-215.

Hendrix G. G. (1979), Encoding Knowledge in Partitioned Networks. In: Associative Networks (ed. by N. V. Findler), New York, 51-92.

Hintikka J. (1975), Impossible Possible Words Vindicated. Journal of Philosophical Logic 4, 475-484.

Hintikka J. (1980), On the **Any** -Thesis and the Methodology of Linguistics. Linguistics and Philosophy 4, 101-122.

Jirků P. (1981), Logical and Linguistic Aspects of Computer-Based Inference Processes. The Prague Bull. of Mathematical Linguistics 35, 41-53.

Joshi A. and S. Kuhn (1979), Centered Logic: The Role of Entity Centered Sentence Representation in Natural Language Inferencing. Presented at IJCAI, Tokio.

Joshi A. And S. J. Kaplan (mimeo), Cooperative Responses: Why Query Systems Stonewall.
Kiss K. É. (1980), A Transformational Generative Syntax Based on the Notions of Topic and Focus. In: Empirische Rechtfertigungen von Syntaxen (ed. by D. Clément), Bonn, 72-84.
Kosík A. and P. Sgall (in prep.), Towards a Semantic Interpretation of Underlying Structures, to appear in Theoretical Linguistics 8
Kuno S. (1972), Functional Sentence Perspective. Linguistic Inquiry 3, 269-320.
Li Ch. N. (1976), ed., Subject and Topic, New York.
Li Ch. N. and S. A. Thompson (1976), Subject and Topic: A New Typology of Language. In: Li (1976), 457-589.
Marciszewski W. (1976), Ot ponjatija temy predloženija do ponjatija ključevogo slova. In: Naučno-techničeskaja informacija. Serija 2, No. 11, 18-25.
Materna P. and P. Sgall (1980), Functional Sentence Perspective, the Question Test and Intensional Semantics. SMIL, No. 1-2. 141-160.
McKeown K. (1979), Paraphrasing Using Given and New Information in Question-Answering. Unpublished Master's Thesis, Philadelphia.
Noonan M. (1977), On Subjects and Topics. In: Proceedings of the Third Annual Meeting of the Berkley Ling. Society, 372-385.
Plátek M. and P. Sgall (1978), A Scale of Context-Sensitive Languages. Information and Control 38, 1-20.
Rylova T. N. (1980), K ispol'zovaniju teorii aktual'nogo členenija v postrojenii odnoj modeli uporjadočennogo smysla. In: Avtomatičeskaja obrabotka teksta, Kijev, 42-59.
Sgall P. (1977), Review of Li (1976). The Prague Bulletin of Math. Linguistics 27, 65-70.
Sgall P. (1980), Towards a Pragmatically Based Theory of Meaning. In: Speech Act Theory and Pragmatics (ed. by J. R. Searle, F. Kiefer and M. Bierwisch), Dordrecht—Boston—London, 233-246.
Sgall P. (in press), Towards a Fully Automatic System of Communication with Data Bases. Presented at the Conference on Artificial Intelligence and Information-Control Systems of Robots, Smolenice.
Sgall P. and E. Hajičová (1977), Focus on Focus I, The Prague Bulletin of Mathem. Ling. 28, 5-54; II, PBML 29, 1978, 23-41.
Sgall P., Hajičová E. and E. Benešová (1973), Topic, Focus and Generative Semantics, Kronberg/Taunus.
Sgall P., Hajičová E. and O. Procházka (1977), On the Role of Linguistic Semantics. Theoretical Linguistics 4, 31-59.
Szabolcsi A. (1980), The Semantics of Topic—Focus Articulation. Presented at the 3rd Amsterdam colloquium on Formal Methods in the Study of Language.
Thompson S. A. (1978), Modern English from a Typological Point of View: Some Implications of the Functions of Word Order. Linguistische Berichte 54, 19-35.
Yuganov V. I. (1979), Tekst i tipy tematičeskich progressij. In Značenije i smysl rečevych obrazovanij. Kalinin, 147-163.
Zuber R. (1978), On Meaning Categories. Linguistische Berichte 54, 44-50.

Hans Karlgren and Donald E. Walker

The polytext system —a new design for a text retrieval system

0. Polytext—a new design for a text retrieval system

During 1979, after preliminary studies in 1978, Kval, Stockholm, in cooperation with SRI International, California, initiated a new research and development project, planned to produce new insights into information science and to yield a useful computerized system for text retrieval, 'The Polytext System'. The project is closely associated with previous and ongoing studies at the two institutions, jointly and independently, on the semantics and pragmatics of question-answering.

By retrieval is here understood the process of locating in a set of given texts those texts or text passages that contain information relevant to a given query. The search, thus, refers to the contents of the texts and not merely to occurrences of words or phrases; on the other hand, the system does not respond by paraphrasing or extrapolating the contents of the input texts as understood by the system. It is text-oriented in that it tries literally to find answers from among the pre-stored texts or text passages rather than to deliver machine-made answers. It reproduces rather than produces answers and may be seen as a reader's guide to the text collection. For many applications, this organization, which may at first sight appear less sophisticated than a question-answering system which coins its own answers, is the only one that allows the system to handle information with a non-trivial complexity and diversity; that is true today and will be true for one or two (human) generations to come. This is particularly so where the users keep developing the concept structure as well as inserting new data in existing slots. The fact that the system does not claim to exhaustively analyze and 'understand' all the information it stores and forwards, does not mean that it does not need high intelligence, including a capacity for dialogue. The relation between analysis, selection, and dialogue will be discussed below.

The present project is an ambitious attempt at creating a radically new system. It will require considerable resources, intellectual and financial, and the necessary time span from now until the system becomes operational will inevitably strain the patience and tolerance of collabor-

Ferenc Kiefer (ed.), Questions and Answers, 273–294.

ators and sponsors. The first obvious question, then, is why we have chosen this hard approach rather than made a series of small amendments to existing procedures, minor innovations which could be tested on a smaller economic scale and in a shorter time range. To answer this question, we must make a short survey of the state-of-the-art, as we see it, and the development that led up to the present situation.

1. Why such radical changes?

Computer-based text retrieval systems are widely used today in many countries for many fields of knowledge and are steadily gaining ground. For many decision-makers they still stand for a new technology, and with the so-called 'full-text systems', which are now becoming common, many trained users feel they are getting into a second breathing. Salesmen and clients alike seem to agree that a lot is happening in this field these days.

At the very same time, people who approach these tools to examine them from a research and development perspective are impressed by the absence of development. None of the commonly used systems is based on retrieval principles which were not all known, published, discussed, and exploited practically in the 1950's. In fact, the thinking behind them is to a large extent much older, since these systems are virtually computerizations of the established reference card file procedures for finding documents. So the miracle is not that they work—why shouldn't they?—but that they can still be competitive. A quarter of a century is a long time in the computer world.

How is it possible that experienced persons can have such different appreciations of the same phenomenon that some find the development overwhelmingly fast and other complain about stagnation? We think the explanation is the following. The actual retrieval services have improved strikingly over the last 25 years and not least during the last few years. The computers and the software have become more reliable, more accessible, much more convenient to use, and, most of all, cheaper. The databanks are bigger and, again, more reliable and better structured. People and routines around the automatic systems have been trained to support them. And in several fields a new corps of professionals has been brought up to live with these systems. In short, the whole field has moved from daring experimentation—those brave men with their fantastic machines—to everyday production. However, these improvements are fruits which have been reaped by any group of professionals using computers on a large scale. It has neither required nor entailed any development of the methods for the computer's search in text databases. It is the hardware and the general systemware that have improved, not the field's own contribution to methodology.

There are two general major improvements that are worth mentioning in this context. One is the capability for interactive processing. An immediate response from a computer terminal instead of a letter arriving on some later occasion does not only mean that much faster delivery of the product, but also a qualitative difference in the end result. It becomes possible for the user, while he still remembers clearly what he wanted to know, to react to the computer's less than responsive answer, so that he can rapidly fire back a modified question.

The tolerance towards irrelevant or otherwise inadequate responses is then drastically increased. From the point of view of the system and hence of the system's designer, this interactive interrogation is merely a rapid succession of independent pairs of questions and answers. This sequence does not form a dialogue in any deeper sense but rather a series of monologues. The computer treats one question at a time, producing the answer it finds best for it, in exactly the same logical manner as in batch processing. It treats the 13th question in a 'dialogue' in exactly the same way as the first one, having learned and forgotten nothing in the process. It is as virgin the 13th time as the first.

The human partner, on the other hand, does change under the impact of the computer's successive performances. He adjusts his wording and his requests as the computer's answers reveal what the database contains and how the stored text is formulated and tagged. He learns from experience, so that question n+1 is made with a different background than question n. The human ability of adaptation is the only intelligent feature of present-day standard 'interactive' search systems. That ability does not logically require interactive operation in a technical sense, but psychologically the shorter turn-around time in the machine enhances human performance.

To sum up: the search algorithms are not improved, but faster and more convenient computer performance produces an environment where the human can make better use of his intelligence.

The breakthrough caused by 'full-text systems' is even more directly an effect of improved computer technology. In fact, it is mainly an effect of a quantitative improvement: the availability of disk storage at reasonable cost has made it possible to record the entire texts of many documents instead of only a heading, abstract, or coded description of the text and its contents. The observation that an increase in the amount of information operated upon could, under certain circumstances, improve the value of the output is hardly very surprising. It is not a methodological achievement in any usual sense. It is quantitative progress of the same kind as when the word length of an arithmetic unit is increased. That does not mean a new method for multiplication, but it does mean that products can be computed with higher precision.

When we said that the search algorithms are by and large unimproved (referring to those in the computer, since, as noted, the users have learned new strategies over these years), we did not mean that they are always unchanged. In fact, the combination of direct access and fulltext availability has often been allowed to justify significantly reducing or leaving out altogether the guiding information—classifying, explaining, or disambiguating the primary text and laying bare the relations among documents, concepts, and terms— which has earlier with such ingenuity and labour been added to the systems in the form of tags to the documents and thesauri or other structural information about the document and the retrieval language used.

The unenriched full-text systems are the information science world's do-it-yourself quick-service offer. And like so many other kinds of self-'service', from supermarkets and filling stations upwards, they have been promoted by salesmen who style the absence of service as quickness (as though staff were necessarily slow) and the user's labour as automation. The resources for mass-storage have made it possible to downgrade the intelligence of the computer systems.

Are there no innovations then to be found? There certainly are, and we shall examine some of them below in section 3. However, neither the rather complex systems implemented for other purposes in the fields of computational linguistics or artificial intelligence nor the ad hoc inventions meant to serve text retrieval on the conditions currently prevalent there have gained wide acceptance.[1]

The explanation for the discrepancy between available or possible innovation and actual practice may be provided by one or more of the following alternatives:

a. An establishment has been created which has vested too much in organization, software, databanks, and training to be responsive to rational suggestions for change.

b. A change would require a transition, but there are no sponsors

willing to carry that load, notwithstanding the fact that innovations are profitable over a longer period.
c. Decision makers do not realize the value of the possible innovations. Or they fear that the advantages that could possibly follow from a proposal would be cancelled by other drawbacks, such as the opaqueness of the system.
d. None of the proposed innovations is good enough to be worthwhile to implement on a large scale. The conservatism is rational: the expected raise of level is not high enough to justify even in a longer perspective the necessary investments in methods, development, retraining etc.

Anticipating what we are going to say below, we must admit that, in our belief, there is evidence to support the three first explanations, but that the stagnation cannot be explained entirely by lack of insight and good will among decision makers the world over. Considering the long time the computer-based systems have had to develop on the market, we believe—and it would require a long treatise to corroborate that belief—that the text retrieval methodology, with its primitive computer procedures and the traditions for human behaviours developed have reached some kind of ripeness where none of the suggested improvements, **taken by itself** is profitable. Should great advances have been possible in small steps, they would presumably have been taken. We draw the conclusion that an essential improvement, if it is to be made at all, must be carried out by a radical change at this stage.

In the following two sections we shall examine to what extent the present technology fails. Following that, we shall mention what we see as the major methodological resources which could be made use of for text retrieval. Thereafter, we shall draw the outlines of a new retrieval system and point at the areas which particularly need be studied to develop it.

2. Shortcomings of Existing Systems

a. Complaints

Suppliers and users of information services are exasperatingly reluctant to volunteer information about failures. That is, of course, very natural, but a reformer or inventor needs to know what ails today to propose some cure better for tomorrow. Thus, if we examine, or elicit, user complaints, we almost always find that only rarely do they concern the basic mode of operation. Beside what could be called quantitative wishes—faster response, larger files, better reliability and more frequent updating—the wish list is conspicuous in that it contains mostly marginal adjustments. The majority of users are a happy and easily satisfied crowd; to such an extent that they become poor informants for those who want to introduce new facilities. They literally cannot think of much they could get which they are not already getting.

This kind of situation creates a problem. An evaluation of the shortcoming of one technology cannot easily be separated from some kind of appreciation of what technology could replace it. It is unreasonable to require of good users that they have so much technical fantasy, and the same goes for most managers and sponsors. And the natural reactions which could at least indicate ergonomic refinement are often trained out of the users by the time they become expert. They are brainwashed by salesmen and by the machine to be skilled and proud consumers. Judging from the satisfaction of the clientele, one would say there is a striking lack of problems in the field.

Let us examine some of the major wishes expressed.

i. Standardization

Typically, the requests that do occur are for more consistency rather than for more niceties. One major complaint, for which remedies are currently sought, is about the rather arbitrary variations of commands and conventions in the existing systems. The user groups look forward towards standardization rather than to development in any scientific sense.

Characteristically, the attempt by the European Community to establish a 'Common Command Language' for all the major databases currently available has met with wide support in user circles and only with perfunctory opposition from the representatives of the various systems. The very fact that such standardization with its necessarily conservative effect on methodware development, is acceptable and technically possible without basic reorganization of the systems or important loss of facilities is an almost alarming confirmation of our conclusion that the field is characterized by stagnation.

ii. Automation

A more fundamental complaint concerns the cost, delay and subjectivity caused by manual analysis of documents. While for some fields this delay is felt as more disturbing than the crudeness of a naked raw-text system so that they prefer to eliminate all input preparation, automatic procedures for indexing are a desideratum for many others.[2]

Now, if we go instead to the non-users to find out why they do not utilize the computerized services, we find, besides just common hostility to any new gadgets, a feeling, not rarely supported by earlier experience, that those systems could not possibly do anything sensible for them anyhow. The kind of answers they provide are either too blunt or too trivial and always too verbose.

Thus, users of computer systems when urged to complain, compare with the best possible computerized system they could imagine, and that is by the nature of things similar to the existing ones. Non-users tend to compare the computer systems they tried or heard about with manual services, finding them too unrefined and uncooperative.

It is only natural, that after a period of a few decades, the clients have ordered themselves into groups, depending on the nature of the tasks they normally face (although one person obviously may belong to both groups with respect to different applications). People with a large number of simple questions, knowing that no human advisor could possibly ever help them, have learned to live with the computerized austerity. People with questions for which more subtle or argumentative answers are called for have realized that they need human help or have to rely on themselves. Neither can imagine any way in which a machine could do essentially more for them, so why complain. The field has, as we said, reached a certain maturity. These observations, if they have the generality we believe, reinforce our conclusion that only a radical improvement over present standards has any hope of being accepted as meaningful.

b. Deficiencies

So much for the complaints proferred. But which is the real situation? Can we as investigators establish a posteriori how well the services perform?

Let us examine briefly the most important points, where in our view the commonly used text retrieval systems fall short of the target.

i. Power of Discrimination

In the central task, that of adequate selection, how well do they perform?

They are exact on a very superficial level in that the system finds all items which happen to have a given wording. But for all this sham exhaustivity— and the noise levels which inevitably go with it—the systems may give incomplete or even misleading answers, since they are misled by the slightest stylistic variation or shift of terminology or perspective, even a misprint. The system does not distinguish between meanings if the wording as specified in the query is the same, and it does not detect similarities when the 'same' thing is put slightly differently. Morphological and syntactical analyzers have made only marginal improvements (in some cases, since they are still surface structure analyzers, even impeded the performance, as demonstrated experimentally by Gerard Salton and verified by an investigation at Kval). Adequate manual indexing may move but not eliminate this fundamental problem: the problem becomes one of finding a meta-expression of the identical foreseen form.

Searching, therefore, functions well as long as the documents are written in a terminology and with essentially the attitude shared by or expected by the questioner. As soon as the questions are put at an angle, the noise level is seen to rise disastrously. Is the number of misses also increasing at the same rate?

This question is harder than it sounds. It is not only difficult in the same sense that establishing the statistics of undetected crime is difficult. It is not, as one might naively assume, even obvious what is a desired answer per se; there are complex feedback mechanisms between the available retrieval procedures and the evaluation of the results they provide. This circularity is not only sloppiness on the part of practical users but is fundamental. Only for very stylized experimental situations can the retrievand be well defined in terms independent of the methods for finding them.

As soon as retrieval goes beyond the most obvious, the concept of 'relevant but not retrieved' items becomes obscure. The fact that a user might a posteriori be able to decide for each item presented to him whether or to what extent it is helpful for his purposes does not imply that a set of relevant items in any reasonably sense 'exists' a priori, independently of the procedure for catching them. It is much more dynamic than that! Many good answers, perhaps the most important ones, are totally unexpected. Rather than 'mechanically' fulfilling the requirements of the question in some foreseen way, they may be more or less at variance with the thinking behind the question, clarifying the issue from a slightly different angel and explaining why. The best answers are often those that set us thinking in a new way. With initiated human librarians or advisors we take a certain independence in answering for granted. Typically, a reasonably well-informed human will, in addition to or instead of direct answers to the question as first formulated:

* ask for clarification or specification;
* correct false assumptions—'presuppositions' and others— as revealed by the question;
* answer questions only implicitly contained in the inquiry;
* provide indirect answers, only implicatively connected with the question;
* supply additional information not asked for but deemed relevant in the inquirer's situation as understood by the answerer;

etc., etc.

Even though the ultimate aim of the search is to provide one item or a few out of a given inventory of prestored documents, the human advisor starts out on a dialogue with counter-questions, meta-answers, indirect answers, etc., thereby making the communication two-way. It is the absence of such deeper 'interaction' which in our view is the major shortcoming in information retrieval so far. Our conclusion is that it is in providing other service than that offered today—in catering for the non-users of today and in serving old users in ways they did not imagine possible—that a new information technology can make a breakthrough.

ii. Hospitality

Besides minor nuisances due to sundry deficiencies in program design, the user encounters two requirements which make the current systems inhospitable. One is the requirement to be meticulously correct, down to the last digit and the delicacies of spelling. Methods for recovering slightly misspelled words are not yet standard, inconceivable though they may seem. Few systems offer any efficient feedback to guide the user over the small inadvertencies.

Spelling may seem a small matter to mention, but, since the demand for exactitude is also valid for the user when putting in information, it must be stated that the systems make quite unrealistic assumptions about human users. There is absolutely no way of making files of many millions of characters correct, and an adequate answer may well be omitted due to a document's spelling 'bord' for 'board'.

More fundamental is the assumption that the user should, in principle, know what he is after. The lack of real interactivity on all levels, but particularly on the so-to-speak intellectual level, is what makes the systems seem so hard to work with; we refer to the discussion above on dialogues to establish the target of the search. In short, the hospitality is reduced because the operation presupposes that the user is more careful than he could be and more rigid intellectually than he should be.

iii. Growth and Aging of the Database

Every manually inserted meta-text, from unsophisticated index terms upwards, has one certain consequence if no other: it creates, as systems are now organized, a delay between the acquisition of the raw document and its use in the system. In practice, the delay caused by indexing groups, term list committees and thesaurus experts can be considerable. Even more serious is that the contents of these meta-items tend to age faster than do the texts themselves. It is a remarkable property of natural texts—perhaps the most important 'naturalness' in them altogether—that we are able to read and reasonably well understand texts with a terminology, fact background, and conceptual framework widely differing from our own. If the author has not followed the latest term definitions or otherwise updated his knowledge and language, we may note this fact, but we can read on. And if the author tacitly introduces new concepts and word meanings, or uses such innovations as have so far passed us unheeded, we can normally catch up without asking for specific definitions or restatements, as long as the distance in some quantitative sense between our language and frame of reference and the one underlying the text is 'small'.

This flexibility often goes lost in the strict hierarchies or clean-cut classifications in the auxiliary 'indexing' information. The enriched database, therefore, ages ungracefully. It exerts a very conservative influence on the usership until a point where it must be discontinuously revised or taken out of use. Manual enrichment, as practiced, therefore entails delay in growth and premature aging. This aging problem is connected with the inherently authoritarian approach necessarily taken. The information added, constituting an interpretation and direction for use of the primary documents, reflects the view of the 'indexer', thesaurus builder, or other helper in the background, who, more or less anonymous to the user, imposes his perspective on the whole system. These helpers sometimes have a very qualified and representative expertise, but even so their views are restricted by whatever experience and ambitions they have, and they necessarily operate prior in time to the moment of search.

In practice, in many organizations, the indexers do not constitute the supreme competence in current knowledge about the field. It is not unusual for engineers who are deemed to be 'less productive' and not extroverted enough to be sales engineers to spend the last few years before retirement in a documentation and library department where they never wanted to go. Assigning to one-year-old documents the labels they find fit, after disinterested samplewise reading on the basis of their 40-year-old theoretical training and discontinued contacts with the projects of the organization, they not unsurprisingly provide a rather weak support for the new engineers reading those documents a couple of months or years afterwards.

iv. Side Effects

Traditional simple methods have other drawbacks besides the possible flaws in their helpfulness to the user. One such effect is the impact on the balance of power in a field. A large database with its particular organization and indexing and pointers tends to create—by its very size, if for no other reason—a de facto monopoly and to vest the 'owner' with a unique influence. With current technology there is no way for the 'owner' to remain impartial: even a decision to omit 'subjective' indexing is a ruling which will favor some types of information at the expense of other information. This 'norm problem' has been observed first in the legal field, where, as is natural, there exists a tradition to be aware of norm problems. Who tells me to look at case x and y and to disregard case z when considering question q? Who said and with what authority that this case is to be read in the light of paragraph so and so? Who included this comment and who was authorized to cancel another one? Who decided that no index term should be added to the case on computer fraud, so that (almost) no one will ever find it? Who is responsible for proof reading and hence for my finding four cases on product liability and missing the fifth case where the concept was mistakenly spelled product liability? Etc., etc. Even the most unsophisticated aids may have a biasing effect! The merely 'technical' problem of finding good keywords is far from as innocent as it first appears. The choice of keywords may well reflect the individual or group background experience, knowledge (or lack thereof), attitudes or intentions, conscious or not, of indexers, editors, and document collectors. The very minute we try to make the system even a little more intelligent, by, say, introducing some kind of automatic procedure for establishing synonymy, we increase the built-in bias to a frightening degree.

One rather often advocated solution of the norm problem is to request the retrieval system to be so transparent that every user knows exactly what is going on and can verify that he is not being manipulated. That requirement would exclude all computational sophistication; in fact, it would exclude even Boolean algebra with nested expressions. Not even a trained logician would be able to recognize completely the semantic characteristics of a document set defined by a Boolean expression with a couple of levels of brackets. It is hard enough to work out what set of required word combinations that expression stands for, let alone to predict, on the spot, the likely nature of the documents in which such combinations occur.

Another side effect worth observing is the detrimental effect on argumentation and even on the style of the documents if a whole professional group becomes tuned to a simplistic retrieval scheme where an over-emphasis is placed on the explicit wording and where implicit reference, shades of meaning, and abstract thoughts are systematically disregarded. The training of young jurists into living with computerized files, substituting word retrieval procedures for more or less intelligent 'reckoning of the mind', may turn out to be harmful in the end. Lawyers may ultimately become as formalistic and unimaginative as popular belief makes them. Exhaustiveness on a literal level will be encouraged, whereas 'analogy', the high-level of legal thinking, will be neglected. A case involving selling a used car with dangerously bad brakes will be checked against a wealth of second-hand, second rate cars, all sold, and possibly also with other failing brakes than those in cars, whereas an obviously relevant analogy (obvious once found, that is) with a house rented out in spite of an almost homicidal chimney flue will be overseen. If the formulation of legal text, even law text, will—as has been seriously proposed!—be adapted to the crudeness of the retrieval procedures of today, the hebetation will be taken one step further. Such undesirable adaptation of the profession and its documents is hard to avoid, since the procedures, once established as the common procedure, will necessarily function as a standard. Documents will tend to be void, unless mechanically retrievable. And the habit of requiring completeness in the survey of surface similarities will, even for those in the trade who would have intelligence and training for more meaningful work, create a work load that will prevent them for sitting down to think.

Conclusion

Raw text methods can produce exhaustive answers to a class of simple questions, but, in order to make them intelligent enough to recognize relevant similarity under variation in grammar, terminology, or perspective, they must be given a more or less elaborated superstructure of man-made meta-statements. With current technology, the more of this kind of intelligence-enhancing information is added, the worse become the other drawbacks: delay in updating, aging of the database, authoritarian attitude of the anonymous System, and the Norm Problem.

3. Idle resources—unused techniques and unheeded insights

Our reason for believing that we can substantialy improve over current technology is that results from other fields could be utilized. Let us briefly list these resources.

a. Artificial Intelligence Systems

Impressive results have been demonstrated in artificial intelligence systems able to answer questions by drawing conclusions from input statements. In current applications, the 'intelligence' of these systems operates on data recoded in an internal form, corresponding to some model for the domain under consideration. Therefore, they can handle only very restricted domains. Natural language, if used at all in AI systems, is a format for input and output, handled by an 'interface'. Text retrieval systems, on the other hand, so far have none of that intelligence but can accommodate texts with any content. Our intention is to use the experience of knowledge representation and deduction-making to add facilities to open-ended text-based systems.

b. Linguistics

Linguists have developed a wide range of well-defined and even computerized procedures for analyzing natural language texts grammatically, semantically and, of late, even pragmatically. Current text retrieval systems make no or little use of this collected experience. Some cannot even recognize inflexional variations of the same lexical unit, and where a syntactical analysis is attempted it is often too amateurish and/or outdated in methodology to produce very helpful results. The interdisciplinary barriers are high!

Also, linguistic insight can help eliminate the prevalent moralizing attitude underlying many systems designs today, that people should learn to be 'logical' and 'exact'. This attitude reflects a technocratic unwillingness to make allowance for human weakness and a lack of understanding of the value of the dynamics of 'natural' growth of language and concept structures. It is often repeated that specialized expert language is not, or should not be vague and that it must build on a rigid 'scientific' foundation. Linguists know that no such rigid language ever existed even as a specialized sub-language, much less as a tool for fluent communication; and there is good evidence that the very fumbling vagueness of more or less natural language is one of its major assets.

c. Dialogue Studies

In later years, theoretical work in linguistics, logics, and psychology has with different points of departure converged towards some fundamental problems of dialogue and what is called 'cooperative behaviour' in communication, problems which are similar to some of the hard problems confronting serious designers of interactive computer systems. A few recent findings give hope that continued work on these theoretical issues will yield result of the greatest practical consequence.

d. Computer Science

Two trends are encouraging: (1) Improved possibilities for modular design where results fetched from different areas can be accommodated. Thus, autonomously developed language analysis, logical deduction, or input/output translation procedures can more readily be incorporated. (2) A technology for computer conferencing and electronic mail has been developed to support a kind of many-to-many interaction among users which could stand as a model for a systems design which replaces the Human-System dialoque with its authoritarian take-it-or-leave-it attitude, by a 'polylogue' among several.

4. Reasonable requirements

a. Text-Based System

The input texts should be stored intact, and copies thereof should normally be the kind of factual answers delivered. Interpretations of the texts in one kind of logical meta-representation or another must never be permitted to replace the texts. Eventually more and larger fields of knowledge can successively be formalized so that they become amendable to qualified AI techniques. However, we do not see formalization of the whole database as even a desirable general solution: in many applications an amount of vagueness and incompleteness is necessary for the dynamics of the field.

Even where a formalization is later possible and desirable, we need tools to handle the intermediate stages while preparing the well-defined conceptual structures which lend themselves to a calculus. For most applications it will probably be a chronic situation that formalization is a continuous process, so that an area of well-structured information is steadily gaining ground at the expense of a wide field of more intuitive knowledge—representable 'only' in natural language statements—which in turn is continuously extended.

We therefore insist that for many applications, including the legal and medical fields particularly studied in this project, one cannot translate oneself out of natural language. Natural language interfaces may be appropriate to make command conventions and formalized subsystems more appetizing, but natural language texts must, intact, be available for operation in the system itself. The formal knowledge representations must be seen as not more than helpful approximations of the given texts and must never replace them or override them.

b. Successive Commenting

A leading specialist[3]) on legal information retrieval in the European Community once said—noting, not quite justly, that the computers do no more than relay legal information anyhow—that there is no excuse for delay in making texts available to the user. No intelligent meta-information should be allowed to delay the insertion of the raw text. Indexing and other comments on the primary texts—and on the comments themselves—must be a continuous process. A text must be available the moment it is acquired, although to begin with only for simple search mechanisms not yet supported by the intelligent reader's analysis. This is our way of handling the problem of delay.

c. Pluralistic Updating

There is no other way around subjectivity than to make it conscious. No guarantees for the quality of the meta-information will make it less authoritarian—on the contrary! The system must be prepared to accommodate the meta-information (and primary texts) submitted at any time by any user or program. The system as such should not take responsibility for the correctness or even the consistency of the information any more than a good librarian warrants the contents of the books he orders on his shelves. It should only administrate the flow of information. We therefore prefer a computer conference system that is endowed with more intelligence to an oracle, no matter how polite it is taught to be.

d. Basic Host Software

The system must include procedures for

i. analyzing texts, from morphological analyzers to powerful semantic interpreters;
ii. AI types of logical operations:
iii. dialogue stategies;
iv. search procedures.

These procedures must be replaceable one by one as research proceeds. This implies that the basic software should be a very robust construct, which can host a large number of interacting programs of diffent design and sophistication. This basic software must be long-lived without hampering the methodological development. It must make few assumptions about the character of the texts or the procedures for their processing. It should, instead, provide an experiment field for testing, in parallel and in an authentic environment with identical users and data, successively new modules for analysis, conclusion making, and dialogue behaviour.

e. Special-Purpose Programs

Text analyzers and AI procedures can hopefully be taken over from other fields, but dialogue strategies and search algorithms have to be developed on the basis of recent theoretical insights and the experience which can be accumulated within the project. The dialogue language should be adaptable to the individual user and will require separate interfaces. These languages should encompass, whenever possible, uniform ways of expressing information which is stored diffently internally according to the needs of different procedures. The dialogue language, then, which may or may not resemble natural language, will help the user to utilize in parallel different semantic models and different sources of information.

5. The polytext message structure

To satisfy the requirements stated in the previous section, we propose the following design.

Successive and pluralistic updating requires the segmentation of the metapart of the database into smaller units, each of which has its own date of insertion and its own responsible author. Thereby the metastatements come to resemble 'the primary statements', or 'documents', and we have decided to treat them alike in the system. The elementary units, whether primary or not, will be called 'messages'; the strength of the analogy with computer conference systems will soon appear.

The databases will be partitioned, thus, into subsets defined by time of insertion and by source, and a user will be given the option to interrogate the subdatabase he prefers and to ignore the rest. The whole set-up could be called a systematic way of handling overlapping databases, or of reading over each other's shoulders, if you like. To produce this effect in a fruitful way, it is essential that the messages are no larger than that each message will be accepted or rejected in its entirety by all users. The atoms we have worked with in our experiments so far have had the order of magnitude of one sentence of running text, one index term's assignment to another message or one subformula in a logical calculus.

a. Agents in the System

The Polytext system's manner of handling these 'messages' places on a par

i. authors of primary documents and those who comment or 'index' them;
ii. information providers and clients—any user may at any time supply new messages;
iii. men and machines—programs may as well as human users of the system read and supply messages.

b. Message format

For these messages we have designed a uniform format:

i. A unique identifier.
ii. The date and time for insertion.
iii. Author, i.e., the person or program who submitted the message.
iv. Modality: the degree of certainty by which the author claims what is stated in the message. This novel item was found to be necessary when authorship was introduced and the trust of the user comes to rely on the credibility of the source. For people to supply under their own name half-baked ideas, which may be the most valuable hints while building up new paths in an unknown domain, they must be given an opportunity to specify the degree of certainty. For some sources, the degree of certainty has been institutionalized by such labels as 'draft', 'draft international standard', 'approved for second reading', etc.

v. Topic: that about which something is stated.
vi. Comment: that which is stated about the topic. The topic-comment relation has been found in recent research to be a fruitful way of describing supra-sentence structures of texts. Often enough, the topic will be an identifier of another message; the comment may also be an identifier but can also be a string of free texts, in natural language or otherwise.
vii. Pragmatics: an instruction to the system telling what to do with the message. The pragmatic item is the one where new strategies can be tested. If a linking is to be performed between a named predecessor and successor the basic system should perform that. If the linking is given as a reference pragmatic item must refer to a program that will perform the matching. Such programs correspond to the search procedures of other systems. We have attempted to keep the basic Polytext software as simple as possible. Therefore, intelligent and short-lived modules are kept outside as programs using the system rather than as parts of it. Thus, text analyzers may take one message at a time, interpret it—using other messages for its own information while so doing (naturally, lexical items should also be stores as messages)—and report the result as a new message, having the analyzed message for its topic and the recoding in some meta-language as its comment.

c. Basic Syustem Functions

The system functions can then be reduced to

i. insert a message;
ii. delete a message;
iii. read a message explicitly specified by its identifier;
iv. supply the identifier(s) of a message (or the messages) linked to a given message;
v. link messages as prescribed by the topic-comment information and by the pragmatic item.

6. The present demonstration system

Recognizing the need for a project of this magnitude to proceed by well-defined steps, the first phase (22 April 1979 to 22 April 1980) included producing a demonstration model by which the soundness of the basic concepts of Polytext could be verified. This demonstration model should be seen as the first in a sequence ranging from a demonstration model, to a prototype for testing the whole set of procedures under simplified conditions with selected interested end-users, to an experimentation system for large-scale operation on authentic data but with no claim to autonomous economy, to a production system.

The implementation was made in INTERLISP because this language permitted the ease of programming and program modification and could host the LIFER package developed as SRI International and placed at the disposal of this project under a separate contract with Kval. For running INTERLISP, the DEC20 computer at the Institute for Information Processing, University of Linkoeping, was selected, following some initial studies on the DEC KL-10 at SRI.

The design and implementation of this demonstration model was made by Staffan Löf who has described his work in a separate report. The demonstration covered four new features:

a. A text database with signed items and thus selection in terms of authorship.
b. Parallel use of different models for describing the same texts: an index term model, a set of hierarchical descriptors, and a propositional calculus, each with partially overlapping and partially incompatible subsets submitted by different users. The study did not aim in finding optimum or very advanced semantic representations but in handling co-existing different sets of meta-information.
c. A unified communication language independent of the internal representations (natural English, as described in a LIFER grammar made for this purpose and this material).
d. Use of the LIFER package for communicating with a text database.
e. Structuring a database by linking messages in topic-comment relations.

This approach, utilizing the intrinsic organizaton of the text and the discourse, was carried out both on natural language texts and on the metatexts in artificial form (propositional calculus and others). The legal text material has been analyzed from this point of view by Mária Heller, Katalin Kiss, and Tamás Váradi, under the direction of Ferenc Kiefer.

7. Plans

It is essential for this kind of project to proceed in parallel with theoretical research and with practical implementation. This fact is reflected in the project planning.

The proposed continuation includes theoretical investigations as well as experimental implementation on the basis of the results obtained.

The moral and/or financial support of a group of future users has been promised, and the cooperation of other institutes besides Kval and SRI has been secured.

a. Theoretical Issues

The theoretical issues of question-answering reach deeply into the fundamentals of linguisitics and logics and AI. Research on pertinent features of human dialogue has only recently entered a systematic phase. While the ideas underlying the original Polytext design have by and large justified themselves, much more penetrating studies are motivated.

The topic-comment relations which seem to be fundamental for specifying criteria for coherence of discourse and hence for establishing criteria for relevant responses, are being studied in conjunction with a group under Petr Sgall and Eva Hajičová at Charles University, Prague. Essentially the same theoretical issues appear in parallel ongoing and planned projects at SRI.

Acknowledgement:

The work reported here was carried out by Hans Karlgren, Don Walker, Ferenc Kiefer, Staffan Löf, Mária Heller, Katalin Kiss, and Tamás Váradi. The work has profited from the suggestions made by the Advisory Panel consisting of Börje Alpsten, Ministry of Justice, Stockholm; Benny Brodda, Department of Linguistics, Stockholm University; Ingvar Gullnäs, Chancellor of Justice, Stockholm; Ferenc Kiefer, Kval and Academy of Sciences, Budapest; Tomas Ohlin, Study Commission for Information Technology, Stockholm; Eric Sandewall, Department of Information Processing, Linköping University; Peter Seipel, Law Department, Stockholm University; Hans Riesel, Department of Information Processing, Royal Institute of Technology, Stockholm.

The work has been supported by Kval Institute for Information Science, SRI International, The Swedish National Defence Research Institute (FOA); the National Swedish Board for Technical Development (STU).

KVAL, Institute for Information Science
SRI International

Notes

[1] Kval has thus been forced to note that good ideas are not stolen, in spite of the fact that they are published and free for the taking. That is true for elaborate models for establishing statistical associations between synonyms, although the model, once constructed, is not computationally complex and has been experimentally proven to give good agreement with intuitive evaluation. That is also true for morphological analysis and dectection of word stems in compound words, the relevance of which has been demonstrated by Kval in studies with material from the ministries of justice in two countries; similar results are well-known elsewhere. The fact that the methods proposed were significantly better than the current ones was noted but no practical conclusions were drawn. When it was found that Kval did not offer for sale a complete system with these features, no one cared to pursue the matter.

[2] We shall not discuss here the many and great problems of classificational structures and indexing languages, since these are normally seen rather as problems concerning the information submitted by man to the machine than as problems concerning the machine-borne algorithms. This view, however, could be disputed.

[3] Colin Thapper.

INDEX OF NAMES

Ajdukiewicz 110, 111, 125, 153
Apostel 149
Aristotle 151, 189
Åqvist 9, 10, 45, 46, 47, 48, 50, 51, 55, 66, 80, 153, 191, 192, 203, 204, 205, 207, 222

Ballmer 122
Bar-Hillel 111, 113
Barri 269
Barth 187
Bartsch 106
Bäuerle 194, 197, 203, 214
Bayer 271
Bayes 78, 80
Becker 187
Běličová 262
Belnap 9, 155
Benešová 257
Bennett 155
Bierwisch 90
Bochvar 209
Boër 45, 46, 51, 53, 54, 55, 61, 62, 63, 64, 66, 81, 82
Bolinger 87, 88, 95
Bressan 152

Callebout 186
Carlson 187
Carnap 82, 160, 254, 259
Chafe 262
Chisholm 190
Cohen 201
Cooper 110
Cresswell 61, 62, 64

Daneš 262, 268
Davidson 97, 154
Davis 13
Dijk 271
Doherty 31
Donnellan 149, 155
Dowty 149

Egli 201, 202
Essler 187

Fine 251
Firbas 262
Frege 155, 259

Gabbay 226
Gazdar 56, 254
Geach 111, 112
Grice 104, 244, 254
Groenendijk 153
Grosz 260, 261, 269

Hajičová 85, 86, 87, 88, 94, 95, 257, 258, 259, 260, 262, 270, 293
Halliday 262
Hamblin 57, 58, 59, 127, 153, 197, 198
Harris 1
Hausser 99, 100, 107, 134, 152, 153, 154, 155, 202, 203, 262
Heller 292
Hendrix 270
Heyting 209
Higginbotham 45, 59, 60, 200
Hintikka 45, 48, 49, 50, 51, 66, 80, 81, 87, 92, 153, 155, 187, 190, 203, 205, 206, 254, 270
Hintikka, M. 187
Hiż 3, 154, 186, 190
Hull 68, 82, 86
Hoepelman 10, 12, 225, 270

Jeffrey 77, 82
Joshi 87, 88, 89, 90, 232, 237, 238, 259, 260, 267, 271

Kaplan, D. 45, 51, 52, 54, 55, 81, 154

Kaplan, S. 232, 267
Karlgren 269
Karttunen 45, 56, 57, 58, 59, 60, 63, 81, 87, 153, 155, 198, 199, 200, 201, 222
Katz 1, 65, 82, 87, 154
Kawashima 255
Keenan 68, 82, 86
Kiefer 87, 92, 93, 94, 95, 292
Kindt 13
Kiss 292
Kleene 209
Kosík 270
Kripke 13, 149, 155, 162
Křížková 262
Kuhn 259
Kuno 258
Kutschera 250, 254

Lakoff, R. 44
Lee 113
Lenzen 254
Leśniewski 111
Lewis, D. 9, 10, 12, 110, 152, 153, 187, 260
Lewis, S. 9, 187
Li 269
Link 81
Lippit 155
Löf 292
Łukasiewicz 207, 208
Lycan 45, 51, 53, 54, 55, 65, 66, 81
Lyons 107

Malone 154
Marciszewski 271
Martin 13
Materna 259
Mathesius 262
Matthews 107
May 46, 59, 60, 200
Mays 232, 234, 236
McKeown 232, 235, 263
Montague 63, 97, 98, 99, 104, 107, 110, 112, 143, 149, 154, 203, 224
DeMorgan 161
Munitz 190
Moore 244

Noonan 269

Olson 9, 187

Panevová 95
Partee 149
Paul 9, 187
Peters 222
Pinkal 251, 255
Plátek 257
Popper 160
Postal 1, 87, 154
Prior, A. 191
Prior, M. 191
Procházka 259

Quine 48, 51, 80, 98, 162, 188

Rantala 190
Rescher 191, 209, 217
Robinson 267
Ross 153
Rozemond 154
Russell 162
Rylova 270

Saarinen 190
Sadock 153
Searle 43, 154
Sgall 94, 257, 259, 260, 268, 269, 270, 293
Spohn 10, 82
Stahl 127, 153
Stalnaker 42
Stechow 95, 155
Stegmüller 82
Stenius 153
Stokhof 153
Szabolcsi 270

Tarski 97, 98, 151
Thapper 294
Thompson 269, 270
Tichý 152

Ungar 190

Váradi 292
Vennemann 106, 155

Walker 269
Wittgenstein 160
Woodruff 13
Wunderlich 81

Zaefferer 153, 155
Ziff 104
Zuber 270

Yuganov 268

SUBJECT INDEX

allegation 86
answer
  complete 59, 60, 180, 186
  direct 4, 87
  false 58
  helpful 73
  informative 46, 68, 70
  partial 59, 60, 180, 186
  possible 1, 2, 3, 57, 58, 71
  pragmatically
    significant 4, 46, 66, 67, 74, 75, 76, 80
  true 1, 2, 46, 57, 58, 76
argumentation
  and questions 191, 192
attitude
  asserted 21, 22, 23, 24
  assertive 28, 29, 30, 38
  epistemic 15, 16, 17, 18, 19, 31
  negative 20, 21, 27, 30, 36, 38
  non-assertive 28, 29, 30, 38
  opaque 31
  positive 20, 27, 28, 29, 30, 34, 36, 38, 40
  propositional
    speaker's 28, 29, 32, 37, 38, 39, 40, 41

background assumption 87, 92

conclusiveness condition 182, 184, 185

epistemic subject 51, 52
existential condition 63

frame 160

individuation
  by acquaintance 50, 51

/knowledge/-desideratum 46, 47, 65, 66, 92, 174, 175, 176, 178, 179, 181, 185

lambda reduction 109

meaning
  attitudinal 18, 26
  epistemic 15, 19, 26, 30, 40, 41
  literal 98, 99, 103, 104, 148, 149
  speaker's 100, 103
model set 160, 161, 162, 166, 169, 170
model system 160, 161, 162, 166, 169, 170, 171
mood
  attitudinal 19, 20, 41
  declarative 100, 101
  imperative 100, 101
  interrogative 100, 101
  responsive 101
mood marker 104, 120, 121, 127, 134

operator
  assertoric 9
  epistemic 9, 48, 92

presumption 87, 90, 233, 234
presupposition
  of questions 85, 86, 87, 88, 89, 91, 93, 175, 176

questions
  alternative 2, 197, 198, 213
  categorial 202
  direct 174, 175, 198, 265
  exhaustive 266
  indirect 163, 165, 166, 175, 198, 199, 265
  multiple 176, 222
  scope of 191, 195, 201, 225
  why- 1, 2, 86, 174, 176, 184
  yes-no- 1, 2, 92, 93, 176, 183, 197, 200, 202, 203, 204, 206, 213

response
cooperative 231, 234, 238
corrective indirect 231
suggestive indirect 232
supportive indirect 232

speech act 100, 102, 103, 122
surface compositionality 109, 110, 111

teleological relativity 55, 62, 64, 66
topic-/focus-articulation 88, 90, 91, 93, 94, 257, 258, 260, 261, 262, 263, 267
translation
imperative-assertoric 10, 11
imperative-epistemic 10